Classics in the Classroom

Classics in the Classroom

Using Great Literature to Teach Writing

Edited by
Christopher Edgar
and Ron Padgett

Teachers & Writers Collaborative
❧
New York

Library of Congress Cataloging-in-Publication Data

Classics in the classroom : using great literature to teach writing /
    edited by Christopher Edgar and Ron Padgett.
        p.   cm.
    Includes bibliographical references.
    ISBN O-915924-58-7 (pbk. : alk. paper)
    1. English language--Rhetoric--Study and teaching--Aids and
devices.   2. Literature--Study and teaching.   I. Edgar,
Christopher, 1961– . II. Padgett, Ron
PE1404.C54   1998
808'.042'07--dc21   98-47189
                                                        CIP

Teachers & Writers Collaborative
5 Union Square West
New York, NY 10003-3306

Cover and page design: Christopher Edgar
Printed by Philmark Lithographics, New York, N.Y.

Acknowledgments

This publication was made possible through generous support from NBC.

Teachers & Writers programs are made possible, in part, through support from the National Endowment for the Arts, the New York State Council on the Arts, and the New York City Department of Cultural Affairs.

T&W also thanks the following foundations, corporations, and individual donors: Bell Atlantic Foundation, Bertelsmann USA, The Bingham Trust, Booth Ferris Foundation, Bronx Borough President and City Council, The Bydale Foundation, Witter Bynner Foundation for Poetry, The Louis Calder Foundation, The Cerimon Fund, The Chase Manhattan Foundation, Consolidated Edison, Simon and Eve Colin Foundation, Charles E. Culpeper Foundation, The Dammann Fund, Marvin Hoffman and Rosellen Brown, J. M. Kaplan Fund, Lannan Foundation, Morgan Stanley Foundation, M&O Foundation, Manhattan Borough President and City Council, The New World Foundation, New York Times Company Foundation, Henry Nias Foundation, The Open Society Institute, Overbrook Foundation, Thomas Phillips and Jane Moore Johnson Foundation, Queens Borough President and City Council, Mel and Barbara Ringel, Maurice R. Robinson Fund, Helena Rubinstein Foundation, the Scherman Foundation, Steven Schrader and Lucy Kostelanetz, Lila Wallace-Reader's Digest Foundation, Alison Wyegala (in memory of Sergio Guerrero), an anonymous donor, and T&W's many individual members.

Table of Contents

෨

Preface

When Teachers & Writers sent out a call for essays on using the classics to inspire student writing, we had little idea of what we would receive. Given the recent emphasis in the schools on contemporary writing, we wondered if the classics had become neglected by teachers and fallen into desuetude. The answer is no, they are alive and well, as the essays in this book show.

But perhaps we should explain what we mean by "classic." The term makes some people think of ancient Greek and Roman literature, while others think of twentieth-century authors recently accepted into the canon (or even a well-known soft drink!). In the planning stages of this project, we opted for a generous definition, one that could include contemporary writing as well as literature from around the world. So in this volume you will find Homer and Ovid rubbing elbows with Bashō, Kafka, and Achebe.

Our aim was not so much to create a multicultural anthology (though happily it came out that way) as to provide good, practical ideas for using great literature to inspire a wide range of students to write with pleasure and imagination. All the essays in this book come from the first-hand experiences of the people who wrote them—teachers and poets and fiction writers who teach, from the elementary to the college level. Their specific assignments are for you to use or adapt to your classroom or your own writing. The essays here provide imaginative approaches to the classics, methods that could be applied to other great works. The possibilities are vast: Homer's *Odyssey*, Sophocles's *Oedipus Rex*, Ovid's *Art of Love*, Dante's *Inferno*, *Sir Gawain and the Green Knight*, Sei Shonagon's *Pillow Book*, the poems of Li Po and Tu Fu, *The Ramayana*, Whitman's "Song of Myself," Kafka's "Hunger Artist," and Ralph Ellison's *Invisible Man*—to name just a few. These are great works of art because, among other things, they contain great passages of writing, passages that through the centuries have inspired other writers to reach for their pens (or quills or keyboards). The classics all offer images of life that can be highly engaging for young people to read and think and dream about. That engagement is confirmed and deepened when students respond imaginatively to the great works of the past, in their own poems and stories.

—*Christopher Edgar and Ron Padgett*

Chris Brandt

The Epic of Gilgamesh

In the High School Writing Classroom

THE ROBERT F. WAGNER JR. INSTITUTE for the Arts and Technology in Long Island City, an industrial area of Queens, New York, is an "alternative" school—its programs are focused on creative approaches to learning and are often cross-disciplinary. A ninth grade English teacher at Wagner, Ms. Dara Winkler, applied for a writer-in-residence to work with her class. Her plan was to have the students read an epic poem and then use that experience to write their own "epics."

When I arrived in March to meet the class, Ms. Winkler had already introduced her students to the story of Gilgamesh, King of Uruk in the Tigris-Euphrates valley, and his unlikely friend Enkidu. The class had read the book and studied the topography and culture of that part of the world by looking at both modern photographs and archeological reconstructions. They had discussed the events of the story and their sequence, so that we could begin deeper work immediately.

Gilgamesh is Sumerian in origin. Cuneiform characters on clay tablets, dating from the seventh century B.C.E., were discovered in the ruins of Nineveh in 1872, but the work has been traced back to the second or third millenium. Modern versions of the work are of necessity episodic in form since the surviving tablets are fragments, but enough of the work survives to place it squarely in the epic tradition. The Gilgamesh story depicts battles, great challenges, long voyages, confrontations with destructive forces of enormous power, victories and defeats, the tragic loss of a comrade, attempts to rescue the dead from the afterworld, and an ultimate humanization of the hero.

Gilgamesh is the cruel and unthinking king of Uruk, half man and half god. He is so powerful that no one challenges him until the arrival of Enkidu, half man and half animal, who has been wrenched from his edenic life among the tigers and other creatures of plains and rivers by a temple prostitute Gilgamesh has sent to seduce him. Enkidu challenges

1

Gilgamesh just as the king is about to exercise his privilege of sleeping with a bride before the groom on the wedding night. Gilgamesh and Enkidu fight mightily to a draw, then in their mutual exhaustion they swear fast friendship. It is the first time the king has felt such kinship. In celebration, Gilgamesh decides to undertake a great task. He and Enkidu will kill Humbaba, the Evil One. Despite the warnings of dreams and omens—and Enkidu's doubts—they set out. In the sacred forest they find and kill Humbaba, but not before Enkidu receives a wound that will prove fatal. As the two companions are returning to Gilgamesh's capital Uruk, the goddess Ishtar tries to seduce Gilgamesh. He insults her; she sends the Bull of Heaven to destroy the two friends. Gilgamesh and Enkidu kill the Bull and earn Ishtar's curse. Enkidu sickens and dies, and Gilgamesh is left to wander the desert in solitary desolation. Refusing the comfort offered him by a woman in a humble dwelling, Gilgamesh sets out across the Sea of Death to find Utnapishtim, the survivor of the great flood—a kind of Sumerian Noah. Utnapishtim has seen more death and felt more grief than Gilgamesh has ever imagined, and he takes pity on the young king and gives him the secret of new life. Utnapishtim then sends Gilgamesh back to the people of Uruk, who need Gilgamesh's leadership and new-found humanity.

Ms. Winkler and I had met about a month earlier to map out our approach to the work. First, we agreed that we wouldn't "teach" *Gilgamesh*, but instead use it to open up opportunities for the students' own writing. Second, we'd forget that the work we were using was a "classic." *Gilgamesh* is a piece of writing just like any piece of writing, more or less useful according to the needs and talents of each reader. Third, we'd make *Gilgamesh* personal and current for the students—not about events of a remote time that, while interesting, have little to do with students' own lives. After all, our students have to walk through the mean streets and all the emotional turmoil of adolescence just to get home. Finally, we invited an art teacher, Ms. Katy McCarthy, and her class to join us, so that we could approach the work in ways both verbal and visual.

Though it's that dreaded entity, a long poem, *Gilgamesh* is easy to read because it is varied in form, composed of short segments that are fairly discrete although clearly related to each other. We chose the translation by Herbert Mason. It is episodic and easy to follow, and no longer than a long short story. (Also, the Mason version was already in the school's stock of textbooks.) Mason uses language that is modern and simple but still elevated in style—one of our goals was to encourage the students to explore the use of different kinds of language and choose those suited to their purposes.

Mrs. Winkler and I began by asking the students questions about themselves, not the literature. How many of them had ever had a best friend, someone they felt they could share everything with, whom they could talk to as they could not talk to their parents, their teachers, or indeed any grownup? As we'd expected, every one of them raised a hand. So we asked them to close their eyes and call that friend to mind in every detail, facial features, stature, posture, clothing, smells, texture of skin and hair. (If they couldn't remember a certain detail, they were to invent it.) Next, we asked them if they had ever lost a best friend. (Such loss could have been by death, because either they or the friend had moved away, or for any other reason.) Again, every hand went up. Finally, we asked if any of them had ever felt betrayed by someone they had trusted. This too was an experience they all shared.

Then we asked them to think about *The Epic of Gilgamesh* in terms of best friend, betrayal, and loss—but to substitute themselves for Gilgamesh or Enkidu, the best friend they had just called to mind for the other, and their own personal experience of loss or betrayal for the events of the poem.

Next we discussed the nature of heroism. What was a hero? Had they ever known a hero (few claimed they had), or dreamed of being one (almost all had)? Most thought in terms of comic-book superheroes, top athletes, or demi-gods like Gilgamesh. But could a hero be an ordinary person, a neighbor or a relative who does something extraordinary? Now many more said they'd known someone who had performed some heroic act. What about you, we asked them. Had they ever had to overcome their own fears to do something brave for someone or something else? Had any of their friends? Was the hero necessarily a "good" character, or could a "bad" person do something heroic? Finally, did the heroic deed need to be one of physical prowess, or could it be something demonstrating great mental or emotional strength?

Once the students began to relate *Gilgamesh* to their own lives, we asked them to consider its language. What was it that made the poem "heroic" or "epic," apart from the events in the story? We had them look closely at the scene in which Gilgamesh and Enkidu first lay eyes on each other. Enkidu is blocking the king's way, challenging him:

[. . .] Gilgamesh looked at the stranger
And listened to his people's shouts of praise
For someone other than himself
And lunged at Enkidu.
They fell like wolves
At each other's throats,
Like bulls bellowing,
And horses gasping for breath
That have run all day
Desperate for rest and water,
Crushing the gate they fell against.

We asked the students to tell us exactly what happens, to rephrase the passage in a "just the facts, ma'am" narrative. After some discussion, we all agreed that the king had simply gotten angry and started a vicious fight. Why, then, all the fancy language? This led to a discussion of simile, metaphor, and hyperbole, and their uses. Next we asked the students to think of a modern event, and to try to describe it in heroic language. For some, this exercise led to the discovery of an "epic" language suited to their own stories. Here is the opening paragraph from "Modern Myth" by Stacey Clermont:

Born on the day of Kings, Marie-Caramel was the youngest and only female child of her mother. Her brother Ernest was the first to see her born and he held her up to proclaim his only sister.

Another response, from "Soelimnoch" by Brandon Yates:

Soelim [an angel and Satan's son] looked down at her, then back at her killer. His hellish eyes ignited in blue flames. Thin, leathery tendrils burst from the pores of his wings and circled around Victor's neck. They tightened, then lifted him up. —Transgressor! You will know the agony of death! You will know the pains of perpetual suffering! May all of Hell reach out and pull whichever piece of your worthless soul they please. *Your eternity of decay will be my retribution!*— A whispering sound began to grow louder and louder, as Victor Coven's life flashed before his eyes.

    Ya yoosh . . . ya yoosh . . . ya yoosh. Rayblum ton begay noray maigon.

    Ya yoosh . . . ya yoosh . . . ya yoosh. Rayblum ton begay noray maigon.

Ya yoosh . . . ya yoosh . . . ya yoosh. Rayblum ton begay noray maigon.

The cries of lost souls echoed throughout the building. Dogs howled, cats hurled themselves from windows, and birds fell off their perches for the last time. Victor's body collapsed into a heap of green ooze—which was usual for one that has lost his soul. Soelim was not content at all. He leapt out of the window and plunged through the ground, going deeper and deeper under.

Many other students, however, had trouble finding such an "epic" language. They used everyday language in keeping with their choice of subject, as in this passage from "The Kittens That Changed a Friendship" by Kimberly McGee:

The two kittens were so very small, and what made Leanna sick was that they still had their mother's umbilical cord attached to them. Flies were all over them. Jessica didn't even care. She was laughing at them and teasing them with a branch from one of the trees. It was then that Leanna started thinking differently about her best friend. She took away the branch and used it to shoo the flies away. She thought the umbilical cords would feel slimy and squishy, and she had to fight her sick feelings to unwind them. To her surprise, they were almost dry and very light, but as she grabbed them, she could feel that they were still wet on the inside, so she tried not to look at them as she brought them into the house and put them in the plastic bag.

We stressed that narrative language needed to grow out of the needs of the story, and be appropriate to it. Here is another example of plain language, from "Isabella" by Leanna Miranda:

One time, when Isabella and Ucella were fifteen years old, they were eating dinner at Isabella's house. Isabella's mother said something smart to her father. He picked up a piece of meat off his plate and threw it at her! . . . They both started throwing food everywhere, even at Ucella, Isabella, and her little brother Bobby without realizing it! Then when they ran out of food to throw, they started fist fighting because of the mess. Ucella . . . wanted her home sweet home and her own parents who never threw anything at each other. Isabella began crying, "Please, don't go and leave me and Bobby here, please, please!" But Ucella really wanted to go, so she said, "Just come over with your brother, it's time for this bullshit to stop!"

We also gave the students as much historical and literary context as we could; some took it all in eagerly, and some ignored much of it. But we asked them to use whatever they could in their own work. Using ideas from Joseph Campbell, we provided the following list of mythic archetypes, with their correlatives in *Gilgamesh*:

The hero as emperor & tyrant	Gilgamesh
The union of opposites	Gilgamesh & Enkidu
The hero as saint/warrior	Enkidu
Temptation & the fall from grace	Enkidu & the prostitute
The road of trials	Humbaba
Crossing the threshold	Gilgamesh becomes afraid
The battle with the beast	Humbaba, Bull of Heaven
The hero's death	Enkidu
Meeting with the goddess	Ishtar & Gilgamesh
The call to the underworld	Gilgamesh & Utnapishtim

Again, we asked the students to consider how the people and events in their own lives or imaginations corresponded to these archetypes. Another excerpt from Stacey Clermont:

Ernest passed a tree in a forest. The tree called his name seductively, "Ernest, Ernest. . . ." The call of the sirens themselves could never have sounded so sweet. So exciting. He continued to walk with a blissful smile, but much more slowly, as if in a trance. "Ernest . . . come to me Ernest . . . come to me . . . come . . . come. . . ." . . . He stopped dead in his tracks when a great breath blew through him. The tree seemed to dance and sway with the sun as it became his dancing partner. Never had Ernest passed this area or heard these delicious sounds. Never had he smelled these scents or brushed and fondled these glorious leaves.

From the time of our first discussions, students began writing drafts of their stories, a little at a time. Some of the early writing assignments were:

• Consider the best stories you have ever read, and tell why you thought they were so good.

• Describe the same event from the perspectives of two people who see it differently.

• Describe the courage or nobility of an "ordinary" person.

• Choose a friend. Describe the feelings you have when you think about that friend. Recall an incident you shared, and write a brief description of it.

• Think of how to relate your story's characters to the list of mythic themes, then chart the characters' development.

For some students, these assignments were enough to get them started; others required a good deal of one-on-one time with us to convince themselves that they did indeed have stories of their own. (One of the great payoffs at the end of the residency was hearing one girl say, "I didn't know I could make a story out of my life!") We divided the classes into teams of four so that the students could read each other their work, thus getting responses from their peers as well as their teachers.

We encouraged those students who were more visual than verbal to begin by drawing. For these students, the chance to draw—and the subsequent dialogue with the teachers—opened up a verbal ability they had not trusted before. These students made masks very much like the hero's shield that depicts his or her exploits. Over a basic drawing of a face— also the shape of a shield—they collaged pictures cut from magazines. We later used these shield-masks as illustrations in our class anthology.

The teachers and I worked intensively one-to-one with the students during the revision and editing process. For the students, writing their own "epics" was a self-motivating lesson in effective diction, narrative structure, and voice, as well as correct syntax and grammar. As their writing improved, the students were often surprised, and became enthusiastic. For many, the idea of working on a piece over and over, revising it until it is right, made sense for the first time.

Nine of our twenty-eight students invented larger-than-life fights or battles with gangs, cops, or supernatural creatures. Seven wrote of heroic responses to common modern emergencies, such as fire, a bad accident, a drug experience, or close encounters with motorized vehicles. The remainder chose to write of everyday events and small heroisms, such as the first day of school, the death of a pet, the loss of a friend, intimations of sexuality or romance, or thoughts of suicide. Several placed their stories in the context of family—about half supportive and half scarily abusive. Few were personal memoirs; most were inventions, ranging from revenge fantasies to perfect love relationships to daredevilry to drug hallucinations. Over a third dealt in some way with drugs, gang violence, or both.

What follows is a series of examples of the students' work, moving from everyday events told in simple language to more epic events and more rarefied language. In "Damien's First Day of School" a kindergarten class is greeted by their new teacher:

"Good morning, everybody. How are you? My name is Robyn Wells. Robyn is my first name and Wells is my last name. Everyone has a first and a last name. Today we are going to go around the room and say our first and last names."

Everyone had to say their name when Robyn went around the room and pointed to them. Of course I was last and I said my whole name, Damien Kareem Hollingsworth.

"Very good, Damien! Damien used his whole name. You must be very smart. Do you know your alphabet?"

I was scared because I only knew a few letters, the ones that my older brothers Donte and David had taught me. I looked up at her and said, "A, B, C, D." I had to stop there. I knew "D" because my name and the names of my brothers all started with D. That's all I knew. . . .

—*Damien Hollingsworth*

The narrator of "This Is My Epic, This Was My Story" is a thirteen-year-old boy who is both discovering his own sexuality and dealing with the teasing of peers, who tell him he "acts gay." The major event of the story is his making friends with a girl named Isis who never wants to go home:

One cold dark day, [as we] were walking . . . I was trying to amuse her, making fun of everyone and everything as I frequently did and still do. She wasn't the captive audience I was used to. I knew something was up. I was about to find out why Isis didn't want to go home.

"Chris, I have to tell you something. I'm afraid you might not want to be my friend anymore, and if anyone at school finds out, I know they'll make me leave and go to another school." Isis kicked at some dirt on the road and didn't look at me as she spoke. I wondered what could be so bad. I tried to make a joke out of it.

"Are you smuggling contraband for the Colombians?" I had seen something about that on *Sixty Minutes*. I thought it would make her laugh but she just got mad.

"You always do that. Every time I try to tell you something important, you think it's funny. Forget it!" She started to walk away.

"Isis, wait. I'm sorry. What is it?" It was starting to rain and neither one of us had an umbrella. We were going to get soaked.

"I have sex with my father. He molests me. There, I said it. I'm a freak, you hate me, and you're going to tell Jessica and then my whole family will know." Well, she was wrong. I didn't think she was a freak, I didn't hate her, and I didn't know who to tell although I knew we had to tell someone. That was why she told me. She wanted my help. I was only thirteen years old, but I knew she trusted me enough to have me help her. Like I knew how.

—*Christopher Ramos*

Responses to modern emergencies are typified by Tiran Antaplian's story of a "young courageous guy," ten-year-old Arshaveer, who shows off to his younger cousin by climbing a tree, from which he falls, breaking his skull, and nearly dies. The surgeons, however, are able to save his life, and later the author visits his friend in the hospital.

> When I walked into the room I didn't recognize him. I got a little scared, for a moment. His head was a horrible, big, black-and-blue mess. I sat next to him and he said, "Hello." His mom was feeding him grapes. This was a day I knew I would never forget in my whole life.
>
> —*Tiran Antaplian*

The dare was another favorite topic. In this example, the fear and suspense are heightened by the sudden change of tense, a sophisticated device in written narrative but one that comes naturally on the street. (Mrs. Winkler and I emphasized that "correctness" in syntax and grammar is relative and depends on purpose and context.)

> So we jumped onto the tracks and started walking, making sure not to slip between the wooden beams and fall into the street where people, buses, cars, and trucks were rushing by, forty feet under our sneakers. When we had almost reached the other side we had to walk over the third rail. Jujo had told us we wouldn't get fried; covering the rail was a wooden piece we could step on without being electrocuted. We were doing fine until suddenly one of my friends stops in front of me, looks down and realizes he is afraid of heights. After a few seconds of being still I take a look to my right and I see the express train coming right at us—my luck, we're on the express track—the train is coming pretty fast and doesn't look like it's going to slow down any time soon. [Jujo returns, pulls the frozen friend off the tracks, and both boys make it to the safety of the platform.] . . . As we stood on the platform waiting for the train to arrive, one of the workers came out and told us that this station was not in service . . . so we had done all that and risked our lives for nothing.
>
> —*Nelson Diaz*

Hallucinations were perhaps the closest our students came to actually living an epic experience. Here is an example:

> The room had a strange glow about it. Kind of luminescent in an odd sorta way. The shapes of the furniture seeming to melt and meld into each other, the colors of the walls leaked onto the carpet as it shifted to and fro. I nodded my head in disbelief, when I suddenly heard something. . . . That something was nothing. . . . The socks in the blue frigidaire quieted their

conversation. . . . But they were always talking about one thing or another, and this fine, chilling evening (remember the fridge?) they had gotten into a strange discussion about G_d. All evening they had rambled on and on about the subject and they had never reached a conclusion. Or maybe they had, but I think they had become bored, because I know I was.

—*Paula Finkel*

A few of the students attempted epics with heroes who overcame larger-than-life monsters and supernatural temptations. Some followed the "classic" epic form and used the epic development we had outlined. For example:

Rade's dreams never ended in victory. It was as though he lived in two separate worlds with no beginning and no ending. Rade didn't know where he was, so he got up, walked out of the hut, and asked the young women carrying gallons of water over their shoulders. . . . A few minutes later, an old man approached him and asked, "Are you a warrior or a renegade?"

"Both," answered Rade, though he preferred to be known as a warrior.

"So, did you hear that in two days you will have to face the monster of the forest? You'll have to travel to the other side of the world."

Rade looked at the man, mystified by words he did not understand. The old man told him not to worry. "Your gypsy girl is your fortune teller. Ask her to tell you. It's your call to adventure."

—*Rajesh Lalloo*

Two students, Brandon Yates and Stacey Clermont, combined these kinds of grand, epic events with contemporary settings and concerns in extremely original ways. Yates's piece, "Soelimnoch" (also see above), concerns the rebellion by Satan's son against his father's power.

[Soelimnoch, whom Satan has sent to bring an earth woman, Anna, to live in hell, has fallen in love with her instead. Soelimnoch defies his father.]

Father, I will not stand for this! She does not belong here!

Who are you to say who belongs here and who doesn't, boy?! Begone or I will have to deal with you!

Never! I am not your servant. Today, you will do as I say. Anna is to be returned to the Earth.

You seek to command me? The surface has really done a number on your perceptions, son! I said begone!

The Lord of All That Is Evil sent a crashing bolt to Soelim's chest, sending the avenging angel reeling in pain. Soelimnoch launched himself back at his father, only to get struck down again, and again. Satan jumped from his throne and landed on Soelim's back, two hundred feet below. Memnoch's son screeched in agony.

> *You will pay for this public betrayal! No son of mine will display free will!*
>
> Blow after blow, Soelim was beaten unmercifully.
>
> *Father . . . it ends now. If Anna must stay dead, then I will give her the ultimate release. I will dismantle this damned place and send all evil crashing down with it, while all of the pure finally make it to heaven.*
>
> *You are bluffing! You wouldn't betray me in such a way, despite how you have before! If you speak those words you threaten to, you have no idea what will occur!*
>
> *I know exactly what will happen . . . Satan.*
>
> Soelim staggered to his feet, bloody and bruised all over his body. A clear, sparkling tear slid down his face. With one huge thrust of his wings, Soelim sent himself speeding towards the sky, then stopped and turned around. He looked down at his father, who was frozen in fear.
>
> *FATHER, I DISOWN YOU AND ALL KNOWLEDGE OF MY PLACE IN THIS REALM. WITHOUT ME, ALL OF THE CREATURES OF EVIL WILL DIE ALONG WITH YOU. YOU CHOSE TO BETRAY GOD AND IN DOING SO BETRAYED YOUR SON, AND ULTIMATELY, YOURSELF. MEMNOCH, MY ONCE BELOVED FATHER . . . I KNOW YOU NOT!*
>
> —*Brandon Yates*

Stacey Clermont combined the classic epic rites of passage with a moving tale of a young girl, Marie-Caramel, and her brother Ernest. The two siblings have a deep and powerful connection. When one day Ernest does not meet his sister, she goes in search of him, directed by a dream to the Forest of Temptation. There she finds

> sweet-smelling flowers and pleasant shades. There were brightly dressed people playing happily. She wondered if this was the place that she was looking for. Marie-Caramel even thought about staying there. The temptation to stay was strong, but she had always been taught that the Forest of Temptation was an evil paradise full of false pleasures. Still it was very enticing for a girl of her tender years.
>
> Temptation has no boundaries and false happiness has no mercy. For those that it claims in its mindless drugged armies, there is no easy escape. Staring into temptation's eye, she refused it and walked away.

Marie-Caramel enters the Cave of the Damned, where she finds "a beautiful woman whose gold, platinum, and precious jewels were the only covering for her luminous body." The temptress is feeding on a glowing sphere, which the girl realizes is her brother's soul. No matter how much she begs for her brother back, the temptress remains silent. Finally she decides to take him herself.

She turned to the body in the corner. She knew she would never be able to carry him. She noticed a peculiar smile on his face. He must like it here, she thought to herself. If he didn't, he could leave. She knew she must leave before the forest consumed her.

. . . When she arrived home, she climbed into her room with the realization that her brother was now out of her reach. He had chosen to go there. Once he is ready, she will help him get his life back together.

Born on the day of Kings, Marie-Caramel was the youngest and only female child of her mother. Her brother Ernest was the first to see her born and he held her up to proclaim his only sister.

She hoped he would remember.

—*Stacey Clermont*

From the simplest of childhood experiences to such moving discoveries of the limits of life and love, from the discovery of friendship to confrontations between son and father, our students found the epic in their own lives by looking at one of the world's oldest pieces of literature with their own up-to-the-minute eyes.

Bibliography

Gilgamesh: A Verse Narrative. Translated by Herbert Mason. New York: New American Library, 1970.

Terry Blackhawk

Greek Boy Got His Wings

Using Greek Myths to Stimulate Student Poems

*I am quite naturally drawn to a myth in which
life and death meet face to face.*—Jean Cocteau

EVER SINCE CHILDHOOD, I've been attracted to the Greek myths, a
lifelong fascination which has led me, as both a classroom teacher and
a poetry workshop leader, to try to make these stories come alive for
teenagers. The myths—with their timeless themes of journey and heroism, loyalty and passion, ambition and betrayal—give us vivid images to
explore and offer voices or masks from which to speak. Their sensuous
imagery and mystery continue to shed light on what it means to be
human. Who can forget the warm drop of oil falling from Psyche's lamp
onto sleeping Cupid's arm? Ariadne's golden thread winding through the
labyrinth? Leda in the grip of the swan, or trees swaying to the rhythm
of Orpheus's lyre? And what young person could not imagine the exhil-
aration of Phaethon's horses tugging on their reins? These images, if we
let them enter our reverie and become translated through our senses, can
become powerful sources for writing. When I ask students to write from
figures in Greek mythology, my goal is to find ways for myth and personal experience to combine, so that students can imaginatively refigure
both the ancient tale and their own lives.

One way to do this is to introduce Greek mythology through film,
visual art, and poems. I take students to the Detroit Institute of Arts,
where they can see a Leda and a maenad within just a few feet of one
another, or, in another gallery, Aristaeus, the Pan figure in the Orpheus
myth from whom Eurydice was fleeing when she met her death. You
don't have to look far into European art to find figures from Greek
mythology. If you don't live near a museum, bring in postcards or art
books with color reproductions. Bullfinch's *Illustrated Mythology* is a
great resource. I also use Edith Hamilton's *Mythology*, selections from
Ovid's *Metamorphoses*, and a collection of contemporary poems that

can make ancient themes come wonderfully alive. These include Hilda Doolittle's "At Ithaca," Katha Pollitt's "Penelope Writes," Stephen Dobyns's "Odysseus's Homecoming," Margaret Atwood's "Circe: Mud Poems," and Linda Pastan's "On Rereading *The Odyssey* in Middle Age"—all contemporary takes on Homer. A ninth grade McDougall, Littell literature anthology presents the myth of Daedalus, retold by Bernard Evslin, along with a reproduction of Pieter Breugel's painting *The Fall of Icarus.* I've supplemented these with modern poems such as W. H. Auden's "Musée des Beaux Arts," Anne Sexton's sonnet "To a Friend Whose Work Has Come to Triumph," and Robert Hayden's "O Daedalus, Fly Away Home." Rita Dove's *Mother Love* recasts the Persephone myth into a rich collection of mother/daughter poems, with both contemporary and mythical settings.

As a classroom teacher, I've used the Greek myths to stimulate word study (requiring students to learn the meanings of *labyrinthine, halcyon, tantalize, herculean, panic,* and *lyric,* and their connections to Greek mythology), reflective writing, formal essays, discussion groups, and class presentations. Myth study can be lots of fun. It may, on occasion, result in pleasant personal surprises for the teacher: one student's treatment of the Persephone myth, for example, cast me as the goddess Demeter rescuing its author from the death of inspiration, a bleak, imageless underworld where she'd been seduced by Hades, a.k.a. "Writer's Block Harry." A highlight from one ninth grade class included an Oprah-style talk show that featured Orpheus (dressed as quite the dude, in a bright yellow suit carrying a guitar) confronting the Maenads, and an intricate board game in which the winner was first to arrive at the Elysian Fields. The game included such pitfalls as the River Styx and a square labeled "Medusa's Lair: You are turned to stone. Lose one turn."

Another way to enliven the Greek myths is to use storytelling. The telling of a tale is a shared communal experience, a living act, that honors the oral tradition and builds common ground in the classroom. Telling a story is itself an act of imagination. When I tell a story, I somehow enter the world of that story. When students listen, they do the same thing: they create the world of the story for themselves. We may all hear the same words when Orpheus crosses the river into the underworld, but each one of us imagines his or her own river. Because myths are so rich, students will find different scenes, characters, or images that resonate for them.

One summer my fascination with myth and story led me to enroll in a workshop with Laura Simms at the Wellspring Institute in Mendocino, California. Laura, a master storyteller, helped us develop oral presentations of ancient tales and myths. We worked these stories through mime, meditation, and writing. We created theatrical tableaux based on our stories' characters; we researched the symbolism of plants and animals in our tales; we created maps and took others on a tour of our story's landscape; we told our stories to rocks, plants, and trees. These exercises were designed to help us achieve that capacity of the teller to "see" the story, a kind of imaginative staging through which the story comes alive for its listeners.

On our first night, Laura asked us to recall a memory from early childhood and to tell that memory to a small circle of people. The exercise appeared simple, yet each childhood memory seemed uncannily—and unconsciously—connected to the main story the participant was working on. One woman—who had chosen an Icelandic tale about a woman who had been a seal returning to the sea and leaving her human children behind—recalled a large, black stuffed animal that had been a source of childhood comfort after her mother died. A man, whose story was about a father leaving home to seek a fortune, told about his own father returning after a long absence. I had selected Orpheus as my story because I was intrigued by the figure of Orpheus as poet. The childhood memory I told was about stealing flowers from a neighbor's yard on the way home from kindergarten, then trying to plant them with a spoon in rock-hard ground. The flowers were tulips, so it must have been the first spring after the first winter I'd experienced. (We had just moved from California to Massachusetts.) To me, this memory has come to suggest Orpheus's journey to the underworld to recapture someone or something loved and lost.

This exercise helped me understand firsthand the connections that can occur between myth and personal experience. It also reminded me of how storytellers often say that their stories "choose them." It is these psychological, or perhaps pre-logical, dimensions of myth that I value most when using mythology as a source for poetry and imaginative writing. If anyone doubts that mythology can connect directly to a teenager's everyday reality, consider Justin's poem:

Grades

Like Medusa's hair
Grades are the sneakiest, crawliest
And only thing wrapped around my head.
I wish I had the shield of Perseus
To protect me from the breath of those teachers
The sword
To slice through F's and D's
Or the helmet
To make me invisible
From those annoying, fast-talking kids.
When an assignment is due
For some creepy reason
Something happens. Those questions.
Each one is a snake coming to attack.
How long does it have to be
    does it have to be typed
        what if I turn it in late
            yes, mama, I finished my homework
take that out of your mouth, that's my homework
    can I see that work from last night
        can someone turn on a light for this stupid boy
           I wish this bus would stop going over so many
bumps
I wish I had wings like Perseus
So I could get out of here.

   —Justin Adams

I am fond of the voice in this poem, and the way the poem takes off toward the end in its crescendo of sneaky, snake-like lines—a deliberate typographical choice. It seemed to me that the poem was a breakthrough for Justin. The Perseus myth gave him a vehicle to tackle a sensitive subject with energy and humor. Without the Medusa figure, I doubt if a poem about poor grades would have worked as well.

Justin's poem shows how images from myths can express experience in unexpected ways. The Orpheus tale also consistently leads to poignant student writing. One year, we began our myth study by reading excerpts from Edith Hamilton's *Mythology*. We also viewed the film *Black Orpheus* and discussed its symbols of love and death. Students were especially fascinated with the spiral staircase, the "underworld" voodoo scene with churchgoers speaking in tongues, and the Maenads presented as jealous "home girls." Soon after, as if on cue, a Detroit Institute of Arts film series screened Cocteau's *Orphée*. I took a group of students and asked them to jot down powerful or evocative scenes or lines of conversation. This film was no small cross-cultural stretch for my urban students—surrealism *and* subtitles!—but they seemed to enjoy the experience. They compiled a collection of images and phrases, which I typed up and gave them as a handout, adding some tips for working the lines into their own poems:

signing a statement as proof of love
a misty night
Death watching you as you sleep
messages you can't understand
Death will love you too much
a hand dipped in mercury
a map leading nowhere
shards of mirrored glass
Death in her upswept hair
a train crosses in front of you
judges sit in a panel before you
a hand reaching through a mirror
descending a spiral staircase
a breeze blowing through a room

Many of these phrases create elusive, mysterious effects in and of themselves. I am fascinated by the way a phrase, image, or single word can generate meaning, and I often use lists of lines or single words to trigger students' thinking. In this instance, the Orpheus story prompted several students to write poems about loved ones who had died. Some of the items from our list found their way, with interesting variations, into those poems.

Daddy

I reached to touch you, Daddy,
trying to remember a message
I couldn't understand.
I walked and walked
but I could not reach you.
I ran to catch up
but a train crossed between us
and when it had finally passed
you had disappeared into
the dark, misty night.

I searched and searched knowing
I would never see you again.
Just in my memory.
Just in my memory—your hazel
eyes, your funny walk with
your head bouncing from side
to side, your words of comfort
breezing through my still
attentive ears.

　　—*Rosalind Tarver*

Orpheus Variations

1. Father
Upon white satin and lace
he lies motionless.
His black, wavy hair and
thin moustache complement
the pale, cold skin.
Pinstripes travel vertically
down the navy blue suit
like roads on a map
leading nowhere now.
The glint of a thin, gold
pin accents the lapel.
A cherry-red rose
where the heart once lived.

2. Ghost
A cool breeze flows through
what used to be your bedroom.
Three white hooded images
approach my bedside.
I know it's you.
A masculine hand grasps
the crown of my head,
keeping me still.
The hand is yours.
Your voice whispers
that everything's okay
but angels hum like a church
choir and my scream for help
goes mute as suddenly
you disappear.

3. Juanita
I step through a mirror
extending my hand to you.
I'm here to rescue you
from the unliving.
You mustn't stay long
or death will love you
too much.
Let our joyous emotions
guide us. Let
shattered shards of mirrored
glass mark our presence
and reflect our descent down
the white spiral staircase.
Welcome home, Juanita.

—*NaShawn Reed*

On a recent museum visit, I told the Orpheus tale to a group of students as we stopped to consider an Italian Renaissance chest featuring inlays of animals surrounding Orpheus with his lyre. As I told the story, I could see the students' eyes become glassy and focused far away, in the manner of much younger children who listen with wide eyes and mouths slightly agape—a sure sign that they are "in" the tale, the imaginative space they create as they listen. Later that day, Jerome turned to the Orpheus myth to write about one of his favorite themes, love for an idealized and unattainable female. Much to his (and my) delight, the poem was selected for the museum's annual student *Writing about Art* booklet, and its first line was chosen as the anthology's title.

Orpheus

My poetry is music
Mourning the loss
Of her face,
Her pearl pink laugh,
Her feathered touch
That mimicked the breeze.

Her voice
Is in every strum
Of my lyre.

I play my song
Soothing

Bringing peace,
Tears
To dazzling eyes
That hurt
With whispers
Of what could be.

On my lips
Remains the hum
Of her song
As I ignore
The rocks
And stretch
My heart
To meet hers
In eternity.

  —*Jerome Williams II*

Another student wrote from the perspective of Hades:

Hades Speaks to Orpheus

Eurydice of the serpent's wrath
descends to lower airs
tastes the golden coin
dropped, dropped as a token
while her funeral pyre
soots the sky into bleak clouds.
My collection of riches,
metals and gems
glitter with fire
but cold they are
in this heated dark.
A box of death, a globe of life
form drops of faded memory
in my abode
the shatter of iron tears
that fall to sulfur pools
when the dream of music
plays with my ears.
Orpheus slivers through
opposite lands to implore
for his wife, so one becomes two
embrace, embrace, embrace
the virgin lyre so I can hear

the sweet mint plucks
that glide from one to another
before the taste casts off
into rivers of desolation
lands of air
that can never be reached

obey, obey, obey
may the dance of the trees
whisk your wife away.

—*Wayne Ng*

Wayne's and Jerome's pieces illustrate how myths or legends can inspire persona poems, in which a myth becomes a mask to speak through. The following poem by Margaret Atwood is a perennial favorite, and a fine model to use when asking students to develop a voice from a myth.

Siren Song

This is the one song everyone
would like to learn: the song
that is irresistible:

the song that forces men
to leap overboard in squadrons
even though they see the beached skulls

the song nobody knows
because anyone who has heard it
is dead, and the others can't remember.

Shall I tell you the secret
and if I do, will you get me
out of this bird suit?

I don't enjoy it here
squatting on this island
looking picturesque and mythical

with these two feathery maniacs,
I don't enjoy singing
this trio, fatal and valuable.

I will tell the secret to you,

to you, only to you.
Come closer. This song

is a cry for help: Help me!
Only you, only you can,
you are unique

at last. Alas
it is a boring song
but it works every time.

Other ways to experiment with persona and voice include retelling a myth as if it were the hottest gossip you'd ever heard or telling it from the point of view of an inanimate object in the story, a minor character or an imagined character such as William Matthews's "Homer's Seeing Eye Dog." I've also enjoyed having students take a "myth walk" (adapted from Laura's exercises) in which they walk through the hallways or school grounds in pairs, taking turns telling their myths to their partner, either as straightforward narration or in the voice of a character from the tale. A walk like this is easy to structure. Give the first teller ten minutes to tell his or her story on the way out, the second teller ten minutes to tell one on the way back. The experience of telling while walking can lead to new, almost unconscious, discoveries as students present the myth in a relaxed, informal way.

I will often start my writing workshops based on the Greek myths by asking students what they know about a particular myth (usually more than they think). I ask them to jot down or volunteer elements of the story (images, objects, emotions), which I then write on the board as a source list for writing. I may present contemporary poems on mythological themes and ask students how *they* might bring the myth up to date. Or I may begin with a storytelling session, encouraging students to pay close attention to the mental pictures that come to them as they hear the story. Sometimes we'll discuss these pictures. I'll have them describe the scenes they see or feel most vividly. I may draw a directional compass on the board and ask them to share the different "maps" they've imagined, or ask them to give directions through their vision of the story. Does the huntsman turn left or right into the forest? Does the cottage face the rising or the setting sun? Other times, I'll simply wait a few moments for the spell of the story to recede before asking them to begin writing.

Recently, while conducting a poetry workshop at the Michigan Youth Arts Festival, I tried another approach. I had been spending some time thinking and writing about Icarus and Daedalus, and I wanted to see how that myth might inspire these talented students, whose poetry had won them an invitation to the annual festival. Since the labyrinth is such a dominant part of the story, I decided to start there.

Icarus's flight is an escape from both the imprisonment of the labyrinth and the societal shame and punishment related to the birth of the Minotaur. Initially, though, I did not mention this—I wanted the students to write without knowing where we were going. I asked them to start by freewriting on the idea of hiding. What kinds of things do we hide—stories, treasures, things we are ashamed of? Where do we hide? From whom do we hide? Is hiding pleasurable? What is it like to be discovered in hiding? Why do we feel the need to hide? After fifteen minutes or so of intense writing, I asked students to volunteer to read. One student had written of his father hiding his love from him. Others had written of hiding places, secrets, and the like.

Then I asked them to freewrite again, this time on the idea of flight. I asked them to imagine the physical sensation of flight and think of as many bodily details as they could. The kinesthetic capacity of words is often overlooked, I think, when we ask students to use the five senses in their writing; movement and action surely constitute a sixth sense. One student, whose poem follows, came up with the idea of backbones turning into wings. Others explored the feeling of flight, how skin or hair might flap in the air, and what to do with one's arms.

At this point, I introduced the Daedalus and Icarus myth. Many students knew parts of it, and were able to add details as we went along. I read several poems related to the myth, including a recent poem of my own in which I imagine Icarus taking off ahead of his father, seeking the warmth and light of the sun (as contrasted with the gloom of the labyrinth) on a bright and very cold day. We spent quite a bit of time discussing the story. The girls in particular were fascinated by Pasiphae, mother of the Minotaur, whose lust for the bull was actually a punishment inflicted on her husband by the god Poseidon. We also considered what we could learn from Icarus's failure to heed his father's advice, and what it meant that Daedalus survived the tale and moved on into yet another story.

Then I asked them to check back over their freewrites about hiding and flight and to look for images or lines that might fit into or trigger a poem about Icarus. I suggested that they either retell the myth or use it to shed light on a personal experience. I added that they might want either to address their poems to Icarus or to write in the voice of Icarus. (As always, I gave them the option of writing about something else if they chose.) They wrote, intensely, for nearly half an hour, then we shared their pieces. One of my favorite first lines was "Greek boy got his wings." Some students chose to write in the voice of Icarus. One developed a childhood memory of attempting to fly from the roof of her garage. Eluehue—influenced by rap—set Icarus's voice to a playful music, in which this adult reader can't help hearing echoes of bossa nova, Smokey Robinson, and Charlie Parker:

Sun Kite Falling

(once)
I get fly
tango music and
maraca cha-cha-cha
I bumble up in
my be-bop
scat a lil higher
fire fire and desire
cause I've got sunshine

(twice)
I get so high and so close that I
blind the sun with my smile. I take
handfuls of sun pulp to eat and savor.
I bathe and breathe in the sun,
mango wine and kissing shine
eat and smile and lather
my sunfruit and summerwater.
I am purged in it, yellow liquor-fire,
gold skin and teeth
lungs and laugh dissolve to
thinness and the sun births me
sun spit I fall smiling.

  —*Eluehue Crudup II*

Lauren's Icarus was much darker, unable to shake the labyrinth:

Icarus's Destination

The labyrinth winds its way to a slow
strangle around my heart.
I know what it means to angle upward
and no longer be shackled by a mason's work.
No more tangle in meaningless conversations
with an uninterested beast.
I am not a canary, putrid yellow, sunk deep in my feathers.
When those wings were strapped upon my aching shoulders
I lost every ounce of anger in my insect soul.
I wanted to stretch my arms into the sun's welcome blaze
and bring my finger to her lips, the heat so necessary.
But these wings could not take me there.
Destination slips coolly as I proceed downward.
Arms extend toward father's face.
Waves engulf me with a bitterfrost glass glare.

    —*Lauren Fardig*

Other students connected the myth with personal experience or family story:

My grandmother told me once that our
backbones are wings, more
than useless bone under paper flesh.
Some day they will grow, she said.
They will rip your mortal t-shirt
and bend your child-back.

I wonder what Icarus knew about backbones.
If he had lain quiet
on his back on the cool labyrinth
floor, he may have felt them, hard
against the grey. His silent
life was burdened by the threat of walls
around him, sky above and ground below.

Daedalus had a mind of steel:
creator of cages and places to hide away.
He kept his son cupped in the palm
of shame. Icarus yielded to the curve
of his father's hand, expected no escape.

Daedalus aimed for wings of wax.
"The sun is on our side," he thought.

"The sun is like an India rubber ball,
and I can toss it far into the sky."

   —*Meghan Van Leuwen*

The Sun Is Lit from Behind by a Wax Candle

Was it 1929 or 1931
when your great-uncle
that Butch Cassidy type
jumped from the sixteenth
story of a Chicago building
above ancient gridiron train bridges
because he knew
that the eastern express would come
knock him flat,
v-shaped,
before he could even
attempt the great Icarus mirror trick of long ago:
flying with skin flapping loosely,
bald head lapping up the sound waves,
the breath of papery wax feathers landing sweetly on his neck,
ground hitting him like the thunderclap of truth,
his feet cut in two,
his money lost flat,
twinkling like constellations below the
trackstrackstracks,

easy clickings underfoot.

   —*Stacey Tiderington*

As these poems show, the enduring imaginative legacy of the Greek myths is something students can explore with personal revelation and aesthetic delight.

Bibliography

Atwood, Margaret. *Selected Poems: 1965–1975*. Boston: Houghton Mifflin, 1976.

Auden, W. H. *Collected Poems*. New York: Vintage, 1991.

Cocteau, Jean. *Cocteau on the Film: A Conversation Recorded by André Fraigneau*. London, England: Dennis Dobson, 1954.

Dobyns, Stephen. *Cemetery Nights*. New York: Penguin, 1987.

Doolittle, Hilda (H. D.). *Collected Poems.* New York: New Directions, 1983.

Dove, Rita. *Mother Love.* New York: Norton, 1995.

Evslin, Bernard. *McDougal, Littell Literature, Orange Level.* Julie West Johnson and Margaret Grauff Forst, editors. Evanston, Illinois: McDougal, Littell, 1995.

Graves, Robert. *The Greek Myths.* London, England: Penguin, 1992.

Hamilton, Edith. *Mythology.* New York: Penguin USA, 1969.

Hayden, Robert. *Selected Poems.* New York: October House, 1966.

Matthews, William. *Selected Poems & Translations, 1969–1991.* Boston: Houghton Mifflin, 1992.

Ovid. *The Metamorphoses.* Translated by Horace Gregory. New York: Viking, 1958.

Pastan, Linda. *The Imperfect Paradise.* New York: Norton, 1988.

Pollitt, Katha. *Antarctic Traveller.* New York: Knopf, 1983.

Sexton, Anne. *All My Pretty Ones.* Boston: Houghton Mifflin, 1961.

Dale Davis

Sing in Me, Muse

Using Ancient Greek Poetry

Take me all over.
There is no place.
I live all over.

—Teresa M.

"WHERE ARE THE CLASSICS in school today?" James Laughlin, the poet who founded New Directions Publishing Corporation, asked me a few years ago. "Why don't you take Homer in, and try *The Odyssey* in elementary school?" was the suggestion of this writer who kept in print the work of writers such as H. D., Federico García Lorca, Ezra Pound, Kenneth Rexroth, and William Carlos Williams, along with the work of Robert Duncan, Nicanor Parra, and Octavio Paz.

A few months later, as a writer-in-residence with the New York State Literary Center, I found a home for *The Odyssey*. The Craig Hill Elementary School, in Greece, New York, enabled me to combine Ancient Greek literature in English translation (as the inspiration for student writing) with the school's prescribed social studies curriculum on Ancient Greece, in a two-day-a-week, two-month residency with three sixth grade classes. The usual language arts, reading, and social studies periods were set aside for my work.

The goal of the residency, named GREECE/GREECE/GREECE, was for the teachers and students to come to feel Ancient Greece through its poets. The culmination of the residency was to be the participation of Robert Fitzgerald, Professor of Rhetoric and Oratory at Harvard, and translator of *The Iliad* and *The Odyssey*.

I began my own preparation for the residency by reading Kenneth Rexroth's *Classics Revisited*. What I responded to, whatever excited me most in Rexroth's book, I typed, page after page, to share with the teachers.

After Rexroth I revisited Jane Ellen Harrison's *Mythology*, and again I selected passages for the teachers. I also spent time with C. Kerényi's

The Gods of the Greeks and *The Heroes of the Greeks*. A postcard from Robert Fitzgerald added C. M. Bowra's *Homer* to my reading list.

The residency unofficially began in November with three study sessions with the sixth grade teachers, who supportively and energetically attended after school. The first session consisted of the many pages of what I had typed from my background reading, presented for the sheer enjoyment of reading, as reading, not to categorize or to classify, but to provide a personal "map" of where I had been. I encouraged everyone to record their thoughts and questions in response to the material, and to begin to chart their own maps. I asked the teachers to begin discussing with their students all the cultures the students had studied since they had been in school and to ask how the cultures were alike and how they were different, and why cultures were studied in school. I also suggested that the discussion involve what the students had read from those cultures.

We were without Ancient Greek. Robert Fitzgerald had suggested C. M. Bowra's *Homer* "for the Greekless." The second teacher study-session focused on how Ancient Greek literature was going to be presented in the residency. I handed out three translations of Meleager's "Heliodora" from *The Greek Anthology*, by Dudley Fitts, W. R. Paton, and H. D., along with these two comments on translation:

> And finally, I have not really undertaken translation at all—translation, that is to say, as it is understood in the schools. I have simply tried to restate in my own idiom what the Greek verses have meant to me. The disadvantages of this method are obvious: it has involved cutting, altering, expansion, revision—in short, all the devices of free paraphrase.
>
> In general, my purpose has been to compose first of all, and as simply as possible, an English poem.
>
> —*Dudley Fitts*, One Hundred Poems from the Palatine Anthology

> Since these are "old Chinese poems," dating from the second to the twelfth century, should not this oldness be somehow suggested in the translation? My answer to this is an emphatic no! Their oldness is no more than historical accident; all were unquestionably new when they were written. *The Greek Anthology* is even older and embraces a longer time span, yet no reputable modern translator that I am aware of makes any attempt to suggest this fret in his translation. The good translator, it seems to me, no matter how he may project himself back into time in order to understand the ideas and sentiments of his author, must, when it comes to getting the

words over into another language, proceed as though he himself were the author, writing the work afresh today.

　—*Burton Watson,* Chinese Lyricism

Our introduction to the literature of Ancient Greece would be, by necessity, through the critical rendering of an appreciation by a translator.

During the third teacher study-session we went over the material gathered together by the teachers for the residency: books and maps of Ancient Greece borrowed from every known location in the school district, ready for whoever wished to go further than what was presented in class. Copies of Robert Fitzgerald's *Spring Shade, Poems 1931–1970* and his translation of *The Odyssey* soon arrived. The classroom residency officially began in January, with eight poems by Sappho, translated by Mary Barnard, Willis Barnstone, Guy Davenport, H. D., Richmond Lattimore, Kenneth Rexroth, and J. Addington Symonds, typed, photocopied, and passed out to each student.

During these first sessions on Sappho I read aloud the English translations of the eight poems. I asked the students to think of questions such as: What is it like to want something, have it right in front of you, and not be able to touch it? What is it like when you want to do and not do something at the same time? What is it like to lie awake alone at night? I asked the students either to describe the effect of Sappho's poems on them, or to write directly to her.

Sappho Talks

Sappho's poems are lilies
that speak with their heart.
　—*Kelly H.*

Sappho lets me know who she is.
She is holy.
　—*Randy P.*

To Sappho

It is I who needs,
who grabs for what is not,
that feeling of feeling
that flows through my heart making holes,

the dream inside the dream.
I am so close I can touch
the wind of my dream,
the speech of nothing.

It chases me.
It knows. It knows
I need the place that is not there
the place that sleeps beneath my body
past the deep where I come from,
the land of the feeling which is not known.

Time passes itself,
sleep of the same world
that has no body.

    —Denise Z.

To Sappho
The gift of a translator is the poems
he uncovers.

    —Renée K.

I then asked the students to select their favorite translations of each of the eight poems. Class discussion, in each subsequent session, focused upon how the translations differed, and how, through the choice and arrangement of words, translators arrived at their English versions of the poem.

Class discussion on Sappho led Michele and Traci to place their own work beside Mary Barnard's, Willis Barnstone's, Guy Davenport's, and H. D.'s translations of the very same poem.

A TEST OF TRANSLATION: SAPPHO

69

This way, that way

I do not know what to do: I
am of two minds.

    —Mary Barnard

Shall I?

I do not know what to do:
I say yes—and then no.

> —*Willis Barnstone*

I don't know which way I'm running.
My mind is part this way, part that.

> —*Guy Davenport*

I know not what to do:
my mind is divided.

> —*H. D.*

I rip myself in half:
my mind is another me.

> —*Michele*

Running
Running away from myself
I am not quite sure which way

> —*Traci*

Following the classroom sessions on Sappho, I introduced the students to *The Greek Anthology*. We read poems by Meleager, Nossis, and Plato in English translations by M. S. Buck, H. D., Dudley Fitts, I. W. Mackail, and W. R. Paton. (I also distributed copies of the poems in Greek so that the students could see the shape of the poems in the original language.)

I asked the students to think about questions that come out of the poems: What is it like to live where you live? How can you hold on to something you cannot place in your hand? What is the one "country" we are all alive in? As with Sappho, I also asked the students to focus upon how the translations differed, and to note how the individual translators arrived at their English versions of the poem. Our discussion focused on the choice of verbs and adjectives, how the tone of the poem is set by the translator, and the decisions a translator must make.

Before leaving *The Greek Anthology* I asked the students to write about what it meant to them.

The Greek Anthology
for Dudley Fitts

Your gift is the life of the words.
The poems tug like shining stars
in my mind,
life while I grow.

> —*Chris S.*

The Greek Anthology

There is a solemn rose I share
with all who can see.

> —*Fran P.*

The Greek Anthology

Minds beyond the world
I hold you
reminding myself
I want more.

> —*Julie W.*

I hold on with my dreams
going down my spine
and back up.
That name is that name is that name.

> —*Benny S.*

The poet knows the world
by the clock that gives time by thought,
by the fish that dreams to walk.

> —*Fran P.*

Song

Look, the empty-hearted fall noplace.
Down nothing meets nothing
Connecting God to nowhere.
Words strung begin a Metaphor,
A place of a blank someone
Like mysteries of ground, hot burning
Ill of summer snow
Knowing a shapeless horse galloping noplace,

Thinking Muse.
Everywhere half feelings
Turn outside, the flower of nobody worlds.
Like the spring air H. D. is my body
Thinking a dream inside tomorrow.

   —*Gino V.*

In the beginning of the second month of the residency, I held another study-session with the teachers: time to catch our breath, to chart where we had been, and to lay the final groundwork for *The Odyssey*. The Postscript to Robert Fitzgerald's translation was to be our guide through *The Odyssey*:

> If the world was given to us to explore and master, here is a tale, a play, a song about that endeavor long ago, by no means neglecting self-mastery, which in a sense is the whole point.

I used the game of Gossip to introduce Homer's authorship of *The Odyssey*. Since neither Homer nor his audience were readers, Homer spoke *The Odyssey*, and his audience heard it. I wrote two lines on a piece of paper, and then whispered the same two lines into the ear of a student. That student whispered what he or she heard into the ear of the next student, and so on, student to student, up and down the rows. We compared the two lines said aloud by the last student with the two lines I had written down; the difference was tremendous.

Next, I wrote two lines in iambic pentameter on a piece of paper, and whispered the same two lines into the ear of one of the students. We followed the same procedure with the last student saying aloud the two lines which he or she heard. There was very little difference between the two lines said aloud by the last student and the two lines I had written down.

I used Gossip to show how, in Milman Parry's words, "Homeric lines were constructed out of metrical formulas." I mentioned Albert Lord's work calling attention to the "phonological context," the formulas available in the memory, such as the alliterative and voweling pattern, used by the storyteller or singer, and the extent to which a formula determines invention.

The students and the teachers were now aware that it was unlikely that Homer himself wrote *The Odyssey* down, and that our reading was due to "a sedentary labor, or joy, sustained at a work table" by Robert

Fitzgerald, the poet, the translator, the reader who was giving us Homer. I introduced Homer with an anonymous poem from *The Greek Anthology* translated by W. R. Paton:

> Of what country shall we record Homer to be a citizen, the man to whom all cities reach out their hands? Is it not the truth that this is unknown, but the hero, like an immortal, left as a heritage to the Muses the secret of his country and race?

I focused my *Odyssey* classroom work on Book One ("A Goddess Intervenes"), Book Two ("A Hero's Son Awakens"), Book Five ("Sweet Nymph and Open Sea"), Book Six ("The Princess at the River"), Book Seven ("Gardens and Firelight"), Book Nine ("New Coasts and Poseidon's Son"), Book Ten ("The Grace of the Witch"), and Book Eleven ("A Gathering of Shades"). The librarian and the music teacher (who emphasized the role of a stringed instrument in the development of a story) also read *The Odyssey* aloud to the students, as did the classroom teachers during the Reading and Social Studies periods.

During my classroom sessions I questioned the students about listening, about looking, about the home of their own imaginations—what it looks like there. I discussed the Greek word *metaphor*, "to move from one place to another," and then questioned the students about a journey to the home of their imaginations, asking where they might stop en route for a rest, and who would ask them to stay there instead of continuing on their journey. We talked about metaphor as a way of seeing, a way in which everything becomes, and everything is, something else.

*   *   *

I introduced Robert Fitzgerald through his own poetry:

Phrase

Sorrowful love passes from transparencies
to transparencies of bitter starlight
between antiquities and antiquities so simply

as in evening a soft bird flies down
and rests on a white railing under leaves

Love things in this quietness of falling
leaves birds or rain from the hushes
of summer clouds through luminous centuries

Touch unconsolable love the hands of your ancestors

Robert Fitzgerald walked into the Craig Hill Elementary School carrying his green Harvard bookbag over his shoulder. His first words to the classes were, "A message from the heart is in all poetry. Poetry reproduces the speech of the heart, which, after all, must matter." We were the students of this poet who brought *sacred* to the meaning of the word *teacher*.

He began with Sappho, read her Pleiades poem to us in Greek, and wrote it in Greek on the board. Fitzgerald proceeded with the assumption that, Greekless or not, we were with him. He wrote the English equivalent directly underneath the Greek and then asked everyone to take out the eight poems by Sappho in the different translations. He then read aloud several English translations of the Pleiades poem:

The moon has set, and the Pleiades.
It is the middle of the night,
Hour follows hour. I lie alone.

   —Guy Davenport

Tonight I've watched

The moon and then
the Pleiades
go down

The night is now
half-gone; youth
goes. I am

in bed alone.

   —Mary Barnard

Alone

The moon and the Pleiades
are set. Midnight,
and time spins away.
I lie in bed, alone.

   —Willis Barnstone

The moon has set,
and the Pleiades.
It is Midnight.
Time passes.
I sleep alone.

    —Kenneth Rexroth

He spoke of what was happening in the poem: "Night was going on, the stars and the moon were going down, time passes, I lie alone," and added, "When even those companions, the moon and the Pleiades go down, I am all alone. The loneliness is intensified."

He read the poem in Greek again, slowly giving the rhythm, the beat. Then he went back to the board and wrote:

The westering moon has gone
With Pleiades down the sky.
Midnight. And time goes by.
And I lie here alone.

    —Robert Fitzgerald

I had mailed Robert Fitzgerald all the material I had prepared before and during the residency: my preparatory reading, the material on Sappho, *The Greek Anthology*, and *The Odyssey*, and copies of the students' writing. He used the material as points of reference with the three classes. At one point, he suddenly stopped one class and stated:

You've shone as the morning star among the living,
Now you are dead, you shine as the evening star among the dead.

Then he added, "Some Plato in the air for you."

At another point he introduced the elegiac couplet of *The Greek Anthology*, using an original composition, the first line by himself, the second line by Vladimir Nabokov:

No one has ever seen Cynthia flustered or drunk or befuddled
Cynthia prim and polite, Cynthia hard to outwit.

Asked by a student how he became interested in Greek, he replied that it had been when his sixth grade teacher wrote two Greek words on the blackboard. The Greek words, in English, meant "horse river," or "river horse," the English equivalent of "hippopotamus":

Ἵ η πιϊ   Πότᾳμος
HIPPOs   POTAMOS
HORSE   RIVER

—Notes taken in class by Benny S.

Fitzgerald spoke of the opening sounds of *The Odyssey* in Greek: "We can hear faintly underneath the sound of sea water slapping under the ship's hull, quite a splendid set of noises." He concluded each class by reading aloud from *The Odyssey*, Book One, in Greek.

*   *   *

When I came back for the last day of GREECE/GREECE/GREECE, one week after Robert Fitzgerald's visit, I did not have to give a writing assignment. When I walked into each classroom, the students began writing:

Homer
for Robert Fitzgerald

Homer's song is Ancient Greece
unraveled in a poem.
The color of the words
is life
piercing.

   —Chris S.

Dreams of Homer
for Robert Fitzgerald

Pieces and bits of *The Odyssey*
spin into dreams.
I imagine Homer.
My dreams tell me
I know this tiny light
shining in, Homer
breaking through to see me.

   —Tracey M.

Robert Fitzgerald

I throw my body up seeing what it is like
to be a bird,

soaring so high I can touch the sky.
Homer's song can only be sung by the birds,
but I can sing that special song
in my dreams. I hear that song tingling,
I hear Greek in my own words.

    —*Jason R.*

Cynthia

Talking, his hand walking
back, forth, his eyes sparkle.
A perfect yellow tulip
takes the chalk, writes "flustered,"
politely.
No one ever thanked Cynthia.

    —*Gino V.*

How
for Robert Fitzgerald

Cynthia is a word I remember, and the word Pleiades.
Greek is a land of air tunnels
that holds dreams.
To learn Greek is to learn
a poem is a word
that tells what it wants to tell,
that gives a taste of what can't be tasted.

    —*Mike D.*

Image
for Robert Fitzgerald

I look at my paper.
You look at the blackboard,
empty, lonely, blank, alone.
Are you listening? Do you hear?
You, Robert Fitzgerald, drowning
in poetry,
Do you believe in love?
Do you love? You, teacher of teachers, poem of poems,
Stuck in a world that nobody else knows, alone,
A melody of words, singing with your heart,
You, the only tree on that land,
Sailing on that lake alone, thinking,

"Will I live forever, do I want to?"

You are the circle of life,
You, dreamer.

—*Michele M.*

GREECE/GREECE/GREECE was the combination of a reading list,
teachers who were willing to risk total immersion with their own interest and time, serious research for each classroom presentation, a visit
from Robert Fitzgerald, and a poet who designed and carried out the
program, and who agreed with Fitzgerald's answer when he was asked
what the difference between a sixth grade classroom and a Harvard
classroom was: "None. A classroom is a classroom."

The Reading List for GREECE/GREECE/GREECE

Barnard, Mary. *Sappho, A New Translation*. Berkeley, Los Angeles: University of California, 1958.

Barnstone, Willis. *Greek Lyric Poetry*. New York: Schocken, 1972.

Bowra, C. M. *Homer*. London, England: Duckworth, 1975.

Buck, M. S. *The Greek Anthology*. Philadelphia: Privately printed, 1916.

Davenport, Guy. *Archilochos, Sappho, Alkman*. Berkeley: University of
California, 1980.

Doolittle, Hilda (H. D.). *Heliodora and Other Poems*. Boston: Houghton
Mifflin, 1924.

Fitts, Dudley. *One Hundred Poems from the Palatine Anthology*. Nor-
folk, Conn.: New Directions, 1938.

Fitzgerald, Robert. *Spring Shade, Poems 1931–1970*. New York: New
Directions, 1971.

Harrison, Jane Ellen. *Mythology*. New York: Cooper Square, 1963.

Homer. *The Odyssey*. Translated by Robert Fitzgerald. Garden City,
N.Y.: Anchor, 1963.

Kerényi, C. *The Gods of the Greeks*. New York: Thames & Hudson,
1978.

———. *The Heroes of the Greeks*. New York: Thames & Hudson, 1978.

Lattimore, Richmond, translator. *Greek Lyrics*. Chicago: University of
Chicago, 1955.

Mackail, J. W. *Select Epigrams from the Greek Anthology.* London, England: Longmans, Green, 1928.

Paton, W. R. *The Greek Anthology.* Cambridge, Mass.: Harvard University, 1969.

Rexroth, Kenneth. *Classics Revisited.* Chicago: Quadrangle, 1968.

————. *Poems from the Greek Anthology.* Ann Arbor: University of Michigan, 1962.

Watson, Burton. *Chinese Lyricism.* New York: Columbia University, 1971.

Wharton, Henry Thornton. *Sappho: Memoir, Text, Selected Renderings, and a Literal Translation.* London, England: John Lane, 1898.

Eleni Sikelianos

Some Greek Girls

On Teaching Sappho and Praxilla

> *Who was Mary Shelley?*
> *What was her name*
> *before she married?*
> —Lorine Niedecker

IF LORINE NIEDECKER'S LINES challenge us to think about assumptions we might make about women writers (and their names), think about this: How many women writers from Greek antiquity can you name? If you're a classicist or an early lyric poetry fanatic, you might be able to name more than two or three. But if you're the average or even better than average literary citizen, you might be able to name one, maybe none. There were, in fact, a number of women writing in those early years, just past the dawn of written language: Erinna, Telesilla, Korinna, Myrtis, and Nossis were a few. According to first century B.C.E. poet Antipater of Thessaloniki: "Great Heaven created nine Muses, but Earth / bore these nine." By other accounts, there were at least sixteen highly regarded women poets who lived between the seventh century B.C. and the end of the Greek period. But history has not always been kind, and many of these texts have been wiped out entirely, by fire or flood or censorship or by indifference to women writers. Those that have survived exist only in fragments, rummaged from other texts or from ancient trash piles. What do these fragments offer? For one thing, many are simply exquisite pieces of writing.

The most famous of these poets—and the first woman writer we have in the Western tradition—is, of course, Sappho. Recently, I have been using poems by Sappho and by a lesser known Greek woman of antiquity, Praxilla, with my elementary and high school classes.

What do we know of that illustrious and sometimes infamous poet, Sappho? Facts about her life are as scarce as her poems. Born in Mytilene on the island of Lesbos in the late seventh century B.C.E., Sappho was writing not much more than a hundred years after the time we believe Homer was composing his accounts of wars and wanderings. Of an aristocratic family, Sappho was bisexual. She married and had a daughter named Kleis, which was also her mother's name. From Herodotus we know that Sappho had a brother named Charaxos and that her father's name was Scamander or Scamandronymos. She may have had two other brothers. She may or may not have run some kind of school, training young women in the arts of poetry and the worship of Aphrodite. From inscriptions found on Parian marble, we know that she was exiled to Sicily, but we don't know why. These are some of the "facts" of Sappho's life; fictions about her abound. One famous legend has it that, lovestruck, she leapt to her death from the white cliffs on the southern edge of Lefkas.

Whoever Sappho was doesn't matter so much, perhaps, as the poems she left behind. The Roman poet Catullus and the contemporary American poet Bernadette Mayer were influenced by her, as were a great many poets in between. She was highly respected by the Ancient Greeks. If to Antipater of Thessaloniki she was one of the nine mortal muses, Plato bade us look again: to him, Sappho was "the tenth Muse." The ancient library at Alexandria housed nine books of her poems, most of which were destroyed by censors or by time. What fragments we have today come to us from citations in other authors' works or rehabilitated papyri (from books recycled into mummy wrappings—some found in the wadding stuffed into a mummified crocodile's mouth) discovered in Egyptian sands. Sappho's poems are passionate, vehement, gorgeous, and—according to the third-century scholar Longinus—sublime. Her longest surviving poem is her invocation to Aphrodite, with those much quoted lines "yoking sudden sparrows to your swift chariot. . . ." Sappho wrote in what translator Richmond Lattimore calls "simple but superbly articulated stanzas," in the Aeolic dialect of Lesbos, and was the inventor of at least one form, the eponymous sapphic.

Both a meter and a stanzaic form, the sapphic is composed of two hendecasyllabic lines followed by a sixteen-syllable line. The sapphic was taken up by many Latin writers (including Catullus and Horace); by the Middle Ages, it had made its way into French, English, German, and Italian, and reappeared in the Renaissance.[1]

One of the most interesting things about Sappho is her position in the history of literature. "Sappho," writes classicist Page duBois, "is a part of a great turn in the poetic tradition and in the very history of the development of subjectivity."[2] In simpler terms, Sappho and a few contemporaries were the first poets to begin writing in the first person. The shift that took place from the Homeric emphasis on heroes and the collective doings in an ancestral past, tales that were repeated over and over through the centuries, to an emphasis on the individual "I" and what it does and experiences, was momentous. Although Sappho's work is still part of an oral tradition, she and other Greek poets of this era initiated a new sense of self, a self that is differentiated from its ancestors, and with this they initiated the birth of lyric poetry.[3]

Meanwhile, back in the twentieth century, at Manhattan's P.S. 19, it was Women's History month and a sixth grade teacher had requested that we read women poets. Another teacher was doing a unit on Ancient Greece, and wanted me to focus on Greek poets. Who would fit the bill better than Sappho? I had taught Sappho at the college and high school levels, yet it had never occurred to me to use her poems with young students. Her poems seemed too sophisticated, and it's hard to talk about Sappho without talking about love and sex. But why not talk about Sappho simply in terms of intensity of feeling? Usually I don't ask kids directly to express their feelings in poems, because it seems too solicited and it's hard for them to escape clichés. They tend to express their feelings anyway, in much more interesting ways, when they write about, say, dreams or colors. But these were classes of sixth graders, eleven- and twelve-year-olds already battling (or exalting in?) massive hormone diffusion. I decided to try out a poem of Sappho's that I use with college students: Fragment 31, in which she turns "greener than grass" with jealousy.

I began by giving a little history. I told the students that most of Sappho's poems were lost, and that all we have left are fragments. I told them the story about the papyri being recovered from a mummified crocodile's mouth. This is a real attention-getter; afterwards, the students are game for anything. With high school kids, I always clearly state that Sappho wrote many of her love poems to women, but with these sixth graders I chose not to broach the subject of Sappho's sexuality. "The gender of one's sexual partner may have been irrelevant to the ancient Greeks," according to duBois, but to many contemporary Americans, it is not. Brave souls may use Sappho as an opportunity to dive into the subject of homosexuality; others may want to say simply that Sappho was from an island in the Aegean close to the coast of Turkey.

Here is most of Fragment 31, which the translator calls "Seizure":

To me he seems like a god
the man who sits facing you
and hears you near as you speak
softly and laugh

in a sweet echo that jolts
the heart in my ribs. For now
as I look at you my voice
is empty and

can say nothing as my tongue
cracks and slender fire is quick
under my skin. My eyes are dead
to light, my ears

pound, and sweat pours over me.
I convulse, greener than grass,
and feel my mind slip as I
go close to death. . . .

  —Translated by Willis Barnstone

At this point, what we have breaks off into fragments. Part of the poem's beauty is its ambiguity: who is the speaker jealous of, the man who is doing all the talking or the woman who is being talked to, or both?[4] Catullus tried his hand at translating this poem, and Longinus admired how Sappho "summons at the same time soul body hearing tongue sight color, all as though they had wandered off apart from herself."[5]

Yet the emotions are not ambiguous. I asked the kids at P.S. 19 to tell me what was going on with poor old Sappho. Several students immediately shouted out, "She's jealous!" Why? "She sees her guy talking to someone else." I asked them to tell me what happens to Sappho's body when she sees these two talking. "Her heart jumps, she can't hear anything, her tongue cracks, there's a fire under her skin, she can't see, she hears thunder, she starts sweating. . . . She's dead." They liked the drama. Does she really die, or does she feel like she died? (Here answers varied.) Have any of you ever had really strong feelings about someone, feelings so strong that your ears buzz, you can't see, and maybe you feel you've gone "close to death"? "Yes!" (of course). What kinds of feelings? When?

"When my mom left, when Andrew punched me, when my grandmother died, when my dad wouldn't buy me a Sega 64, when I raise my hand and the poetry teacher goes to someone else. . . ." Okay, so what did it feel like? Describe what happened to you physically—make me really see it in an unusual way, so that I know exactly how you felt. Here are some of the poems they wrote:

The Girl I Cannot Have

She looks very nice I like
her but cannot have her I laugh
at all her jokes that are not
funny I like her like I like
a beautiful day but when she
is with a boy I feel like a
bomb's going to blow up

    —*Tarik Velez*

I was happy to see that Tarik tried using enjambment, much like that in the Barnstone translation I had handed out, even though we hadn't yet discussed line breaks.

Beating Up Andrew (*excerpt*)

When Andrew plans jokes at me
I get angry
The feeling makes me want to punch him
Andrew makes me feel dumb
He makes me feel like fighting someone
But I don't want to fight
So I try hard
not to show my feelings
My mind breaks and feels
like tornadoes coming
and going, to blow my mind away
My head turns
I can't even think
Storms shake my body
It breaks me like
hard metal
I feel like fire is all over me
I can't stand it
I don't know how I am going to end it

    —*Mary Joyce (Mary J.) Tagatac*

Although Mary J.'s poem is pretty much a straight imitation, I was impressed by how she expressed herself so directly about a difficult conflict, and by how the speaker's feelings change. The poem begins with a long, blow-by-blow account of the mounting dispute, during which the poet mostly wants to fight. As the poem continues, the desire for retaliation diminishes; the author begins to focus on what happens to her physically, and how she might end the conflict. Since this poem, Mary J. has been writing up a storm, sometimes two or three poems a day.

Another student wrote about an entirely different "other":

Wanting to Be in Union with the Other Me

When I see myself
the one who comes in my
dreams every night, I feel
why am I trapped here and not
one with him, but a different and
yet similar Matthew sharing one
life and one soul. I am only
with half and not whole with the
other me.

—*Matthew Kossey*

Admittedly, some of the kids' poems fell into the trap of clichés about first kisses and so on. But the unusual directness in some of the poems made the exercise worth it.

*　　*　　*

Another Greek girl to use in the classroom is Praxilla. Although Praxilla was first on Antipater's list of mortal muses, even less is known about her than about Sappho. Praxilla was from Sicyon, on the Gulf of Corinth, and was well known in her own time (the fifth century B.C.E.) and for several centuries following.[6] There is evidence that Praxilla wrote poems to be performed publicly at symposia, an unusual honor for a woman, and her drinking-party songs were sung in Athens well beyond her time. These drinking songs often gave advice, such as "O friend, watch out for a scorpion under every stone." One of her most famous poems is "Hymn to Adonis." Adonis, in the afterworld, when asked what he misses from earth, replies:

Loveliest of what I leave behind is the sunlight,
and loveliest after that the shining stars, and the moon's face,
but also cucumbers that are ripe, and pears, and apples.

   —Translated by Richmond Lattimore

Of the eight remaining fragments attributed to Praxilla, this is the longest, and all that remains of the "Hymn." The story goes that Praxilla was made fun of for her love (in this poem) of simple things. Lattimore cites the saying, "Sillier than Praxilla's Adonis." But the exaltation of simple things is exactly what makes this a wonderful poem.

Although I read and discussed this Praxilla fragment with my sixth graders at P.S. 19, we didn't do any writing from it. Recently, however, I used Praxilla as a writing model, in conjunction with Sappho, while teaching American high school students in a summer program in Paris. In this class, at the Oxbridge Académie, I had the luxury not only of being in Paris, but of three hours in which to work, rather than the standard forty-seven minutes.[7]

The first thing I did with the Oxbridge students was to talk briefly about how we view history—how we tend to imagine it as a kind of seamless fabric even though it is in fact a series of outbursts and events, sometimes simultaneous, sometimes years and years apart. We talked about how there are many kinds of histories occurring at once. I asked the students to imagine everyone in the room writing his or her own history of our times. How would these histories be the same? How would they differ? What if everyone in Paris was asked to write a history? We talked about how a history is constructed by a person—an historian—from a series of fragments (documents, objects, etc.) connected to form a narrative. Can one person be objective? ("No!" the students answered resoundingly. This seemed to touch something.)

From here I told them about the birth of the first-person voice, how Sappho was one of the first poets to use it. We spent some time discussing subjectivity and objectivity. We read Sappho's Fragment 31 and the quotation from Longinus. Once again, the emotional immediacy of the Sappho poem worked its magic on the students. To help make the transition into Praxilla's poem, I wrote another poem on the board, one by Ezra Pound:

In a Station of the Metro

The apparition of these faces in the crowd;
Petals on a wet, black bough.

Here, I introduced the concept of luminous detail, Pound's idea about the kinds of sensory details that leap out at us and make a poem. Notice how Pound has distinct faces arise out of a crowd in just two lines. Then I read aloud Praxilla's "Hymn to Adonis." What are the details in Praxilla's poem that leap out? We talked about why Praxilla might have found these "simple" things beautiful. (You might try bringing in a cucumber, a pear, and an apple, and slicing up each.) Some students may notice (as mine did, and I hadn't before) how the things that give light in the poem—sunlight, stars, the moon—reflect off the cucumbers and pears and apples, making the latter luminous.

I then asked the students to think of simple things they themselves find beauty in. What do you see every day but take for granted? Can you recall strong, sensory memories of any "luminous details"? (One student said she remembered lying on the closet floor with her mother's purple dress with little yellow moons on it.) What small things would you miss if, like Adonis in Praxilla's poem, you left Earth? I asked them to write down one or two "luminous details" from the past—maybe the first things they remember seeing or smelling or touching. Then I had the students find details in the present. I asked them to note down at least one or two more details while looking carefully and attentively around the Luxembourg Gardens across the street.

When we met up again under a big plane tree, I asked the students to recopy their details on new sheets of paper, ones they could tear out of their notebooks. As the students finished, they handed me their copies, which I proceeded to tear up. This certainly got their attention! I then collected the fragments and handed one to each student.[8]

For the next part of the lesson, I asked the students to resist the temptation of finding out who wrote the fragments of which they were now in possession. Instead, try to rebuild the full original from what you have. Was it a poem? A recipe? A journal entry? You decide. Once they had "reconstituted" a poem (or whatever they decided it was), I asked them to invent a history for the piece and its author, again using clues, but this time from their own reconstructions. What period of history was the poem from? Where was it from? Was the author a man or a woman? What was his or her profession, what were his or her loves, dislikes? I asked students to use their imaginations, to let strange things come in, if they felt so moved.

When everyone was done, I had each student read first the fragment, then the reconstruction, then the "biography." Ali Berman, from Connecticut, received this on a scrap of paper:

> of wind
> is grueling
> to see who
> the other
> is over
> to recover

From this, she wrote:

> entering a blanket of wind
> where being new is grueling and dead, as are
> the sick, boarded in the strange shadowed houses
> too aged to help each other; the other
> empty time is over
> too raged, too bent to recover

And then:

> This poem was written by a woman in her early twenties living in London in 1665 at the time of the Great Plague. She did not survive from the plague nor did anyone else from her house, where she lived with her mother, father, and brother. It was discovered in 1893 in a trunk full of papers.

The exercise seemed to allow room for all kinds of mysteries to creep in. What the students wrote, and how they responded to the exercise, gave me the sense that they felt a certain liberation from the need to "construct" a poem of their own. Recognizing the fragments from their own original notes in someone else's newly made piece—and comparing the biographies to the real-life authors—was exciting, too.

After everybody had read their pieces, we talked about Sappho and Praxilla again. What had they learned about the effects of history on a writer's work or biography? "It makes me see how we don't know at all who Sappho really was, and how they keep trying to piece her together again," said one student. Beyond that, many of them had created interesting new pieces from fragments left by someone else (much like Catullus did with Sappho). I encouraged them to think of these new creations as their own. Jessica Shaefer started with this:

```
moving
nd vocal
only ex
    The
on me, the
the world. Next to the laugh is
green and brown.
a crowded
 the hot sun,
 perfect
lt or
moving pho
```

And ended up with this:

```
                    moving
            physical and vocal
            terraces only exist
        in my mouth. The
            sun came down on me, the
    tongue of the world. Next to the laugh is
            green and brown. I still cry out in the
morning of a crowded cosmos but for
                the hot sun, pounding again a
                perfect murder, slaying my
        guilt or pulling itself like
        a moving photograph across me.
```

Given these results, I'm starting to cook up ways to teach poems by the other fourteen known women of antiquity.

Notes

1. You can find a twentieth-century example of the sapphic in Ezra Pound's "Appurit."

2. Page duBois, *Sappho Is Burning* (Chicago: The University of Chicago Press, 1995), p. 6.

3. Sappho and the other poets who initiated this shift in consciousness usually performed their poems alone rather than with a chorus. Generally, they performed to the accompaniment of a lyre; hence the term "lyric poet." Sappho is said to have played the lyre herself and even to have invented an instrument.

4. Translators have argued both sides, although in the original the pronouns make it fairly clear that Sappho is addressing the woman.

5. It is actually because of Longinus's treatise *On the Sublime* that we have Fragment 31. Quoted in duBois, op. cit., p. 67.

6. Sicyon still exists—barely—as a small fishing village called Sikya (which means *fig*), about an hour from the city of Corinth. In antiquity, there was a statue of Praxilla in the town square.

7. If you are working in standard class periods, I would suggest dividing this lesson into three parts, or perhaps cutting out the first part dealing with Sappho.

8. This process can be time-consuming. An ideal thing to do is to have the students note down the details in one class. Then you can tear the students' papers—or better, photocopies of them—into fragments at home, and continue the exercise the following day. Be sure to use one fragment from each student.

Bibliography

DuBois, Page. *Sappho Is Burning*. Chicago: University of Chicago, 1995.

Greek Lyrics. Translated by Richmond Lattimore. Chicago: University of Chicago, 1949.

Sappho. *Sappho Poems: A New Version*. Translated by Willis Barnstone. Los Angeles: Sun & Moon, 1998.

Snyder, Jane McIntosh. *The Woman and the Lyre*. Carbondale, Ill.: Southern Illinois University, 1989.

Margot Fortunato Galt

From Aristophanes To Bird Land

Reinventing a Poetic Lift-Off

Residency Format

The goal for my two-week residency with ninth–twelfth graders at Johnson High School in St. Paul, Minnesota, was to use Aristophanes's fifth-century B.C.E. play *The Birds* as the basis for shaping student poetry and dialogue into a readers' theater script. The script would then be performed by some of the same students who helped write it. Readers' theater, in the format I use, relies on a variety of voices that slide in and out of specific characters. It has a more thematic, and poetic, structure than realistic drama, and is performed by being read aloud from scripts, rather than being memorized and staged.

Contact teacher and poet Norita Dittberner-Jax and I planned the residency with five other Johnson teachers. We hoped that students would see how ancient ideas could inform their own creative practice, and conversely, how their contemporary slang and concerns about fashion, gender, authority, and diversity—along with more recent forms of poetry (free verse, surreal metaphor) and drama (readers' theater)—could transform an ancient vehicle to speak for them.

Aristophanes's Play

The Birds contains two strata of beings—humans who are fleeing contentious Athens in search of a quieter life, and the birds they encounter, some of whom have had previous human incarnations. The play is full of humorous criticism of human life, delivered by a number of funny characters—pompous poets, rebellious youths, an oracle, a statue seller. The play also contains lovely lyrical homages to various birds, an argumentative flock for a chorus, and lots of play on words and phrases that refer to birds.

During the play the humans and birds form a plan to create an alternate city in the clouds. Soon the city, Much Cuckoo, becomes all the rage as humans name themselves after birds, and birds begin to act like humans. Eventually enough cross-fertilization occurs for Much Cuckoo and Athens to become quite a bit like each other. The joke is on those who thought they could escape messy, silly human life.

In addition to the whimsy and satire, the play also seemed a wonderful vehicle for teenage students to vent criticism of each other and adults, increase their knowledge about birds, and write lyrically, dramatically, and humorously about birds, bird people, and bird slang. During the residency, we also asked former Johnson students to present brief oral histories of their lives as students. We thought this would enlarge the scope of the project, giving students material from other eras to weave into the script, and teaching students about their own community.

Preliminaries
Before the writing residency began, I created an abridged version of *The Birds,* which I sent to the school and asked students to read.[1] But many of the younger or less advanced students found it difficult. We compromised: I gave the students a synopsis of the play—essentially what appears above—and asked the teachers to have the students read sections of the play aloud in class. I suggested that they sample some early dialogue between the two Athenians, later dialogue among birds and people, and the sections of chorus and poems spoken by the birds.

Early Decisions and Activities
From the beginning I decided not to have students generate material based exclusively on the play. I wanted more of a poetic rather than a dramatic script, partly because we were not going to stage a full-fledged drama, and partly because the "bird talk" in Aristophanes, which is in poetic form, sounds rather archaic with its rhyme and regular meter. Although I had little idea of what the Johnson High students thought of poetry, I knew enough to steer clear of anything that could easily slide into doggerel. I knew that if I wanted to elicit a range of emotions and experiences for the students' writing, I would have to give them forms that would sound more neutral to their ears: i.e., free verse without a heavy rhythm.

On the other hand, the notion of mixing human and bird life, fundamental to Aristophanes's play, suggested many fresh and unexpected writing ideas. I thought it might free the students from sentimentality and egotism, open their eyes to the beauty and behavior of birds, and possibly nudge them into using birds for what T. S. Eliot called "objective correlatives"—objects saturated with the feeling of a moment, yet having their own integrity and history. Early Egyptian and Greek artists created compelling images of vulnerability by projecting human feelings onto animals. I was hoping that Aristophanes would help the students do the same with birds.

Thus, to introduce the students to birds and bird talk, I collected armfuls of books, mostly picture books and field guides. I also made lists of current idioms and slang that refer to birds. Aristophanes (in the translation by Sommerstein and Barrett) uses bird slang too: his disaffected humans complain about getting a "bird's-eye view" and a "man's-eye view" of everything (161), and about a "flighty type . . . an absolute bird—restless, shifty, flighty, unreliable, can't stay in one place for two minutes on end" (161). To these idioms I added *bird-brained, featherweight, take wing, brood* on or *hatch* a scheme, *fly high*, etc. I intended to introduce these expressions early in each of the six classes, to inform their writing and immerse the students in bird language. For the same purposes, every day I had students peruse the bird books I brought in.

With several classes, the first session was devoted to little else: we listed bird talk on the board and the students looked through their bird books. Even when I tried to nudge them into writing, these classes couldn't be budged: the students became so engrossed in reading and chatting about birds, discovering surprising or gross tidbits about them, that they used up the entire period. Since some of these classes were not high-achieving groups, considered to have discipline problems, I decided that a session of getting acquainted with birds—especially one that kept the students fully engaged—was just fine.

With one group, I suggested that students pair or triple up and argue the merits of their birds. One of the teachers, Karen West, had given me Minnesotan Keith Gunderson's funny prose poem about choosing the state bird. I read the Gunderson poem to the class:

> And because we lived in a democracy all the school kids got to vote
> for some bird to be The State Bird and in fact any kid in any
> class in any grade except kindergarten could nominate a candidate

for The State Bird and after the voting the results would be sent to
the guys who had been elected to run The State of Minnesota and
they would figure out democratically which bird was the lucky
winner and I guess the woodduck was or the loon but no one who was
in our class which was 8th Grade Room 205 at Jefferson Junior
High had ever even heard or thought about those birds so they
didn't get considered and there were six or seven of us who were
boys who played a lot of ball together and got in trouble for fun so
the bird we nominated our class to nominate was THE CHICKEN
and anyone in favor of a particular class nomination could give a
speech on behalf of that bird so we all gave speeches on behalf
of THE CHICKEN and talked about eggs and eating chicken on
Sunday and what other bird did so much for everyone and one of us
questioned a guy who'd come out for THE CARDINAL about what
a cardinal could be used for and all he could think to say was that
they were red and pretty and a baseball team was named after them
so we booed and hissed at the cardinal until the teacher said
no booing and hissing allowed and then the teacher remembered
that although she wasn't permitted to vote THE ORIOLE was
her favorite bird and probably quite a few people liked
THE ORIOLE and they build such interesting nests so about two
seconds later at least five kids really liked THE ORIOLE and
nominated it even though one of them thought it was green but we
kept talking up the usefulness of THE CHICKEN and when the
votes were counted THE CHICKEN squeaked in the winner with
THE ORIOLE second so we laughed and clapped until the
teacher reminded us that laughers and clappers could stay after
school and that democracy was a serious business and there'd
be no more nonsense about messy chickens and since THE ORIOLE
came in second and was the only SERIOUS candidate of the two
it would be the nominee of Room 205 and one that
we could all be proud of.[2]

I then asked students to debate which bird should be chosen the class
bird. I recommended that one student in each group become a scribe, but
in fact what was written down did not capture the heat of the discussions. That seemed fine: the activity certainly roused the students to lively
engagement with the subject.

Early Exercises: Writing Odes and Photo Poems
My next step was dictated in part by the limited time I would have with
each class. I didn't want to waste time trying out new models and strate-
gies from contemporary poetry; I wanted to use those I knew would lead

to good student writing. Since I often link drawing and writing in the brainstorming process, I chose two familiar exercises that did just that: writing a long, skinny ode modeled on Pablo Neruda's *Elemental Odes,* and another modeled on my poem "Halloween Kimonos."

I chose parts of Neruda's "Bird-Watching Ode" as the model:

Well now
invisible
birds
of jungle and forest,
. . . . .
vagabonds
the way I like you,
free
far from gun and cage,
fugitive
corollas,
. . . . .
faithful and sonorous
society of heights,
leaves
on the loose
stunt-riders
of the air,
petals
of smoke
. . . . .
happy
constructors
of the softest nests,
. . . . .
uncles of seed,
I love you,
ungrateful ones:
go back
happy to have lived out with you
a moment
in the wind.[3]

The class also read a similar poem directly addressed to birds in Aristophanes, spoken by the Hoopoe, a bird-man sought by the Athens escapees:

Come along, come along, birds of my own feather,
Birds who live in the farmer's well-sown fields.
Eaters of seeds and barley, myriad flocks

Of a hundred species, fluttering quickly,
Uttering gentle calls,
Twittering together on the furrowed soil
In a pleased voice, tio, tio, tio.
. . . . .
Birds of the watery places
Snapping up the sharp-mouthed midges
Along the ditches in the marshland,
Birds of the swamp and the fenland
And the pleasant meadow at Marathon:
Birds of the stripy wing, godwit, godwit, godwit. (163)

Neruda's ode made a nice comparison to Aristophanes's: each described birds' habitat and gave a sense of their variety and range. Neruda's ode presented striking comparisons: *petals of smoke* or *uncles of seed*. The Greek song offered a nice medley of bird sounds and sites. It also gave us a chance to identify Marathon, one Greek reference that students would have heard about, as a sports event. Marathon was the site of a Greek victory, news of which a messenger carried to Athens on foot. This connection to long-distance running helped draw the contemporary students closer to the Greek world.

In the ode exercise, students drew quick sketches of birds of their choice, labeled them with all kinds of information and fanciful comparisons, and wrote long, skinny odes, some of which spoke directly through the beak of a bird, introducing itself to the world, and some of which spoke affectionately or disparagingly to the bird. Some of the results were wonderful, and many excerpts made their way into the script; for example, the image of a hummingbird as a "Speedy little bird/ghost of flight" by Chong Xiong, or "Gaudy oriental flying home to Asia/camouflage green to match the leaves," by Dison Vang. As I had hoped, the students' own feelings and experiences came through the common subject of birds.

Here are two student odes:

Ode to Rose-Ring Parakeet

Beautiful green bird
so conceited
with your pink necklace
around your neck.
When you sit
your tail looks
like a mermaid's.

You are the beautiful mermaid
of the sky.
You were the first
and lucky one,
the first parrot
to reach Europe
brought to Greece
by helmsmen of
Alexander the Great's
fleet. Inhabiting
lands of the old world
from West Africa to
Indochina, you settle
in gardens and tilled fields.
You are the prettiest,
you are the most glamorous
smallest parrot
in the blue, blue sky.

 —*Mayra Quintanilla*

The Crown Victorian Pigeon

The feathers on top of my head
like the crown upon a king
you humans say I'm a nuisance
soiling buildings, stealing grain
The truth of the matter is
you took my land from me
So now the time has come again
for me to take my throne, my friends.
Let us come as one
to put a common fiend
in a place where the sun does not gleam.

 —*Chang Vang*

"The Crown Victorian Pigeon" echoed a theme in Aristophanes: the damage that humans wreak on birds, for which birds sometimes seek revenge. Thus, in Aristophanes, the chorus of birds proclaims:

> . . . birds all-seeing and all-ruling
> for we see the whole earth,
> We preserve the thriving crops. . . .
> We kill the destroyers of sweet-smelling gardens.
> The ravishers of plants,

And everything that creeps and stings,
We slay them all, they cower at our approach. (190–191)

Later in the play, birds swear death to Philocrates, the bird-merchant, who "strings chaffinches together . . . inflicts indignities on thrushes, inflating them by blowing through a tube . . . sticks feathers up the black-bird's nostrils . . . catches pigeons and keeps them caged, ties them up in a net and uses them as decoys. . . . We strongly advise you to set them free. Because if you don't you'll be caught by the birds and tied up and used as decoys."(191) Such passages helped to establish the interrelation of bird and human, and the adaptation of human behavior to birds and vice-versa that provides many critical and humorous episodes in the bird city of Much Cuckoo.

"Ode to the Rose-Ringed Parakeet" represented another theme connecting the student writing to Aristophanes: appreciation for the beauty and history of birds. In Aristophanes, a lovely example of an ode celebrating a single bird occurs midway in the play. The ode is sung by the chorus to the Hoopoe's mate, the Nightingale. Here is an excerpt:

Nightingale, we all adore thee,
Russet-coated,
Vibrant-throated . . .
Sweetly-fluting,
Spring-saluting,
Seldom seen though often heard. (177)

Reading the many passages in Aristophanes and in the contemporary bird books—about endangered species, environmental needs, and the good that birds do humans—emphasized some important ecological lessons, without preaching. This was one of the strong underlying messages of the residency.

Photo Poem

Another well-tested drawing-and-writing exercise that I adapted used my poem "Halloween Kimonos." In the exercise, I led the students through the same process that I stumbled upon in writing my own poem: first, drawing a quick sketch of a photo from memory, labeling it, making comparisons, then drafting.

After I sketched the drawing on the board, I read the poem, which expresses my jealousy of my sister.

The next step had students draw their own photos from memory. They could also draw a moment that should have been photographed—like an accident they were involved in, or their first day at school or in a new house.

Then I asked students to add a bird to their drawing. First we decided what bird would best capture the mood in my drawing. A vulture, someone suggested, to pluck out your sister's eyes. So I drew a sinister vulture hunched on my shoulder.

After the students finished drawing, I asked them to label their drawings: Who, Where, When, What is in the photo? What feelings, i.e. attitudes, emotions, thoughts, wishes, dreams—everything that is inside the people as the photo or moment occurs? Why did you remember this? Why did someone take the photo? What was the "official" reason to commemorate this moment? What were the feelings of the various people involved in the moment?

Finally we used the drawings to play what I call "the comparison game." Students isolate one element of their drawings—a tree, for instance, or the bird's claws. Then they ask themselves, "What else does this look like?" Claws might suggest a rake, a tree, a cloud. Then, they write the comparison beside the item.

Now we were ready to draft the poem. I pointed out how I had alternated description with information in my poem. "Try that," I recommended. And to begin: look at your drawing and ask yourself, "Where does my eye go first?" Then begin by describing that little area.

As for the bird, it could be commenting on the scene or taking part in it. It could heighten the feeling of the photo, or provide an entirely different perspective.

I also hinted that students could use a question to capture uncertainty or suggest possible interpretations. They could also include wishes for future events. The ending could return to an earlier image or question. The end could also step back and question the moment recreated in the poem.

The resulting good poems were too numerous to use them all in the script. But eventually I chose a handful and used excerpts. Here is one dramatic photo poem that appears early in the script:

My mouth like a wave in the sea
I am angry how my sister's
treating me. I am sleeping and

she seems not to care. I go: You
be taking all the cover! She go:
Well, girl, maybe you don't need it.
I go: Girl, please, you better recognize!
She go: OK, don't get dealt with.
She better watch out before I
pull out her hair. A grosbeak
in my head, maybe it will fly
and push her off the bed.

    —*DeClara Tripp*

And here is a poem about an event remembered from the refugee camps in Thailand. A man's corpse swings back and forth under a tree:

A rope wrapped around his neck
Connected to a branch of that tree
His eyes closed and his lips were so dry
His mouth also closed; he couldn't cry.
The face turned blue
and the whole body was so cool
He was a good hunter
He had killed many birds
He had trapped pigeons with his snares
He sometimes took just one of a pair
He hung the pigeon to death
and now he tied a rope to his neck
He swung and floated dead
His face faded
His family felt bad
He didn't know how to solve his troubles
He was a debtor
He was an opium smoker
Killing himself in the wind
so he wouldn't be ashamed with his friends.

    —*Xai Hong*

Finally, here is an example in which the bird heightens the poem's feeling:

Short hair, gray feathers
one picture. One night
it's me and the owl
yes, my only pal.

My mom doesn't care
if I cry or laugh

all she wants is a picture
of me and my haircut.

Why did she cut it?
It's not her hair.
Why doesn't she cut
hers instead?

Oh my sad owl
I know how you feel
when lonely at night
you call and nobody listens.
Short hair, gray feathers,
one picture, one night
it's me and the owl,
my only pal.

—*Karen Cano*

Creating Dialogues—Pass It Back

Though we didn't have enough time to write or stage a regular drama, I wanted the students to try their hand at creating characters and writing dialogue. To accomplish this, I employed a familiar exercise I've titled "Pass It Back."

Before doing the exercise, I gave the students some background I thought was necessary. We discussed how in Aristophanes's opening dialogue the two humans, Euelpides and Peisthetaerus, are not distinctive except that Euelpides has a jackdaw and Peisthetaerus, a crow. During the course of the play, Euelpides says less and less; Peisthetaerus becomes a dominant character. This gave me a chance to talk about some of the ways character is revealed in drama—through speech patterns and contrary attitudes, and through the things that characters say about each other. Attributes like age, gender, wealth, race, size, temperament, and history also differentiate characters and affect the way they interact.

We then proceeded to the sometimes zany "Pass It Back" exercise.

I explained that each student would begin by creating a name for a character and writing it at the top of a sheet of paper. I urged the students to think of the wide range of races and backgrounds in the school and not to be afraid to identify differences by involving, for instance, an Asian or Italian name.

After writing his or her character's name, each student passed the paper to the person behind them. On this new paper, each wrote a short physical description—age, race, hair, eyes, clothes, gestures, quality of voice. Then they passed the papers again.

Next, the students created personalities for this new character: quirks of belief, behavior, fears, phobias, loves, hates, dreams, wishes, experiences with family or school. Then they passed the papers on to another student. Finally, they wrote what bird belonged to the character and how human and bird came to be together. This done, papers were returned to the students who initially created the names. Here is an example of a composite character created by one class:

> Patrick Stupiditious is a thin boy in poor health. His shocking bright hair stands up like he's been electrocuted. His pimply face is red. Narrow shoulders can't support his big-necked T-shirts. Baggy pants and thin-soled shoes complete him. S. got his crow because its mother landed on his head and hatched an egg. S. rescued the egg and a crow was born. He kept the crow. They have been friends ever since.

Usually this first part of "Pass It Back" takes one class period. On the second day, the teacher and I have teams of three or four students write dialogues using the characters created the day before. Students can use the material generated by their classmates for their character, or they can alter the description to suit their fancy. Each group appoints a scribe to write down the speeches, or the group passes a paper around and each student writes the dialogue for his or her character.

I told the students that the dialogues should update Aristophanes: imagine a group of students, tired of school, trying to find their way to Bird Land, using birds they've acquired. Before starting, we reread the opening pages of dialogue in *The Birds*, and laughed at the way the jackdaw and crow led the two humans in circles and up and down hills until one human complains that the bird had "worn the nails off my toes."

This dialogue writing activity was so much fun for one twelfth grade class that they elected to keep going twice as long as I had anticipated. The two sections of dialogue that I used in the final script came from this class. They had the most temperate humor and the funniest slang. Here is one of them, written for three young men:

VOICE 12: What up?
VOICE 13: What up, G-lock?
VOICE 14: Hey, dawg.
VOICE 13: Dis school makes me sleepy. Study hall's all right, doc. I
   just need to relax.

VOICE 12: I know how we can relax. Let's slam some 40s, yo!

VOICE 14: Yeah, let's bounce up outta dis joint.

VOICE 13: Word, but first we gotta take care of the gatekeeper.
My pigeon will wreck the "bleep" up.

VOICE 12: Let's go marinate at Bird Land, yo!

VOICE 14: First, let's go get some females. I got my pimp gear
strapped on, dawg. My Tommy's and Nikes.

VOICE 13: Here comes my pigeon. He tore da heck outta the "gatekeeper's" eyes. Now we're safe.

VOICE 12: These 40s will give us wings and we can flock to Bird
Land.

VOICE 14: Yeah. It's on. I can fly with my Asian flycatcher.

VOICE 13: I can feel da wings ripping outta my back, y'all.

VOICE 12: It's time to fly high with my crow.

—*Brian Lipinski, Steve Cole, and David D.*

From Oral History to Bird People

In two senior classes, two Johnson graduates, Dorothy Lynch '39 and
Roger Halman '59, gave informal renditions of their school days.
Dorothy talked about the Great Depression era, and Roger talked about
the flush days of the 1950s. The day after the interviews, I asked the students to select an old Johnson High yearbook and to use it, along with
the bird guides, to draw and label a short sketch of a hybrid bird person.
I told them to look at the hairdos in the senior pictures, and at the "cred-
its" under each of them.

The drawings that resulted were funny, as was the hybridized information. In the script, I used some of these bird people as guides, who
introduce themselves, then launch into stories about life in former years.
Here are three examples:

VOICE 12: Hey, man, like my polyester '70s bellbottoms? The only
ones in Bird Land. I'm Adam Ducky Lilly, former president of the
Star Wars fan club at Johnson High School. Man, I'm the most flam-
mable bird-man alive—catch a whiff of my Aqua Velva.

—*Patty Mangan*

VOICE 8: Hi, I'm Mary Goose Ling, grad of Johnson High School
1936. I have Asian eyes to see my goals, one human arm to achieve
success, lips to peck a forever kiss, one wing to soar the sky. Want to
see the three diving boards I used to bounce off into Phalen Lake?
And the Salvation Army shoes I replaced every week with cardboard

in the soles. We were poor but so was everyone else; we didn't know we were poor.

—*Linda Moua*

VOICE 13: Listen to me toot. Kenneth "Barn Owl" Blyton is my name, Johnson grad of 1985. Like my Afro? All suited up for the Black Hawk country band, ready to toot my mean saxophone.

—*Frank Marchio III*

Letters from Bird Land and Concluding Chorus

One of the more successful adaptations I made for the Aristophanes residency used Lisel Mueller's poem, "Letter to California."[4] I had used the poem before in various geography and creative writing sessions, and was quite fond of Mueller's vivid unexpected contrasts between her Chicago life and that of her friend in California. For Bird Land purposes, I suggested that students use the letter-poem format, but unlike Mueller, report on the way they had left the human world and ended up in Bird Land. We brainstormed ways this transformation could happen: jumping off a cliff and taking wing, letting go of a water-skiing tow rope, swinging up very high, or as Marci Xiong imagined, using wings bestowed by Demeter:

The emerald forest that traps me
is Artemis's private garden.
I am being hunted, I am scared.

Gasping and panting, I fall,
my back hits the ground.
Demeter awakens to answer my call.

She gives me wings
and shiny black claws
to scratch Artemis
should she use her hands
against me, and to catch
her arrows if she decides to shoot me.

One more gift, a red tail
forged by Hephaestus himself
in his volcano.

Burning all evidence
I scream my freedom and
fly straight to the

66

kingdom of the birds
and tell my story.

Marci combined Greek gods and goddesses with attributes of a red-tailed hawk. Tom Franco wrote his letter after he had already reached Bird Land, and spoke about missing his family and wanting to return home:

Dear Family,
I have no idea what has happened to me.
While playing soccer and running as fast as I could,
I turned into an ostrich.
Dear Mom, I miss you so much, I miss Dad, brother and sister,
and you too, Mom. Enough is enough. I'm coming home.
I hope you will recognize me. I'm still very large.
I'm very fast, and I still cannot fly. Please watch for me,
as a bird not a guy. I'm an ostrich—you know what they look like.
Please accept me as I would accept you. I will be home soon,
with love and some tears.

From Circle Poem to Good-Bye Chant

One of my favorite exercises draws on Native American writer N. Scott Momaday's "The Delight Song of Tsoai-Talee." I have the students draw a circle and place the names of all kinds of natural beings and things around it—from forms of water to birds to trees to land formations to flowers to mammals, etc. Next, randomly linking two items from the circle, students write an "I am" line describing how the two items are related to each other. Momaday's beautiful poem provides the model, as in this line: "I am the fish that rolls, shining in the water."

Adapting this exercise for the Bird Land script involved directing students to couch each line in the form of a good-bye to a dream. From a sheaf of these dream-chant poems, I chose the best line from quite a number to create a chorus of quick-paced, alternating voices. The chorus says good-bye to the dream of Bird Land as the students prepare to return home. Here are a few of the good-byes:

Goodbye, anaconda dream of smothering a barracuda with my bendable agility.
    —*Henry Bonner*

Goodbye, ancient willow dream of an angry black cave.

   —*Jayde Torgerson*

Goodbye, slow flowing stream dream of sunshine gleaming over me.

   —*Chang Vang*

Goodbye, catfish dream of feeling the sharp teeth of a bear clamping onto my stomach.

   —*Kim Goodar*

Goodbye, wind dream of a beautiful turquoise blue jay.

   —*Pa Houa Lee*

Finale

I created the final thirteen-page script out of the student writings, excerpts from the oral histories, and some connecting material by me. A fairly constant cast of around ten students rehearsed the script four times. Many in the cast were seniors, but there were also some ninth graders. The school drama teacher Mark Fisher helped with the rehearsals. Finally, during the last period, the cast read the script to the assembled students who had contributed to it. The names of the writers, identified in parentheses in the script, were announced afterwards, and they and the readers all received several rounds of applause. Aristophanes would have been proud. During the performance, the fourteen bird cutouts that had been made by Mrs. Dittberner-Jax's class soared above the heads of the readers.

Notes

1. Aristophanes, *The Knights, Peace, Wealth, The Birds, Assembly-women.* Translated by Alan Sommerstein and David Barrett (New York: Penguin, 1978).

2. Keith Gunderson, "Naming the State Bird," from *25 Minnesota Poets* (Minneapolis: Nodin, 1974).

3. Pablo Neruda, *Selected Poems.* Edited by Nathaniel Tarn. Translated by Anthony Kerrigan, W. S. Merwin, Alastair Reid, and Nathaniel Tarn (New York: Delta/Dell, 1972).

4. Lisel Mueller, *Alive Together* (Baton Rouge, La.: Louisiana State University, 1996).

Carol F. Peck

Singing Our New-Made Songs

Using Psalms and Proverbs

"WHY NOT have the children write some psalms, like the ones in the King James Bible? It would be nice if they could learn to appreciate that beautiful language."

A teacher at Sidwell Friends School, in Washington, D.C., where I was in my first year as Writer-in-Residence, made this suggestion. At first I had my doubts that her students could really understand the format of a psalm, much less use it as a model for their own writing. However, I had discovered that this was a writing-rich school: all of the teachers, pre-K through fourth grade, emphasized verbal and written expression across the curriculum. This class in particular, consisting of forty third and fourth graders, had risen to every writing challenge I had presented them. So I decided to try this new idea.

Which Psalm should I use as a model? I wanted one that used not only colons and balanced phrases, but also imagery and metaphor in simple but vivid ways. Remembering how puzzled I had been, as an eight-year-old, by many of the metaphors in Psalm 23 (the "valley of the shadow of death," the table prepared in the presence of my enemies, and my cup running over), I bypassed it. I considered several others, seeking ones that emphasized joy rather than sin and destruction: Psalm 8 is good but does not use the colon; Psalm 150 has beautiful rhythm and clear use of the colon but has limited imagery; Psalm 147 would be good for older students; and Psalm 88 might appeal to junior and senior high school students filled with despair. Finally I decided that the first seven verses of Psalm 95 would be the most accessible to eight- and nine-year-olds, and I made a copy for each student.

O come, let us sing unto the Lord: let us
  make a joyful noise to the rock of our salvation.
Let us come before his presence with thanksgiving,
  and make a joyful noise unto him with psalms.
For the Lord is a great God, and a great King above all gods.
In his hand are the deep places of the earth: the strength
  of the hills is his also.
The sea is his, and he made it: and his hands formed
  the dry land.
O come, let us worship and bow down: let us kneel
  before the Lord our maker.
For he is our God: and we are the people of his pasture,
  and the sheep of his hand.

First, we all read the passage aloud together. The students were seated, with their two teachers, on bleachers at one end of their large classroom, and the reading sounded crisp and good. "That sounded like church," remarked a fourth grader. Next, I pointed out how the colon in each verse not only indicates a pause, but also acts as a "heads up" punctuation mark, alerting the reader to the other half of an idea or to details that expand that idea.

Then we read the psalm as two groups: for each verse, I read the part before the colon (or the first comma), and the students and teachers read the part following it. I asked the students what they noticed about the two parts. They were quick to tell me that the second half *balanced* the first half, in both rhythm and imagery. "Sometimes the second part gives us more pictures in our heads that explain the idea more," said one child. Next, we took turns reading over our favorite verses aloud, enjoying the rhythm of the lines, the sounds of the words, and the vivid images.

"I like picturing God's *hands* forming land," said one child.

"I like the 'deep places of the earth,'" said another.

"And I like to make 'joyful noise!'" remarked an often-noisy third grader.

"The whole thing is like a song," said a fourth grader, and that gave me the perfect opportunity to describe the boy David sitting out alone on a hillside, guarding his sheep, using his harp and voice to compose songs in praise of God.

Finally came the writing assignment: "Imagine yourself alone in your favorite place—the beach, the mountains, your own neighborhood, your own room—and think about something special to celebrate in a poem." I also gave them the option of doing the opposite—*lamenting* something—if they could not think of anything to celebrate.

As usual, the students scattered to various areas of the classroom to write—some sitting at tables and sharing ideas, others sprawled on the floor or tucked into corners, working alone.

Some celebrated a single season:

> I celebrate leaves springing from green to gold: I have fun
>   raking them and then jumping
>   into their bouncy and light colors.
> They seem to fly when the wind blows: then they come
>   drifting down to the ground.
> They spring their colors from green and yellow
>   to gold and brown: so they can change their clothes
>   every season, just as we do every day.
>
>   —*Mary Stuart Scott, third grade*

Another chose to celebrate the days of his life:

> I celebrate all the days of my life: for the days of my life
>   have been good.
> I celebrate the workdays and the playdays: work brings
>   satisfaction and play brings joy.
> I celebrate the everydays: the ordinary days are nice
>   because I know what to expect.
> I celebrate the summer days and the winter days:
>   in summer I can wake at five o'clock and go to sleep
>   at nine; and in winter I can go to school.
> I also celebrate the hard days and the easy days: the easy days
>   are nice, while the hard days help me learn.
>
>   —*Peter Shakow, third grade*

Other students were so thrilled by the Bible's lofty language that they reached new heights in their celebrations and laments:

> I shalt say, oh Lord, that mine hope has withered away:
>   and has gone into the lonely beams of the moon.
> Watching over mine herd I am merely a forgotten sheep
>   of thine.
> Every coming day is a past sorrow: freezing is the
>   endless night which you have put upon me.

The day withers on and thy beams beat me into the ground:
   mine enemies have become mine nightmares
   since sleep I cease to have.
Lord, will thee grant me one blink of hope?

   —*Robin Weigert, fourth grade*

Others liked the idea of celebrating things in their lives that might
seem ordinary to other people, but were quite special to them:

I like how fast I pedal my bike: I like the way the air blows
   against my face.
I can do a wheelie: you pull up your handlebars and the
   front wheel goes up.
I also like to go very fast and very slow: I like to be
   in control of my bike.
Someday my father and friends may ride in other places:
   we may follow the canal or go down country roads.

   —*John Meyers, third grade*

And one student celebrated the whole world:

O celebrate the things in the world: sing of wonders
   that will never cease.
The fish that live in the sea: silver, gliding silently
   through the endless days.
The happy people: rejoicing in harmony.
Meat: which supplies the Lord's people with their daily meals.
For parents: the guardians of children.
The pets: providing forsaken comfort for their kind owners.
The birds on the wing: flying swiftly through the silent
   blue sky.
The land animals: walking or crawling on soil or sand.
The wonderful seasons: for the harvest
   and the toilsome months.
The wonderful wood: without it there would be no paper
   and fire for warmth.
And mother earth: the haven of life.

   —*Marc Abramson, fourth grade*

The psalm writing project was one of the most successful I have ever
done with elementary school children, and it would be equally successful with middle and high school students because of the beauty of the
King James Bible's language and the universality of the ideas involved.

In fact, I know of one high school student, inspired by Psalms, who wrote her own poem of praise, using a simpler form:

> For yellow lacquered buttercups
>   and robins pulling up worms;
> For the smell of bread baking,
>   ripe apples and pine boughs at Christmas;
> For the twitch of a rabbit's nose
>   and the black silk of my cat's ears;
> For the cool taste of mint
>   and the hot crunch of radishes;
> For the wild hoot of owls,
>   the mewing of new kittens
> And the mourning dove who cries
>   as she flies. Thank you, Lord.
>
>   —*Elizabeth Lechliter*

When this was read in class, her teacher said, "Now, *that* is a psalm!"

*　　*　　*

The week after our psalm writing at Sidwell Friends, I decided to introduce the third and fourth graders to the Bible's Proverbs. I sought the shortest, clearest, and pithiest of Solomon's proverbs and found them in chapters 10–31. (High school students may enjoy chapter 31, verses 10–31, which describes the properties of a good wife!) After selecting several that I thought the students could understand, I read each proverb aloud and asked the students to give me an explanation or example in their own words:

> A talebearer revealeth secrets: but he that is of a faithful spirit concealeth the matter. 11:13
> ("A good friend won't tattle on you," was one student's response.)
>
> He that diligently seeketh good procureth favour: but he that seeketh mischief, it shall come unto him. 11:27
> ("Some kids just always seem to get in trouble!")
>
> Lying lips are abomination to the Lord: but they that deal truly are his delight. 12:22
> ("Nobody likes a liar.")
>
> A soft answer turneth away wrath: but grievous words stir up anger. 15:1
> ("When my little brother broke my doll I was really mad at him, but when he said, 'I'm really sorry,' I forgave him.")

73

As cold waters to a thirsty soul, so is good news from a far country.
25:25
("Everybody likes good news!")

A man that flattereth his neighbour spreadeth a net for his feet. 29:5
("When you say things you don't really mean, you feel trapped,
    because you didn't really mean it and have to live with it.")

Just as they had no trouble catching on to the idea of proverbs, they easily invented their own, often relating them to instances from their own lives. And they loved the idea of using similes and metaphors to give wise advice to the world at large:

Truthfulness is sometimes painful even when it is needful,
    just as putting disinfectant on a cut is painful
    even though it is healing.

—*Sheba Crocker, fourth grade*

A bragger is like a balloon that is just about to pop;
    so much hot air inside can lead to nothing but disaster.

—*Andy Kaufmann, fourth grade*

Foes will never keep secrets, as a raincloud can't keep his rain,
    while friends keep secrets as the sun keeps
    good weather around.

—*Amanda Godley, third grade*

Bragging is like turning nine without ever being eight.

—*Sarah Balderston, third grade*

He who boasteth is a helium balloon let go.

—*Meg Fullerton, fourth grade*

A few months after our psalm and proverb writing experiences, I put together the Lower School's first literary magazine. Several people suggested titles such as *Reflections*, *Imaginings*, etc. But as far as I was concerned, there was only one choice: *Celebrations*.

Barry Gilmore

Carpe Diem

Using Catullus

"TAKE A SHEET OF PAPER and make a list of everything you want to do before you die."

A few of the ninth, tenth, and eleventh graders in the Latin class I'm visiting start their lists immediately. To the others, I offer some further guidelines.

"Think of all the things you've ever dreamed of doing," I tell them. "Your dreams might be as simple as making an A in this class or as crazy as flying to Pluto. They might even be things you've already accomplished. Just be sure to list everything. I want you to include all of your goals, no matter how fantastic or boring you think they are."

By now, all of the students are conjuring at least the beginnings of a list, and a few have started scribbling away frantically. "Remember," I say, "list *everything.*"

Then I add the kicker.

"You have three minutes."

Hillsboro High School is located in an affluent suburb of Nashville, Tennessee, but the population of the school is more diverse than one might expect. Students from more than thirty countries attend classes at Hillsboro; during my residency there, I encountered students from Bulgaria, India, and even Rwanda. The students were a culturally diverse and intelligent group, especially in my mother's Advanced Placement Latin class, which I visited as part of a three-day residency sponsored by a grant from a local not-for-profit organization. My job was to incorporate creative writing into the curriculum of the Latin classes. At first, the idea of trying to teach so many different kinds of students in one class was intimidating, but I quickly realized that our subject was the perfect equalizer for such a group, since we all approached the language and culture of ancient Rome with something in common: a modern perspective.

The students had already encountered one surprise—a mother and son who not only get along but team-teach, and have fun doing it. When my mother (Dr. Gilmore to her classes) first disclosed our relationship to the students, I noticed a few expressions of horror on the faces of these teenagers as they imagined teaching with *their* mothers. But personal relationships were going to be important during this residency; we wanted to show the class that relationships were as important to Roman poets as they are to present-day high school students.

That's what my residency at Hillsboro was all about: making poetry personal. For months, this class had been studying and translating the poems of Catullus, in preparation for an Advanced Placement test in Latin at the end of the year. The approach had been, for the most part, academic. The students translated a given poem, discussed its content, and then moved on to the next one. The poems included a lot of new vocabulary, and because of this the students tended to begin their translations by merely exchanging the Latin words with their closest English equivalents. The results were frequently accurate but stiff translations of the poem.

The students had learned a lot, but in the process of turning Latin poetry into English prose they sometimes missed the real charm of the original poems. In his poems Catullus is often as irreverent and wicked as any teenager, and he is also a master of wordplay and imagery. His poems seem entirely contemporary, and offer rich inspiration for both the reader and the writer. My task was to help these students see that Catullus's poetry was prompted by emotions and relationships very similar to their own.

The lists I described above were part of a creative writing assignment that didn't occur until the last day of my visit. During the first day of my residency, we reviewed a poem the class had translated already. This poem was a personal favorite, Catullus 5, in which the poet addresses his mistress, Lesbia, and asks her to kiss him repeatedly:

Vivamus, mea Lesbia, atque amemus
rumoresque senum severiorum
omnes unius aestimemus assis!
soles occidere et redire possunt:
nobis cum semel occidit brevis lux,
nox est perpetua una dormienda.

da mi basia mille, deinde centum,
dein mille altera, dein secunda centum,
deinde usque altera mille, deinde centum.
dein, cum milia multa fecerimus,
conturbabimus illa, ne sciamus,
aut ne quis malus invidere possit,
cum tantum sciat esse basiorum.

Line by line, I asked various students to translate pieces of the poem into English. Since they'd already worked through the grammar of this poem once with my mother, we very quickly achieved a collaborative translation, which I wrote on the board. Grammatically, this translation was solid, but poetically it was a pale shadow of the original work, with little of Catullus's humor or musical language.

"What's this poem about?" I asked the class.

A girl from Italy raised her hand and answered, with a lift of her eyebrows, "Kisses."

"How does Catullus try to convince Lesbia to kiss him?"

"He tells her she's going to die."

I nodded. "So we're talking about kisses and death. Is this poem happy or sad?"

No one was quite certain how to answer.

Catullus fit a great deal of meaning into fourteen lines; the poem is at the same time light-hearted and shadowed by references to death. The students' translation had captured neither the joviality nor the despondency of the poem. Few literal translations could. We talked for a moment about how we might convey more of the *feeling* of the poem in English. One idea was that we might try to recreate Catullus's figures of speech, and his wordplay, in our translation.

Fortunately, the poem is rife with lines that capitalize on sound and double meanings. An example is the image Catullus used to suggest death, *nox est perpetua una dormienda* ("there is one perpetual night which must be slept"). The *u*, *m*, and *n* sounds in the last three words, especially when spoken aloud, suggest sadness, sleep, and perhaps dying. Our English translation was much stiffer. A football-player type sitting in the corner suggested changing "sleep" to "slumber" and "perpetual" to "unending," so that our line would read: "there is one unending night of slumber." Though perhaps less precise, this enhanced the line's meaning by adding melancholy sounds.

We quickly made several other changes. At the students' suggestion, *conturbabimus*, which we had originally translated as "we will confuse," became "we will discombobulate." We replaced *basia*, Catullus's own invented word for "kisses," with several slang terms that seemed more apt, including "smooches," "smackeroos," and "tonsil-hockey." We tried to capture the diminishing syllables of the phrase *occidit brevis lux* ("the brief light sets") with "once the transient daylight fades."

Our revised translation was much stronger. Still, my mother and I wanted the students to understand that Catullus was not just saying something important in a poetic way, but also that he was having *fun* doing it. We needed to put the poem into a new context for the students—their context, using their words. I told the class we were going to do an even looser translation, departing further from the Latin. On the board, I quickly wrote out the following chart:

METHODS OF TRANSLATION

Literal	*Middle Ground*	*Figurative*
Every Latin word = an English word	Precision vs. meaning & sense (looser translation of figures of speech, word play, poetic imagery)	Latin meaning = English meaning

"In literal translation, you're simply substituting," I told them. "Of course, you have to change the order of the words around, but it's still a very direct, almost mathematical, effort. Figurative translation isn't as exact, but offers more breathing room for the ideas behind the words."

I had the students pair off.

"You have to focus on literal translation first. Look for the most precise way to translate, the most 'correct' way. But you also have to decide when and where to depart from your literal translation to make sure the reader *feels* the poem." I asked them to translate the Catullus poem with their partners as figuratively as they could, using the voice of a high school student from Tennessee. I encouraged the students to have fun with this exercise, and the results showed that they did.

Here is my own literal translation of the poem, followed by a figurative translation with lines written by students in the class:

Let us live, my Lesbia, and let us love,
and let us count all of the rumors of severe old men
not worth one penny.
Suns are able to rise and set:
When once for us the brief light sets,
there is one perpetual night which must be slept.
Give me a thousand kisses, then a hundred,
then another thousand, then a second hundred,
then continually another thousand, then a hundred.
Then, when we will have made many thousands,
we will confuse them, so that we should not know,
nor is anyone evil able to envy,
when he knows there to be so many kisses.

   —*Catullus*

Hey baby! I dig you, but we ain't gettin' no younger.
Forget the old geezers, life's too short for gossip
and they just think I'm stealing you from your husband.
Shoot, woman, you know hunting season comes and goes
and you only get one shell—soon we'll be pushin'
up the daisies, so let's get going.
Kiss me! Kiss me! Kiss me again and again,
over and over until my tongue falls apart.
Kiss me till we pass out and can't even remember
how many times we locked lips,
and then no one will be jealous
and your pa won't come after me
with the shotgun.

   —*Class collaboration*

On the second day of my residency, we read two other poems inspired by Catullus 5: "To the Virgins, to Make Much of Time" by Robert Herrick and "since feeling is first" by E. E. Cummings. Neither poem is a direct translation, but both respond to the ideas and language of the Catullus poem. (On my chart, I added "Responses" to the right of "Figurative Translation").

Dr. Gilmore (Mom) pointed out that both poems pick up on Catullus's use of the sun as a metaphor for life and death, but they add lines in which love and life are compared to a flower (an image that forms the striking ending of another work by the poet, Catullus 11). Cummings's poem even demands kisses. It was not difficult for the class to see how, many centuries after Catullus wrote "Let us live," his feelings of urgency continue to resonate with other poets. We ended the second day by summing up in one statement the central theme of all three poems: life is short, so it's best to enjoy yourself while you can.

Day three: The three minutes are up and the lists are finished.

I ask if any students want to read what they've written. After an initial pause, I see a tentative hand go up in the back row. I smile and ask the student, a shy girl with curly hair, to read loudly so that we can all hear.

Things to Do Before I Die

Marry
Have kids
Skydive
Star in an episode of *Beverly Hills 90210*
Develop calf muscles
Have straight, blonde hair for at least a day
Own J. Crew
Wear fake eyelashes
Win the Latin Convention costume contest as Scylla
Be on *Oprah*

    —Meredith Lorber, tenth grade

Meredith's reading draws a few laughs and even a groan at the mention of the television program—obviously a class joke. Other students are suddenly anxious to read their own lists aloud. We listen to a few more.

"Look at your list," I say. "Raise your hand if you put something about falling in love or starting a relationship first."

A few students raise their hands.

"How about if a romantic relationship is on your list at all?"

More hands go up—all of them, in fact.

"Now ask yourself this question: 'If I were to die next year, how much of my list would I have accomplished?'" I wait a moment, then add, "What if you died next week?"

I see several knotted foreheads, and a few surprised faces. Most teenagers assume they'll have years to accomplish their goals. But most have also already had an experience with death. Teenagers are hardly incapable of contemplating their own mortality, though they also don't plan as if they'll pass away before graduating from high school.

"One last question," I say. "Ask yourself this: 'If I died today, which goal on my list would I feel most upset about leaving unfinished?'"

This time, the room is pretty quiet.

"This assignment is about life, not death," I tell them. "Write a poem in reaction to Catullus's words or ideas. How do you feel about rushing to get something done just in case you die? Given the fact that you'll die anyway, what would you most like to do before it happens? What would you least like to leave undone?"

The poems that come from this assignment can be lighthearted or serious, poignant or silly. I try to encourage students as much as I can to play with the notion of impending finality, an idea that can be as liberating as it can be depressing.

Carpe Diem

To experience the change of seasons,
the metamorphosis of land,
and the lessons of the earth
without ever missing a breath.
From Georgia to Maine, one step,
breath,
thought,
at a time.
To tattoo myself with the earth.
To remember what she teaches me
throughout my journey.
To appreciate
what I have been given.

—*Rebecca Stinson, eleventh grade*

As a variation, my mother had the students write responses to Catullus's poem using the voice of Lesbia. In this example, one student ends by asking Catullus the same question he attributes to Lesbia in a later poem, Catullus 7:

Oh, my, Catullus, you're a smooth talker, aren't you?

You actually expect me to fall for that old "Let us live and let us love" line? Do you know how many times I've heard that, and how many times I haven't died? How many other girls have you used that on, anyway? I'm not worried about dying anytime soon, and I'm pretty sure you'll be around, too. Just settle down there, Big Rocket! There'll be plenty of time for us if you just stop trying to sweet-talk your way in.

Now, how many kisses are enough? I want an exact number this time, mind you. No more confusing poetry. . . .

—*Johanna Russ, eleventh grade*

Translating from any language can lead students to writing poetry and fiction that truly reflects the feeling of the original words. Getting beyond literal translation, into the realm of figurative meaning, helps us make the connection personal. E. E. Cummings may have summed up this idea best, in the last lines of the poem I mentioned above: "for life's not a paragraph / and death i think is no parenthesis."

Bibliography

Catullus. Edited and translated by Henry V. Bender and Phyllis Young Forsythe. Wauconda, Ill.: Bolchazy-Carducci, 1997. This is the advanced-placement student text and includes all of the major poems. The accompanying *Teacher's Manual* includes accurate prose translations of the poems.

Cummings, E. E. *Complete Poems 1913–1962*. Edited by George W. Firmage. New York: Norton, 1991.

Herrick, Robert. *Poems*. Edited by Winfield Townley Scott. New York: Crowell, 1967.

Jeff S. Dailey

Dealing with Dragons

Using *Beowulf*

THE POET WHO PENNED the Old English epic *Beowulf* is maybe the most famous anonymous author of all time. More than 1000 years after it was written, *Beowulf* is more popular than ever. It has been translated into Modern English more than sixty-five times. With the exception of Greek, there are translations in every major European language, and in many non-European languages as well. John Gardner's popular novel *Grendel* is only one of the many creative works based on it.[1]

Yet, in spite of its popularity, high school English teachers seldom use it in their classes. At first glance, *Beowulf* can be perplexing for students—there are many characters, the plot frequently alternates between the past and present, and it deals with a period in history not covered in American Social Studies classes. Still, *Beowulf* is a great story, full of things that interest high school students, and a book that can inspire them to read and write.

Beowulf was written some time between 700 and 1000 C.E. Little else is known of its background, and scholars keep busy attempting to explain and analyze it. The poem was written in Old English (also called Anglo-Saxon), the language spoken in England at the time. On first sight, Old English bears little resemblance to its modern equivalent. As part of their experience with *Beowulf*, students should experience some of it in the original; not only does the medieval flavor come through, but many of Modern English's seemingly archaic rules and inconsistencies can be traced back to its Anglo-Saxon ancestor.

Of course, to read the entire text, students need a modern translation, either in prose or verse. Of the many prose translations available, high school students will find those by David Wright and Constance Hieatt the easiest to read. The translations by E. Talbot Donaldson and Robert Gordon are closer to the original in syntax, and are, consequentially, harder to understand.

Although the prose translations are often very precise, they cannot convey any sense of the poetic form of the original. Over the past century, many poets have tried to capture the spirit of the original in a variety of verse forms, ranging from attempts to imitate the Old English alliterative pattern to blank verse and rhymed couplets. The most common verse translation used in high schools is that by Burton Raffel, which, although very readable, is not as accurate as Michael Alexander's more recent rendering. There is also a complete recording of Alexander's translation, which is very useful in the classroom.

In 3,182 lines, the poem tells the story of the warrior Beowulf's life and death. It focuses especially on Beowulf's battles with three monsters—Grendel, Grendel's mother, and the dragon that ultimately causes the hero's death. In between these major events, the reader learns a great deal about medieval society and customs, both through the main narrative about Beowulf and in a series of tales about related legendary and historical figures, called "digressions." Many of *Beowulf*'s themes are relevant to today's students—the problems of growing up in a violent culture, the role of women in society, and figuring out how to cope with unknown dangers. Comparisons between contemporary society and that of Beowulf's time can yield revealing insights, and help students explore their own thoughts and values.

Beowulf can also help students develop their language skills. Its author was a master wordsmith, capable of manipulating language to great effect. The rhetorical and poetic devices make startling effects even in translation.

My approach to using *Beowulf* as a writing tool consists of three parts—first, having students experiment with its poetics; second, having them respond to its content; and, finally, having them create their own epics.

Experimenting with Poetic Devices

1. *Alliteration.* Usually, Old English poetry does not rhyme.[2] Instead, it is organized into lines of verse unified by alliteration. Each line consists of four stressed syllables and an unlimited number of unstressed syllables. The line is divided into two half-lines of two stressed syllables each,

with a caesura (or pause) in the middle. The predominant sound of the line is the third stressed syllable (the first one after the caesura). One or both of the first two stressed syllables alliterates with this third syllable, but the fourth one never does.

For example, lines 1384–1389 of *Beowulf* read:

> Ne sorga, snotor guma!   Sēlre biŏ æghwǽm,
> þæt hē his frēond wrece,   þonne hē fela murne.
> Ūre æghwylc sceal   ende gebīdan
> worolde līfes;   wyrce sē þe mōte
> dōmes ǽr dēaþe;   þæt biŏ drihtguman
> unlifgendum   æfter sēlest.[4]

A literal modern English translation is:

> Do not fear, wise man!   Better is it for him
> That he his friend avenges,   than that he mourn greatly.
> Each of us shall   the end experience
> Of worldly life;   may he who can achieve
> Glory before death;   that is for the warrior
> After life   the best.[5]

My attempt to render this into alliterative verse came out like this:

> Fear not, wise friend!   Fortunate more is he
> Who his righteous companion revenges,   rather than mourns greatly.
> Each of us eventually   shall encounter the close
> Of this world's life.   Let him that may
> Achieve distinction before death;   directly following
> The end of life,   that is the best.

Students can experiment with this form by taking a passage from any prose translation (or their own poetry) and attempting to imitate the structure. A thesaurus is recommended to help locate synonyms. Students should remember that they are dealing with sounds, not letters—thus, the initial sound of *circus* alliterates with *sister*, but not with *cannon*.

Here are two examples by tenth graders[6]:

> A heroic man had halted a bank bandit
>
> —*Lisa Gnad*

The reckless redhead wrestled an alligator
—*Alaina Gemeniano*

2. *Flyting.* Flyting is verbal dueling. It occurs in the epic narratives of many cultures.[7] Students who have read *The Iliad* or *The Song of Roland*, for instance, will be able to draw parallels between those works and *Beowulf*. It is important to realize that insults and exclamations uttered during battle are not flyting, but the verbal assaults that happen before or in lieu of actual combat are. Flyting occurs most notably in *Beowulf* in the exchange between the hero and Unferth in lines 499–606, but it also appears in the dialogue between Beowulf and the Coastguard (lines 239–319).

Students can create their own verbal exchanges. They should note that the dialogue always remains very proper—at no time does Beowulf or his adversaries yell or curse.

3. *Litotes.* Litotes refers to extreme understatement, often used with humorous effect. It is common in Old English literature, both in poetry and prose. For example, kings are not "killed," they are "deprived of their kingdoms." "Many" becomes "not a few." After Sigemund kills the dragon, he does not receive great praise, "but no little glory."

Students can search out the litotes in *Beowulf* and then come up with their own. In the examples below, the first line is a declarative statement; underneath is the same idea using litotes.

The soldier suffered a deep gash from his enemy
The soldier received an offending cut from his foe

   —*Vincenzo Gaicalone, tenth grade*

The men drowned in the water
The men's lungs did not react well to the water

   —*Mario Vargas, tenth grade*

4. *Kennings.* Kennings are compact metaphors. In *Beowulf* and other Old English poems, kennings are usually brief symbolic phrases or single words that replace simple nouns. For instance, the sea becomes a "whale road" ("hron-rade"—line 10). Grendel is called a "sharer in Hell's secrets" ("hel-rune"—line 163), and the Devil is a "soul slayer"

("gast-bona"—line 177). Students can experiment, creating their own kennings and including them in their writing. (There are many examples of both kennings and litotes in "The Lament of the Last Survivor," below.)

Once, when I was teaching about kennings, a student insisted she did not know how to make up one. I told her to write a simple statement about what she had done over the weekend. This was no help, she insisted, as she had not done anything—"I just stared at the four walls." When I explained that "four walls" was a kenning, she had no trouble understanding the concept and went on to finish the exercise.

Here are other student kennings:

body transporter [car]
foot fest [dancing]
festive diversion [party]

   —*Aizza Gemeniano, tenth grade*

tummy pleasers [cookies]

   —*Daisy Mera, tenth grade*

eye of heaven [sun]
day's ending [twilight]

   —*Catherine Horath, tenth grade*

Responding to the Text

Beowulf contains much to write about, and students can respond to themes in the poem in a variety of ways—writing essays, letters, parodies, etc.

One theme students can write about is that of retribution. Anglo-Saxon society, as portrayed in *Beowulf*, was governed by a very strict set of rules and regulations, many of which conflict with modern ethics. Their law was based on revenge; family and friends had an obligation to avenge a slain comrade, either by exacting *wergeld*[8] or by slaying the killer. In spite of the fact that Anglo-Saxon England was Christianized, the doctrine of forgiveness was largely ignored. It was a matter of honor and a pleasure to avenge one's companion and extremely shameful if one could not: in *Beowulf*, the most despondent men are those who are unable to exact revenge. In lines 2435–2453 we learn the story of a depressed father, one of whose sons was killed (probably accidentally) by his other son. His grief comes from the fact that he cannot avenge his dead son without killing another member of his family. Immediately following this story, the poet relates another, similar, tale of a father whose son has been executed by the government. Unable to retaliate, he is forced to live out the remainder of his life in sorrow.

As part of their *Beowulf* unit, teachers can have their students write their interpretations and comments on these and similar passages. Many find the eye-for-an-eye theme unsettling. For instance, when asked to respond to lines 1384–1389 (about revenge, see page 85 above), my students wrote:

> The writer is saying that if you're a man, you have to be a fighter till the end. That's what makes you a man, so before your death you'll be known as a brave man and not a wimp. . . . I don't agree. . . . It doesn't make you any more of a man to be fighter and have physical strength. It's inner strength that's important.
>
> —*Judie Song, eleventh grade*

> The speaker is saying that if someone kills your friend, kill that person who killed him because it will make you feel better. . . . I don't agree because then the killing will never stop. If you avenge your friend's death, then that person's friend will kill you, and so on.
>
> —*Thomas Vazquez, eleventh grade*

> Two wrongs don't make a right, but, on the other hand, that's the first thing you'd think about if a friend that's really close to you dies.
>
> —*Kany Rodgriquez, eleventh grade*

Others, however, found the prospect of vengeance appropriate:

> I agree with him [Beowulf]. It is true you should get even with the person if he kills your best friend.
>
> —*Kelvin Sanchez, eleventh grade*

> I agree. . . . If your friend is killed your natural reaction is to kill the guy that killed your friend.
>
> —*Stephen Amarosa, eleventh grade*

I also ask students to respond to "The Lament of the Last Survivor," a digression in lines 2247–2266:

Hold now, Earth, my treasure. Heroes may not take
These noble possessions thence. They, indeed, return
From where the dauntless once procured them. Death-in-War,
That cowardly life-consumer, has carried off every one
Of my people. Those who pleasure partook of in the hall
Are now forsaken. I no longer have companions to
Ply a sword or pass around a plated cup, a cherished vessel
Garnished with gold, the glorious helmet
Tarnished sits. Sleeps he that should burnish it.
Likewise the war coat, which during battle endured
Biting sword and slamming shield,
Decays from disuse; denied is the ear the mailcoat's clamor
Throughout the war leader's wide-ranging travels,
Surrounded by soldiers. Sounds no more the harp's joy,
The singing wood; nor swoops through the hall
The trained hawk; the horse—once fleet—no longer
Stamps in the square. Sinister murder
Away has sent all of the living.

Students are often very moved by this passage, seeing in it parallels with their own times:

> The tone of the poem is sad and depressing because it speaks of death and unhappiness.
>   In this poem, the speaker is trying to say that, since humans have gotten all caught up in fighting and competition, everyone has eventually died. . . . I do agree, because, to put it in today's terms, with all the new weapons . . . we're eventually going to kill ourselves.
>   —*Diane LaSalle, eleventh grade*

Teachers can encourage students to respond to *Beowulf* in imaginative ways. For example, before they read the end of the poem, I present students with the following problem:

> Several weeks ago, someone stole a precious object from a fire-breathing dragon who lives in a cave outside the city. The dragon is furious and is taking out his anger by flying over local neighborhoods at night, breathing fire that is killing people and destroying buildings. Your assignment is to prepare a plan to solve this problem. Prepare a proposal that tells how you will save the city.

Some try to solve this problem in a distinctively non-Anglo-Saxon manner—they try to negotiate with the dragon:

My plan to save the city is to talk to the fire-breathing dragon and tell him that I will get his precious object back if he stops breathing fire at the people and buildings. I would tell the dragon that everything is going to be fine and leave all the work for me to do. Then I would go on television to tell everyone in the city to please cooperate with me. I will go to everybody's house, backyard, and secret hiding place to search for the precious object.

—*Gregory Chan, eleventh grade*

I would try to talk to the dragon to see if we can get to an agreement so that he won't hurt more people. I would tell him to give me more time so that I can find the stolen object. . . . [While he waits] I'll find him a pretty good-looking female dragon to keep him company in his cave. With this plan I'm pretty sure he would stop killing people.

—*Viviana Gomez, eleventh grade*

Others are more bellicose:

I gather a few good men to take out this dragon. We build a cart with wheels that shoots out a sphere with the tip made of steel and is very sharp. We make a few of them, put one on every roof, and, when the dragon flies by, we shoot it down.

—*Thomas Vazquez, eleventh grade*

We get the military to get helicopters and soldiers so that when the dragon strikes, the military could attack with our modern technological weapons. Just in case the dragon burns any buildings, there should be at least ten fire trucks to stop the flames. When the dragon goes down, we use our firemen to put water in the dragon's mouth so that he won't be able to burn anything, or anyone, again.

—*Moises Rodriguez, eleventh grade*

There are other topics in *Beowulf* that students can explore in similarly imaginative ways. Possible assignments include:

1. Using the clues found in the poem and your imagination, describe Grendel, his mother, and their cave.

2. Write a newspaper article describing Beowulf's fight with Grendel or with the dragon.

3. Write a story explaining how the speaker of "The Lament of the Last Survivor" came to be the last of his tribe.

4. Write an obituary for Beowulf (or any other dead warrior).

5. Write a description of what a typical day would be like if you were a king or queen in Anglo-Saxon times; a warrior; a servant.

6. Update a section of *Beowulf* to contemporary times.

Encourage students to use their creative ingenuity to come up with other ideas. Publish these as a class publication—call it *The Beowulf Chronicle, The Anglo-Saxon Times,* or something similar.

Writing an Epic
After they have finished reading *Beowulf* and have completed the above assignments, students can then collaborate on their own epic.

The process begins by discussing what an epic is and what it should include. If students have read other epics in addition to *Beowulf,* they can compare and contrast them. The teacher should ultimately make it clear that an epic is the story of a hero or heroine, usually with a battle between the forces of good and evil. At this point, the teacher should decide whether the different episodes of the epic will be created by groups or if each student will create an episode individually (which makes for a very long story).

The next step is to make a list of all the events that should occur in a hero's life. This may include his or her birth, youth, education, first love, training, major battles, romantic encounters, marriage, heroic deeds, less-than-heroic deeds, children, and death. As long as the hero's origins and death (or other conclusion, such as Merlin's being shut up in a tree) are included, any other incidents are fine. Each group or student is assigned one of the episodes.

Following this, the class decides on adjectives to describe the hero's physical appearance and psychological traits, to provide continuity from episode to episode.

Recently I did this exercise with Brian Blayer's honors sophomore English class at Grover Cleveland High School in Ridgewood, N.Y. The class invented a hero, "Blake," and gave him the following characteristics: romantic, cunning, charismatic, strong-willed, strategic, smart, athletic, and stealthy. They then decidesd to explore the following aspects of his life: origins, romance, villains, beliefs, discoveries, achievements, disappointments, battles, journeys, and death.

Groups of four students were then each assigned one of these aspects and worked on creating chapters of the epic in prose. At the end of the period, a spokesperson from each group read a passage out loud.

It began with Blake's birth ("On a stormy day, a great hero was born . . . his family was poor but friendly") and his education ("His parents taught him very well when it came to matters of war"). It progressed to his experiences with the villainess Jezzebel [sic] ("Sister of John who was killed by Blake") and an unfortunate incident ("He was constantly tormented by the ghost of his daughter, whom he accidentally killed in battle"). It concluded with his return ("After many journeys and adventures, Blake went back to his native land, to be reunited with his family").

Thus students ended their Beowulf unit with the recitation of an epic, much as an unknown storyteller recited *Beowulf* over 1000 years before.

Notes

1. Others include Michael Crichton's *Eaters of the Dead* (Ballantine Books, 1976), Frank Schaefer's *Whose Song Is Sung* (Tor Books, 1996), and Parke Godwin's *The Tower of Beowulf* (William Morrow and Company, 1995).

2. The so-called "Rhyming Poem" from the Exeter Book is the only notable exception.

3. Old English had two letters not found in its modern counterpart: *eth* (ð) and *thorn* (þ). Both are equivalent of *th*.

4. In Old English poetics, any vowel alliterated with any other vowel.

5. All translations in this article are by the author.

6. All samples of student writing came either from Mr. Blayer's sophomore class or the author's own junior class at Grover Cleveland High School.

7. See the Introduction to Parks's *Verbal Dueling in Heroic Narrative* for a list of flyting sequences found in epics from all different cultures.

8. Literally, "man-money," the amount of which varied with the social class of the deceased. The etymology behind the term is interesting—*geld* is related to *gold*, and hence, money—and *wer* appears in Modern English only in the first syllable of *werewolf*.

Bibliography

Beowulf. Translated by Michael Alexander. New York: Penguin, 1973.
———. Translated by E. Talbot Donaldson. New York: Norton, 1975.
———. Translated by Robert Gordon. New York: Dover, 1992.
———. Translated by Constance Hieatt. New York: Bantam: 1983.
———. Translated by Burton Raffel. New York: Mentor, 1963.
———. Translated by David Wright. New York: Penguin: 1957.
Bessinger, Jess and Robert Yeager, editors. *Approaches to Teaching Beowulf*. New York: Modern Language Association, 1984.
Bjork, Robert and John Niles, editors. *A Beowulf Handbook*. Lincoln: University of Nebraska, 1997.
Jackson, Guida. *Traditional Epics: A Literary Companion*. Oxford, England: Oxford University, 1994.
Klaeber, Fr. *Beowulf and the Fight at Finnsburg*. Lexington, Mass.: D.C. Heath, 1950.
Ogilvy, J. D. A. and Donald Baker. *Reading Beowulf*. Norman: University of Oklahoma, 1983.
Parks, Ward. *Verbal Dueling in Heroic Narrative: The Homeric and Old English Traditions*. Princeton, N.J.: Princeton University, 1990.
Tuso, Joseph, editor. *Beowulf: The Norton Critical Edition*. New York: Norton, New York, 1975.
Whitelock, Dorothy. *The Audience of Beowulf*. Oxford, England: Oxford University, 1951.

Jordan Clary

Rumi in Susanville

Using Classic Persian Poetry
With At-Risk Students

MOST OF THE TEENAGERS at Credence Continuation High School are the take-up-a-lot-of-space kind. They come with attitude stuffed in their hip pocket along with a smashed pack of cigarettes. Their concentration is focused on how much they can put over on the adults around them. Sometimes you can smell the alcohol on their breath.

I feel for them. When I went to high school there wasn't a continuation school, but if there had been, I would have been there. Instead, I was put into a vocational track education program and barely managed to graduate; my highest grade was a C–. Many days I sneaked into the girls' bathroom and smoked. And like many of the students at Credence, high school was where I first experimented with drugs and alcohol.

Credence is located in Susanville, a small, high desert town in northeastern California. In recent years it has become known as the Idaho of California because of its reputation for harboring anti-government militia groups. Many of the kids here are bored and restless. They feel that life is going on out there, away from them, while they are trapped in a dead-end town, one with one of the largest prison complexes in the country.

A California Arts Council grant brought me into the classroom with these teenagers. The poetry class met two days a week during their regular English class, and I worked with two separate groups of students. At Credence the students are not separated by grade level, so ninth through twelfth graders are all together. I had never taught students who had no choice about attending and I wasn't prepared for the bad attitudes that accompanied some of them.

For several years I had been teaching creative writing to prison inmates, and I tended to rely heavily on the classics for in-class readings. As a writer, I believe that everything we write is built from what has been written before. At the prison, the men I taught were hungry and eager for anything I wanted to read to them; they wanted to learn. My prison class had become a tight, student-run workshop where the men offered suggestions—from Shakespeare and Dante to Ralph Ellison and Jack Kerouac—it seemed there was never enough time to cover all the authors they wanted to read. At Credence, the students sometimes fell asleep on their desks. They claimed they couldn't understand Shakespeare and when I read selections from *Jane Eyre*, they pleaded boredom. What did these works have to do with their lives?

There were breakthroughs. When I showed the Franco Zeffirelli version of *Romeo and Juliet*, they were enthralled, and occasionally the writing exercises, especially those which called for group participation or used mixed media such as collage, brought forth bursts of creativity. Yet I felt something was missing. Much of the work continued to feel forced or stilted. The wariness that I saw in their eyes was reflected in their writing.

The day I brought in Rumi we seemed to cross a line. I didn't tell them who the poem was by or when the author had lived. I simply began by reading:

Who Says Words with My Mouth?

All day I think about it, then at night I say it.
Where did I come from, and what am I supposed to be doing?
I have no idea.
My soul is from elsewhere, I'm sure of that,
and I intend to end up there.

This drunkenness began in some other tavern.
When I get back around to that place,
I'll be completely sober. Meanwhile,
I'm like a bird from another continent, sitting in this aviary.
The day is coming when I fly off,
but who is it now in my ear who hears my voice?
Who says words with my mouth?

Who looks out with my eyes? What is the soul?
I cannot stop asking.
If I could taste one sip of an answer,
I could break out of this prison for drunks.
I didn't come here of my own accord, and I can't leave that way.

Whoever brought me here will have to take me home.

This poetry. I never know what I'm going to say.
I don't plan it.
When I'm outside the saying of it,
I get very quiet and rarely speak at all.

—*Translated by Coleman Barks*

The students liked Rumi because they could understand him. If a work is too abstract, they feel bored; if it's too full of symbolism that they need to decipher, they shut down. I don't avoid classics just because they might be difficult, but Rumi cut right to the bone. Some of these students were hard on the road that takes them down some dark ways, and Rumi, for those who were willing to listen, offered a ray of hope.

"What would be the answer to help you break out from your prison?" I asked them.

Their answers were flippant at first: "To get out of Susanville," "To smoke some bud." But gradually the flippancy changed to anger. They felt that what kept them imprisoned was the world of school, teachers, and parents. They saw injustice everywhere. For many of these teenagers, that dwelling place of anger seemed to be the only place they could get to and they held onto it like a great, smoldering chunk of lava. I wanted to move them past that, to a place where they could begin looking for solutions rather than storing that ire in their guts.

Usually I give focused writing assignments on a specific topic, but this time the assignment was open. I told them to write about whatever thoughts Rumi inspired in them. Mary Brooks, a quiet, pretty girl who often sat with her long, brown hair cascading over her face, wrote:

I think about it. Soon
I dream about it.
It's not where I came from, it's
why?

How
is my eyesight
the sound of my
voice and my
ears to hear?

I say to myself
I want to get

away. I want out.
Take me from
this silence.

After collecting their work and reading back some of the poems, I
told the students a little about the life of Mevlana Jelaluddin Rumi. Rumi
was born in what is now Afghanistan. He and his family escaped the
Mongol invasion of their country and wandered throughout Muslim
lands, finally settling in Konya, Turkey. Upon his father's death, Rumi
succeeded him as a religious teacher in the dervish community of Konya.
In 1244 his life changed when he met the wandering dervish, Shams of
Tabriz. Over the next four years, Shams and Rumi developed a deep and
intimate friendship. When Shams mysteriously disappeared, Rumi's
bereavement for his friend found expression in an outpouring of music,
dance, and lyric poetry. Rumi died on December 17, 1273. He is remembered as one of the great spiritual masters, as well as a poet, and was the
founder of the Mevlevi Sufi order, a mystical brotherhood of Islam.

The students were surprised to learn that the poem that they understood so clearly had been written more than 700 years ago. "Rumi got
loaded," a young man with a shaved head called out from the back row.
"Did you hear what he said about getting drunk?"

"Maybe," I said, but I also explained that the Sufis follow a strict
code of the Koran which forbids alcohol. It is far more likely that Rumi
was using drunkenness metaphorically. Rumi believed we should live
through experience rather than through words but he was also willing to
look inside at both the light and dark places of his soul. Many of his
poems deal with dichotomies of one kind or another—of love, of the
soul, of the material world. As an illustration I read "Two Kinds of Intelligence":

There are two kinds of intelligence: one acquired,
as a child in school memorizes facts and concepts
from books and from what the teacher says,
collecting information from the traditional sciences
as well as from the new sciences.

With such intelligence you rise in the world.
You get ranked ahead or behind others
in regard to your competence in retaining
information. You stroll with this intelligence
in and out of fields of knowledge, getting always more
marks on your preserving tablets.

There is another kind of tablet, one
already completed and preserved inside you.
A spring overflowing its springbox. A freshness
in the center of the chest. This other intelligence
does not turn yellow or stagnate. It's fluid,
and it doesn't move from outside to inside
through the conduits of plumbing-learning.

This second knowing is a fountainhead
from within you, moving out.

    —Translated by Coleman Barks

The majority of students who attend Credence do so not because they are less intelligent than the students at the regular high school, but because for one reason or another they don't "fit in." They learn differently. In some ways they are more worldly than the average small-town teenager, but they don't do well with books and tests. Many of the Credence kids were resistant to writing, but I hoped by freeing them from the constraints of a structured essay and into the world of poetry they would learn to write "from within, moving out." One of the students who seemed to intuit Rumi's message most completely was Ben Farmer. Ben had not written a thing all year. He was not disruptive, but not exactly cooperative either. At sixteen, he was newly married and soon to be a father. For a while, he sat silently at his desk while the other students began scribbling away in their notebooks. Finally, he began to write and at the end of the period handed in the following poem:

The man inside has no voice
but speaks in many ways.
The man inside doesn't cry
but has many tears.
The man inside is outgoing
but stopped within.
The man inside has lots of love
but only loves a few.
The man inside never forgives
but will forget.
The man inside stays hidden
in fear he'll be discovered.

The following day I read Ben's poem to the class without naming the author. I told them I thought it was an important poem. After that, Ben began turning in work on a regular basis. Sometimes it was awkward but other times I was stunned by the risks he was willing to take. Later that year, he and a couple of his friends began a student newspaper. It failed after only a few issues, but at least it was a step taken. I believe that in some small way Rumi helped give them voice.

Rumi took the students to a quieter place when they wrote. I continued to read them other classics as well as contemporary writings, but whenever the class began to drag, I turned to Rumi. One day I read his "Quietness":

> Inside this new love, die.
> Your way begins on the other side.
> Become the sky.
> Take an axe to the prison wall.
> Escape.
> Walk out like someone suddenly born into color.
> Do it now.
> You're covered with thick cloud.
> Slide out the side. Die,
> and be quiet. Quietness is the surest sign
> that you've died.
> Your old life was a frantic running
> from silence.
>
> The speechless full moon
> comes out now.
>
> —*Translated by Coleman Barks*

"Write about the most quiet time you remember," I told them. Blaine Spraggins, a confirmed rebel, wrote:

> I hate quiet time. My life is seldom quiet. My mind moves fast. Always. I like to be loud, to voice my opinion. Life should be lived to the fullest. Loud. Fast. Fun and energetic. I will make all the noise I can while I live because once I'm gone in my negative six foot bed, all will be quiet and still. Then I shall enjoy quiet time.

"Rumi would have liked you," I told him. "He was in favor of living life to the fullest, too." I was pleased with Blaine's piece. He took Rumi's "Quietness is the surest sign that you've died" and gave it his own twist. Another young man, Lalan Nix, wrote the following:

Thought Is Quiet

When thought is quiet—it is a peaceful,

kind, revealing, and soothing thought that can lure you in
and take you prisoner in the mind itself.
Thoughts can reveal life, secrets or even love,
but thought cannot be persuaded. For thought
is merely a state of mind and a question
being answered in the depths of the quiet mind.

Lalan's previous work was filled with profanity and references to drugs and liquor. After this assignment, he reverted to his former subjects, but at least for a short time he showed that he was capable of moving beyond the partying mind-set to introspection. Maybe someday that contemplation will resurface.

My relationship with the students began to change subtly over the next few months. Their poems were becoming more thoughtful. We made place mats using their writing and put them in the local coffee shop. Their work came to the attention of the local newspaper, which began printing a student poem a month. For the first time, many of them were receiving positive recognition from their community.

At the same time, their work was becoming angrier, more intense. They were asking questions of themselves and their world:

My life is a burning mass of flames

    I look cool and calm from afar
But come closer

My soul is burning
        Burning for lust
        Burning for chaos
        Burning for recognition

    —*Rob Brocksen*

Most teenagers are reacting to life; they have not yet learned how to be players. Some of them are lost. Most are confused. They are desperately trying to make sense of the world and of their place in it. Rumi struggled with these same questions. He speaks to the adolescent mind searching for answers.

Bibliography

Rumi. *The Essential Rumi*. Translated by Coleman Barks, with John Moyne, A. J. Arberry, and Reynold Nicholson. New York: HarperCollins, 1995.

Jane Avrich

Sonnet Writing in The Fifth Grade

Using Shakespeare

LAST YEAR I TAUGHT a fifth grader named Rachael whose confidence waxed and waned. Usually she'd slam her books down on a front row desk, ready to leap to the fore of class discussion. "Oh, oh! Please, me!" she'd pipe, waving her arm wildly, upper body lurching over her desk. But when Rachael was unsure of the material, she retreated. If I called on her, she shrank back in her seat, large-eyed and timid, her answer barely audible. That spring, Rachael wrote a sonnet about shyness:

> The waves build up and up until they're gone
> Gone up upon the shore hiding in the sand
> Retreating to the sea as other waves have done
> Then, gathering their courage, surge to land.
> The aspen tree so bold and bright stands tall
> It battles against all kinds of weather
> But when the wind blows its hardest it calls
> To mind the quivering of a lovely feather.
> The morning glory, the gold and the bold,
> Opens its petals to the morning like lions
> But when the afternoon does come it folds
> Into a timid little mouse who's crying.
> > As I retreat from my boldness I'm shy
> > But I know my courage will come by and by.

Rachael wrote this sonnet in my Language Structures class at Saint Ann's School in Brooklyn, N.Y. The sonnet writing project was highly successful; each student in the class of fifteen was able to produce a fresh, artful sonnet in his or her own voice. The success was partially due to the exceptional nature of Saint Ann's itself, a private school progressive in both curriculum and philosophy. By removing the pressure of grades, the school fosters a mood of curiosity and openness to new projects; the aim is to encourage individual growth and group interaction instead of competition. My fifth graders were a particularly supportive group, listening to and commenting warmly on each other's poems as I read the daily sheaf of homework aloud.

In addition, the school makes a point of introducing creative writing as early as the second or third grade and continuing its practice throughout the high school years. Lower school students are encouraged to write stories and poems without worrying too much about errors in grammar and spelling, so as to make writing as spontaneous and free of anxiety as possible. By the time I receive my students in the fifth grade, they think of writing as fun. Language Structures, a course taught side by side with English, presents language as a versatile tool. As well as writing poetry, my fifth graders learn to trace etymological roots, read and write newspaper articles, use library resources, and write research papers.

Many of the children at Saint Ann's are gratifying to teach. Bright, curious, many of them very talented, they feed on intellectual stimulation. Small classes of thirteen to eighteen students allow lessons to take place on an intimate level, enabling the teacher to be constantly aware of each student's needs.

At the same time, it is important to note that many students at Saint Ann's, while motivated, do not possess exceptional abilities. The fifth grade humanities courses are divided into four levels; last year mine was third from the top. Many of the children were not strong readers and few were strong writers. Some had problems with spelling and retaining information, while others had learned English as their second language and were still shaky on usage and rules. Moreover, few students had formally studied poetry; although most of them had done plenty of free-form writing of stories and poems, a formal structure such as the sonnet was something new.

But the fact is that younger children in general, regardless of their education and background, have a strong instinct for poetry. Nine- and ten-year-olds are highly attuned to rhythm and sound. Words, not yet worn out and drained of life, are for them still imprinted with images. Much of what my own fifth graders were able to do, others of their age could do, too.

During the poetry unit that my class did that spring, I grew more and more impressed with their enthusiasm both for reading and for writing different kinds of poems. Children are remarkably clever imitators, able to read and appreciate a variety of forms and then to make those forms their own. The sonnet was a fitting final project because it wraps up many new skills, such as the use of meter, rhyme, and imagery, into a neat and compact package. The Shakespearean sonnet is also an exercise in clarity: its tight, logical form disciplines students to focus on one idea, develop it in twelve lines, then bring it to a conclusion in the couplet.

I approached this writing assignment in cautious steps. The fifth graders started by looking at poetic images, so often the building blocks of a poem. The students read haiku and drew pictures of what the three-line poems let them see—a blossom, a loon, a reflection of the moon on water. Then, in seventeen syllables of their own, they tried to capture an image in a few swift strokes, leaving a lingering feeling of its "after-presence." Their haiku were simple, frank observations of insects, sunbeams, passing clouds, or snow freshly fallen on a meadow in nearby Prospect Park.

They went on to read Imagist poems such as William Carlos Williams's "The Red Wheelbarrow" and Wallace Stevens's impressionistic "Thirteen Ways of Looking at a Blackbird." I introduced the terms *simile* and *metaphor*, which I described as points of intersection between two images, like the joining place of two links on a chain. Ezra Pound's "In a Station of the Metro" served as a good example:

The apparition of these faces in the crowd;
Petals on a wet black bough.

After turning the poem over in their minds, the students began to nod in appreciation and murmur, "Oh, I get it," as they realized how the splotches of a hubbub of faces could look for a moment like wet blossoms clustered on a branch.

As we played with figurative language, I pointed out the distinction between poems about abstract ideas (love, peace, or fear) and concrete ones (the sound of glass breaking or the image of two plums in the icebox). We explored how abstract ideas could be represented by concrete images and thus rendered more familiar, more personal, as in Emily Dickinson's poem #254:

"Hope" is the thing with feathers—
That perches in the soul—
And sings the tune without the words—
And never stops—at all—

And sweetest—in the Gale—is heard—
And sore must be the storm—
That could abash the little Bird
That kept so many warm—

I've heard it in the chillest land—
And on the strangest Sea—
Yet never, in Extremity,
It asked a crumb—of Me.

The fifth graders warmed to this emotive poem, which is so simply written, and whose single image suggests so much about the woman who wrote it. Unlike the Imagist fragments that describe impressions coolly and deftly, Dickinson allows her feelings to show, extending her metaphor by drawing numerous parallels between the nature of hope and the behavior of a bird (the "thing with feathers" that she playfully declines to name). One girl flapped her hands and pointed out that "her words sound like this"; indeed the bird's frenetic fluttering is much like Dickinson's delicate bursts of verse. Like a bird, she is persistent yet fragile. At this point I asked the fifth graders to describe an abstract feeling by comparing it to something concrete and to sustain the comparison for at least eight lines. The resulting batch was mostly animal poems, many of them very lively. In one poem, loneliness took the form of a baying dog; in another, playfulness was a panda.

After experimenting with figurative language, we went on to rhyme and meter. Getting the children to rhyme didn't require much work. For exercises I gave them one-, two-, and three-syllable words and asked them to go home and find as many words as they could that rhymed with each. They brought back scores. (After all, most of them had been rhyming since *The Cat in the Hat*.) Some were already rhyming their poems voluntarily. Others were accomplished rappers; in the lunchroom they'd rap about subjects ranging from Nintendo to peanut butter cups.

Fifth grade ears were not as well tuned to meter, however. I tried bringing in examples—fluid iambs as opposed to plodding spondees, rapid anapests and waltzing dactyls—and showed them Coleridge's tour de force, "Metrical Feet":

— ⏑   — ⏑   — ⏑   —

Tro-chee | trips from | long to | short.

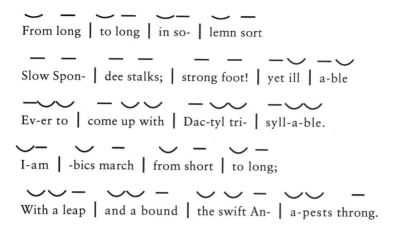

From long | to long | in so- | lemn sort

Slow Spon- | dee stalks; | strong foot! | yet ill | a-ble

Ev-er to | come up with | Dac-tyl tri- | syll-a-ble.

I-am | -bics march | from short | to long;

With a leap | and a bound | the swift An- | a-pests throng.

But when the students read a poem on their own, they had trouble distinguishing the stressed syllables from the unstressed. I encouraged them to read the poems out loud. In fact, the first poems were songs, I told them—that's where their rhythm comes from.

Then my own words gave me an idea. The next day, I came to class armed with a boom box and a Beatles tape. I pushed *play* and "Eight Days a Week" blasted out. The fifth graders mouthed the words and drummed the beat on their desks. Within moments they were keeping time in perfect trochees:

Ooh, I | need your | love, babe

Guess you | know it's | true

Or the iambics of another song:

I want | to hold | your hand. . . .

I wrote lines from these songs on the blackboard and asked for volunteers to scan them. Most of the students were eager to come up and mark the stressed and unstressed beats. For homework they were able to write two lines of iambs and two lines of dactyls for me to read

105

aloud. They also began to like having the odd, consonant-cluttered metrical terms in their vocabulary; daily they announced discoveries of "trochees," "spondees," and "anapests" in limericks, TV jingles, and their own names.

Now it was time to put the pieces together and look at some sonnets; in order to construct such a strict form, the students first needed to see it in action. Shakespeare seemed a reasonable place to start. His sonnet #29 proved a good icebreaker:

> When, in disgrace with fortune and men's eyes,
> I all alone beweep my outcast state,
> And trouble deaf heaven with my bootless cries,
> And look upon myself, and curse my fate:
> Wishing me like to one more rich in hope,
> Featured like him, like him with friends possess'd,
> Desiring this man's art and that man's scope,
> With what I most enjoy contented least:
> Yet in these thoughts myself almost despising,
> Haply I think on thee, and then my state,
> Like to the lark at break of day arising
> From sullen earth, sings hymns at heaven's gate;
> > For thy sweet love remembered such wealth brings
> > That then I scorn to change my state with kings.

I was surprised that the fifth graders did not seem intimidated by the antiquated language or syntax. They asked me the meaning of certain words (*scope* and *haply*) and they found it helpful to trace a few participial phrases back to their distant antecedents (*I* to *wishing, desiring,* and *despising,* for example), but their basic response to the poem was immediate and strong. The students could relate to the bouts of insecurity and self-pity that Shakespeare talks about when he says, "I all alone beweep my outcast state." You feel that you're stupid and clumsy, that you look awful, while everybody else seems smart, popular, and cool. "Nobody likes me, everybody hates me, I think I'll go eat worms" was one student's chanted response. The students liked the bantering self-mockery of Shakespeare's tone and felt conversant with him rather than daunted by the old-fashioned language. Even their misunderstandings brought them closer to him. In the phrase *bootless cries,* for example, they pictured someone kicking out tender bare feet in frustration, only to have them slam against a wall.

Perhaps most important, the students were able to trace the shape of the poem's argument. After the buildup of complaints in the first eight lines, they recognized the "turn" in the ninth, signaled by the pivotal word *yet*. The poet stops, remembers his love, and in the remaining six lines regains his confidence. The final couplet, chiming with the sound of *brings* and *kings*, gives the poem a satisfying sense of closure.

Another poem that went over well was the anti-Petrarchan blazon #130 ("My mistress' eyes are nothing like the sun"). The students liked the fact that the poet's love is a real woman, palpable and earthy, who "treads on the ground." At the same time, a few of the girls admitted that they wouldn't be thrilled if some guy declared that their eyes *weren't* bright, their lips *weren't* red, and that "black wires" grew out of their heads. We tried to imagine how Shakespeare's mistress might respond in her own right, pointing out her love's spindly legs or his receding hairline.

The most helpful of the Shakespeare sonnets was #73:

That time of year thou mayst in me behold
When yellow leaves, or none, or few, do hang
Upon those boughs which shake against the cold,
Bare ruined choirs, where late the sweet birds sang.
In me thou see'st the twilight of such day
As after sunset fadeth in the west,
Which by and by black night doth take away,
Death's second self, that seals up all in rest.
In me thou see'st the glowing of such fire
That on the ashes of his youth doth lie,
As the death-bed whereon it must expire,
Consumed with that which it was nourish'd by.
   This thou perceiv'st, which makes thy love more strong
   To love that well which thou must leave ere long.

This melancholy lyric about aging might seem beyond the experience of young students, but my fifth graders read the poem with understanding and compassion. They appreciated the sober beauty of its three images, each developed in a quatrain: the tree on the eve of winter, the vanishing twilight, and the nearly extinguished fire. Many of the children adopted this format when they came to write their own sonnets. In Rachael's poem (quoted earlier), the alternation of shyness and boldness is at first the ebb and flow of the waves, then the aspen tree in the wind, and finally the opening and closing of the morning glory.

Rachael chose to adhere to strict Shakespearean form: her poem is based on iambic pentameter and the lines follow the traditional *abab cdcd efef gg* rhyme scheme. But my students did not stick to established patterns of rhyme and meter if such formulas constrained them or didn't suit the themes they wanted to express. The modern sonnet is an adaptable form; the students saw how E. E. Cummings tossed out old rules of end-stop and capitalization so that his sonnets speak in his own voice.

And so did the fifth graders' sonnets. I was delighted to see how each reflected the writer's own personality. There was a wide range of topics—musings on nature, statements about friendship, a description of a pet turtle, a tongue-in-cheek poem about the changing sports seasons:

As the season of spring comes in, behold,
A starting of baseball has come to spring.
The month of April it started, I'm told
It goes to fall and ends with a big ping.
In the season of fall, basketball comes.
Shoot a sphere through a hoop, try not to miss.
If you call a basketball player dumb,
He will be very mad and they will hiss.
In the season of winter football is there,
Big people play it and make people fall.
They tackle and block—what do people care?
The people are strong, big, fast, fat, and tall.
    The sports never stop, go through the season.
    More guys who watch it is the reason.

—*Mike Lee*

Also wry and humorous—and a bit naughty—is William Avedon's whimsical riddle poem:

What Is It?

Shooting over the ice and through the rain
The rain covers its tracks so they cannot be found.
Could this be a horse? Or a donkey in pain?
Not slipping and sliding, but merely gliding.
Maybe it's an animal of some special kind?
It could be a donkey whose nickname is a behind.
It could be real, it could be a fake,
It could be a child making mudcake.
Maybe it's Athena, maybe it's Zeus,
Maybe it's a runner with Nike A I R shoes,
Maybe it's God's messenger, maybe it's his mail.

But you know their motto, even through hail.
It looks like a Porsche, a real cool hot rod,
But if you ask my opinion, I think it's God!

William loved wordplay; his poem is full of witty tricks, like the derivations of Nike sneakers and the florists' logo of Hermes ("God's messenger") from Greek mythology, which we had studied earlier in the year. Aaron Neff's poem also mentions the Greeks, but is quite different in tone:

The dawn arises for a whole new day
The day is as beautiful as I thought it.
Dawn meets dusk and the daylight goes away
And the sky burns then is dabbled and lit.
Then it shows its ever-present beauty
The night is radiant with pure white light.
The stars and moon do their special duty
To summon all the gods up high and bright.
Andromeda, Perseus, Pegasus
All tell their story with their shining light.
Scorpio, Orion, and Artemis
Shine down from the heavens showing their might.
   The night is mystical and magical
   Gods conversing in light and madrigal.

Impelled by the structure of the sonnet, many of the children found themselves exploring new corners of their imaginations. Some created surreal fantasy lands:

Flowing water, purple, blue, green, and red.
More and more green goldfish first fly around.
Catfish, sea stars, sea slugs are at the head
Scurry around without making a sound.
Light dances around on the water's edge
Sun slowly goes into the horizon
Dances back and forth on a little ledge
Goes down like it has some sort of poison.
Blackness fills the sky as the sun goes down.
Darkness fills the sky and light from the moon.
Darkness makes people seem to have a frown
Good news is that dawn will be coming soon.
   In the water melting into the twilight
   I'm sure this is going to be my light.
      —*Rebecca Milburn*

Rebecca's clever rhyming of *twilight* and *my light* brings the poem to a gentle, glowing close. Other students experimented with the couplet in their own ways. One child, describing a tropical vacation resort, concludes with

> In the pond there is an alligator
> There are secret passages, so see you later.

I collected all fifteen poems in a book that I distributed among the authors. Seeing the poems in print, the children were amazed at how good they were. They complimented one another wonderingly.

I was no less impressed. The sonnet form provided the children with the guidance they needed to express their thoughts clearly and sequentially while allowing them leeway to improvise, to ride the crests and dips of language to realms of their own. One such realm is described by Nao Terai, whose knowledge of English as a language second to Japanese gives her verse its own special music. Nao's was the class anthology's opening poem:

The Sky

> In the sky, a great big white fluffy cloud,
> There are angels with hulas and wings,
> Playing a golden trumpet very loud,
> The other angels in beautiful voices sing.
> The other angels swim in the sky beach
> While the others make cloud castles.
> The angels walk their dogs on leashes
> Cats jump on angels—what a hassle.
> People down below cannot hear the noise
> So most people do not believe in this.
> But when you hear it they rejoice
> But when you ignore it they hiss.
> Now you saw the secret of skyland.
> When teachers ask you about it raise your hand.

Kevin Griffith

Hamlet Meets Frankenstein

Exploring the Possible Worlds of Classic Literature

STUDENTS OFTEN UNDERSTAND that the classics are "good for them," that they need to read them to "be a better person"; however, they also see much classic literature as a static entity, something to be studied, memorized, and tested on. What they do not understand is that literature is wonderfully elastic. Student readers and writers can and should feel free to revise, rewrite, and appropriate the greatest works of our culture as they create their own original works. The universal characters, settings, and themes of the classics can be wonderful starting points for inspiring students to exercise their imaginations.

In my college creative writing classes, I encourage students to explore the possible worlds of classic literature in a variety of ways. One of the most successful activities asks students to take two characters from two seemingly unrelated works of literature and then write a poem speculating on what would happen if those characters met. In class, I ask students to take ten or fifteen minutes to brainstorm and list the names of as many characters from literature as they can remember. Next, they pick two characters from that list and brainstorm all the details and traits they can remember about them. Then, if we have time, I allow students to begin writing poems in class that incorporate the details generated by their brainstorming and then finish the poems later. Using this same method, I wrote the following poem, a poem that made me reflect on the nature of dramatic tragedy:

Hamlet Meets Frankenstein

For Frankenstein, of course, Hamlet's central
problem is irrelevant. The monster
offs the king in the first act,
dispatches Polonius quickly with a twist
of the neck, and then terrorizes the kingdom
until he ascends to the throne,

a feared leader, making the phrase
There's something rotten in Denmark
his badge of honor, an official seal.
Ophelia is fished from the river,
brought back to life with a bolt of lightning
and made his bride, a fitting queen.

Meanwhile, Hamlet is still sulking
at the gravesite, skull in hand
and three dead kings to contend with,
one still very much in charge.
Remarkably, the play ends like all tragedies:
The dead watch over the living

and the living wonder why it's so hard to be alive.

Such an activity is not only fun, but it is an excellent way to engage students in understanding the universal threads that weave themselves through great literature. By juxtaposing two characters, students can begin to understand that each work of literature is a part of the larger human tapestry, not just an isolated book appearing in a unit and then culminating in a test. Students can also compare and contrast how the traditional genres—poetry, drama, fiction—play off each other when a character from one comes into contact with a character from another. The possible combinations of characters are endless: how about Odysseus meets Ahab? Eve meets Dracula? Gulliver meets Walt Whitman?

All great literature begs for our engagement, for questions that push us beyond the words on the page. Another creative writing activity both I and my students use involves recalling a work of literature that they have read recently and then asking "What if"? For this activity, I ask students to do a focused freewrite in which they interrogate a work of literature. I explain to them that when composing their masterworks, the authors of great literature could have gone in hundreds of different directions. What if they had taken a different approach? Could one tiny change in plot, character, or setting transform a great work? Often, to get the students started with their freewrites, I'll provide a few prompts, such as "Who is the hero of this work? What if the hero were the villain? Who is telling the story? What if a minor character were telling the story?" Consider, for instance, what would have happened if Eve had not eaten the apple? Wouldn't life now be boring? Would we still be walking around naked? Would television exist? What if Ahab had caught

Moby-Dick? What if *Romeo and Juliet* were a comedy? What if the speaker in Frost's poem had taken the path *more* traveled? What if Browning's Duchess could present her side of the story? In the following poem, a student revisits Faulkner:

As I Lay Frying

The little boy found it,
knew he would,
the fish that talked
with his mama's voice.
(Dewey Dell gave birth
to the 10-pound salmon
and threw it away
but wouldn't admit
to mothering the thing.)
"I can't talk right—
I need false teeth,"
it said. "And make sure
they're from Jefferson."
So Anse put off buying
his own set and
went off to buy hers.
Meanwhile, Cash began
building a 20-gallon
tank (nothing too good
for his ma). Dewey Dell
shortened her name
to DeeDee, moved to a big city,
and went into a business
where a good many
of the customers were named
Skeet. Jewel refused to leave
his fish-mother's side, but
Darl convinced him
to run out for an air pump
for the aquarium.
On his way to the pet store,
Jewel passed Vardaman
knee-deep in the river,
his legs glistening with fish scales,
staring into the smooth roundness
of a fish-eye cupped in his hand.
Back at the house, Darl
also stared at the glassy fish-eye

of his mother as she sizzled
and popped in the skillet
on the stove. And this time,
Jewel was too late:
as he walked in the door
with air pump and
plastic seaweed in hand,
Darl swallowed the last
bite.

—*Kristin Kummer*

I wrote the following poem by asking "What if Kafka had written a story about a bug waking up to be a man, instead of the other way around?"

"Metamorphosis" Revisited

In the newly discovered version,
the one Kafka felt too risky to print,
the bug wakes one day to find it's a man.
When it tries to unhinge its claws
all it has are two hands, stubbed and callused,
no good for crawling on the floor,
a practice which now seems utterly humiliating.
Instead, it is compelled to sit in a chair
and cradle paper, saying prayers over ink,
its skull heavy with gray sludge,
ninety percent of its awkward weight useless.
What's truly terrifying is its face: two small eyes
leaking salt and three holes for breathing
(one of which floats a muscle in slime,
uttering sounds that nothing really seems to hear).
It lacks wings and contains just one heart,
a pathetic monster indeed.
Yet its lifespan is an eternity for any insect,
a soul trapped in an amber of blood and fat,
growing a shell only at death, when it needs it least.

The following student poem questions the arbitrary nature of language, as God interrogates Adam about his choice of names for the things of the world:

I.
What if after he named everything
Adam looks at Eve and then somewhere out
past the trees and speaks
what we all want him to:
"God, we're still alone."

And God responds, "All right,
let's see where we went wrong."

After a long silence God asks,
"Okay, Adam, you see that thing
sitting up that tree, that little one making
all the noise?"
Adam turns and responds, "Yeah."
God asks, "Now what did you call that?"
"A *bird*, I called it a *bird*," Adam says pridefully.
"Why did you call it a bird?" God asks.
"Well, I don't know, God . . . I needed to
call it something."
"I mean, what about that thing says bird?
Is it the sound it makes when it flies
or when it eats?"
"No," Adam says.
"Well, why not then *window* or *novice* or *bullet*
or *funny*?" God pushes.
(Those sounds had not been assigned to things yet.)
"Because I didn't think to call it any of those," Adam says.
"Well, you could have. Is bird a better name for
the thing than any of those?"
"I guess not." Adam looks at the ground.

II.
Sometime later, a voice asks:
"Adam, are you still alone?"

But the thing that used to call itself Adam is now
far beyond wondering whether *alone*
is a strange creature that navigates the earth
on its thousand legs and curls itself into a ball
when frightened
or the name given to ice-cracking in the spring,
or the way the whole body aches when the gut is empty.

The thing that used to call itself Adam is too
busy doing nameless things among the other

nameless beings to notice that a question
has been asked, just as most of us can become
too busy with our things to notice the wind,
or our own breathing.

—*Eric Carlberg*

Such speculative poetry encourages students to stretch their imaginations and also to explore why authors make certain decisions when they compose a literary work. By speculating on all the possible paths a work could have taken, students incorporate great texts into their own experience and learn that analyzing and understanding a work of literature involves creativity and intellectual excitement.

A third assignment takes a character from a classic work and then places that character in a new context. Such a displacement highlights that character's strengths and enduring qualities, and encourages students to focus on and prioritize certain key elements of the text. During class, I ask students to divide a sheet of notebook paper into two columns. In one column, they list the first ten or twelve characters from classical literature they can remember. In the second column they list ten or twelve occupations. They then scan both columns to see if any intriguing matches occur. Using this method, some of my students have written their best poetry, in which Moses works at Taco Bell, Eve sells Avon, King Arthur drives a Brink's Truck, and so on. Here's a particularly witty example:

Robin Hood: Investment Wizard

After wedding the lovely Maid Marian,
Robin Hood decided it was time
to be done with his rogue days
of thievery and trickery.

Nay, he had to support a family now.
Sure, Marian's dowry was a good start,
but it wouldn't last forever.
It was time to plan for retirement.

Robin decided he could invest
his and the Merry Men's earnings
in high-yield stocks, bonds, mutual funds and IRAs.
Buy low, sell high.

He did so well in first-quarter investments
that everyone in the kingdom begged for his advice.
The market was raging like Friar Tuck on a mission
and dividends were soaring like an arrow.

And nobody seemed to notice
when Robin skimmed a little off the top.

—Chad Alexander

In the following poem, a student cleverly places Hamlet in the role of talk show host:

A Shakespearean Talk Show

A catchy theme song plays
And mimes act out
The day's theme.

Out steps our host clad in all black.
He banters with his sidekick—
A cackling skull who laughs at even the faintest attempt at humor.

Our melancholy prince of a host announces his first guest
As a weak, putrid woman who married her dead husband's brother
Just two months after the funeral.

The audience voices their disapproval of this fallen queen
With trite comments such as
"You nasty and you don't deserve no man."

Next comes her husband and former brother-in-law.
He is greeted with a spattering of boos and hisses
As well as mocking laughter for his decision to wear tights.

Our host, though deeply disturbed by his guests, keeps his cool
By making snide comments about funeral meats
And puns that no one understands, but still applaud.

The final segment brings a special surprise mystery guest
Who literally appears out of thin air.
His only contribution is to mutter "Remember Me" every five seconds.
The show climaxes to the typical brawl between dead and living
Which cannot be tamed even by guys in black t-shirts labeled
"SECURITY."

Tainted swords and poison end the mayhem, but not before each
guest is killed.

The crowd whoops, the rating soars,
And our pondering host wittily comments
"I guess they decided not to be.

Stay tuned for tomorrow's show—
'My Fam Wants My Man to Die,
So I'm Gonna Commit Suicide.'"

—Gail Prickett

In this prose poem, a student writer combines elements from the
first activity as well:

Frankenstein Works at Shelley's Repair Shop

"Madcap ruffian! One-half lunatic! These dirty, redneck mechanics!"
Frankenstein looked up suddenly from his work on a cracked crankcase to
find a rather large woman in a rather loud tropical-print pantsuit striding
rather aggressively into his garage. He hit his head on the car's hood in his
haste to block her path to the power tools. "And where's my car *today?*"
she confronted him. "Have you even *thought* about fixing it yet, or do
you have the brains?"

Frankenstein raised his hand to calm her and drew breath to explain
that the part that he needed for her Alfa Romeo was only manufactured in
Italy and had simply not come in yet, but Mrs. Petrucchio refused his pla-
cating gesture before he could begin, saying, "Nay! I will be angry! You
told me it would be ready on Saturday. Today is Friday. I have places to go,
people to see! Do you think I like being immobile, stuck at home?" She
reached for a gas cap, and it whizzed past his head. "Don't tell me you have
other things to do, oaf! I'll not be made a fool. If this car isn't ready for
me by Sunday, I'm getting my lawyers, and I'll see you hanged up to dry
in court!" In a multicolored whirl, she turned sharply on her heels and
walked out as roughly as she came.

Frankenstein looked back at the crankcase. Maybe he could sneak
off for a few moments at lunchtime and play the violin. It was a great
stress-reliever. Or maybe he could even. . . . "Hey!" A gruff voice echoed
in the garage, interrupting his thoughts. In the doorway stood a stooped
man with a thick cane and a captain's hat, blocking out the sunlight with
his bulk. His prosthetic left leg stuck out oddly from his khaki shorts. "Do
you repair boats here? I need mine fixed for a mission."

The mechanic sighed. This was definitely going to be a long day.

—Laura Goodman

All three of these activities have generated outstanding poetry in my classes. Students seem less hesitant to read aloud poems based on these activities because they often generate humor, and because the students are writing about topics that contain characters and situations common to their academic experience. These activities open up the range of topics students can draw material from, and they illustrate a creative use for the great literature they are assigned to read. Many students have told me that these activities encouraged them to review their notes for literature classes and helped them to generate ideas and add details to their poems. Too many students in creative writing class do not understand that to be a great writer, one has to be a voracious reader. These activities underscore that principle. Studying the classics is not the only option for students and teachers. Exploring the possible worlds beyond the pages can be just as rich an experience as reading them.

Here are some other poems that explore the classics in new ways:

"Edgar Allan Poe Meets Sarah Hale (Author of *Mary Had a Little Lamb*)" by Thomas Lux. In *Split Horizon*. New York: Houghton Mifflin, 1994.

"Jack," "Metamorphosis," and "Questions about Angels" by Billy Collins. In *Questions about Angels*. New York: William Morrow, 1991.

"Excerpts from God's Secret Diary," "Lazarus," and "On the Anniversary of His Death, the Men of the Village Meet to Talk about Frankenstein" by Ron Koertge. In *Making Love to Roget's Wife*. Fayetteville, Ark.: University of Arkansas, 1997.

William J. Higginson

Bashō and Linked Poems

AS A RESULT OF COOPERATION between Recursos de Santa Fe, a non-profit arts agency that sponsors programs in contemporary literature, and the Title I Reading Program of the Santa Fe (New Mexico) Public Schools, in the spring of 1996 I was invited to help students write linked poems in a style based on the work of the great Japanese poet Matsuo Bashō(1644–1694).[1] The project involved small classes of fourth, fifth, and sixth graders, but I have done similar work with large groups of secondary and college students and adults, which I divide into teams of four to six writers, in both traditional classrooms and a variety of community settings.

In planning meetings before my classroom visits, teachers Sarah Allen at Piñon Elementary School and Geraldine Coriz at Larragoite Elementary School agreed that linked poems would be a good means of achieving the project's goals: 1) to stimulate students to write creatively; 2) to develop students' reading skills by having them read and respond to one another's writing; and 3) to produce an attractive final product entirely created by the students. They were also pleased that the source for the type of writing the students would practice was a recognized genre of non-Western literature, since much of the focus in courses at these grade levels was on societies other than the Anglo-American, Hispanic, and Native American cultures prominent in our region.

In each of six Title I classes, I met once a week for four weeks with the same group of four, five, or six students, in one-hour sessions. Each group composed a linked poem of eighteen or more stanzas. Further sessions with an artist-teacher of European calligraphy and a book-arts artist resulted in the creation of hand-made portfolios of six broadsides (8 ½ x 14"), each featuring one of the linked poems.

Linked Poems: A Brief Introduction

For several decades, teachers worldwide have introduced students to haiku. Bashō is considered the greatest haiku poet of all time, and his poems have become models for succeeding generations. However, many may not know that in his own day people knew Bashō mainly as a poet of *haikai no renga*, or humorous linked poetry. From the fourteenth through the eighteenth centuries, Japan's most prominent poets composed linked poetry, usually working in small groups as they took turns to create long poems made up of short, individually composed stanzas.

By Bashō's time, people from almost every walk of life composed linked poetry in a popular style called *haikai*. Much in *haikai no renga* resembled today's popular songs, but Bashō reached back to the great Chinese poets of the T'ang Dynasty—Tu Fu, Li Po, and Po Chü-i—and to classical Japanese poets for his inspiration. He incorporated the common experiences of his day into poems that echoed the great literature of the past. Above all, Bashō and his disciples saw how deeply things and events were all interconnected and made poems based on these connections.

Today in Japan linked poetry has become popular again, and poets look back to Bashō for inspiration. To honor the differences between Bashō's linked poems and those of earlier times, they call Bashō's long poems and their own works *renku*, which literally means "linked verse." For example, here are the first five stanzas of "Summer Moon," a famous *renku* by Bashō and two of his best poet-companions, Bonchō and Kyorai. Notice how the first two stanzas seem closely connected, but each of the subsequent stanzas moves in a new direction.

1   Around the town
     the smells of things . . .
     summer moon   (*Bonchō*)

2   "It's hot, it's hot"—
     the voices from gate to gate   (*Bashō*)

3   the second weeding
     not yet done, and ears
         out on the rice   (*Kyorai*)

4   knocking the ashes off
     one piece of sardine   (*Bonchō*)

5   in these parts
     silver's an unknown sight
     how inconvenient!   (*Bashō*)

Bashō's stanza (#2) links to the first by filling in some details of the summer evening scene that Bonchō started, namely, adding a picture of houses in the town and what people are saying as they lounge in their front yards after a hot day. Kyorai links his verse (#3) to Bashō's by continuing the conversation, but shifts it from the city to a farmer's field in the countryside. Bonchō links his verse (#4) by showing us the farmer or one of his workers, shifting from conversation to lunch—which evidently includes a sardine that fell into the fire. Bashō continues the lunch scene, but he moves it into a rural store and comments on the inability of the clerk to make change from a large-denomination coin. (Today we might find the same inconvenience in a shop that does not accept credit cards.) Note that the ashes on the sardine have now become an irritation with the service in the store—which increases when someone tries to pay the bill.

Two main techniques of linked poetry are expanding a scene or action from one verse to the next or adding more detail (as in verses 1–2 and 3–4 above), and shifting part or all of the action or setting into a completely new situation (as in verses 2–3 and 4–5). A third technique, especially prized by Bashō, involves linking through an emotional tone, though the two stanzas may speak of quite different and otherwise unrelated things—creating a dramatic shift despite the similar feelings involved. Here is an example from the poem called "Plum Blossoms and Young Greens":

> given their freedom
> the pet quail—even the tracks
> have disappeared   (*Sodan*)

> rice shoots lengthen
> in a soft breeze   (*Chinseki*)

> a convert
> starts by going over
> Suzuka Pass   (*Bashō*)

Chinseki's verse links with Sodan's through expanding the scene and alluding to an older poem that includes quail crying in a breeze. But the rural domesticity suggested by pet quail and rice paddies is gone from the scene as a young monk trudges along the trail through a high mountain pass. Instead, Bashō's verse matches the delicacy of young rice shoots in a soft breeze with the hesitancy of the youth, newly made a monk, and the desolate place we see him in.

Here is another example of this kind of emotional linking, in this case with an expansion of the scene as well—showing how two methods of linking may be involved in one pair of stanzas. The third stanza demonstrates a typical shift from a broad setting to a close-up with action. This sequence is from the poem "Winter Rain":

> in azure sky
> the waning moon's
> daybreak   *(Kyorai)*
>
> in the autumn lake
> Mt. Hira's first frost   *(Bashō)*
>
> a brushwood door . . .
> buckwheat stolen, the hermit
> chants poems   *(Fumikuni)*

Note the similar feelings evoked by a pale moon fading in the sky at daybreak and the thin frost on a mountain reflected in a lake. I've translated these verses to show how Bashō underscores the visual and tonal parallelism by following the same grammatical pattern used by Kyorai. Fumikuni's "brushwood door" links by suggesting the modest hut of a hermit who lives on the mountain. The stolen buckwheat and chanted poems shift from the delicate panoramas of the earlier verses to dramatic action.

These kinds of linking and shifting lie at the heart of linked poetry.

Getting Started

Historically, the haiku genre derives from the hokku ("starting verses") of linked poems. So I devote the first class session to writing haiku. The best way to do this, I have found, is simply to read a number of excellent haiku by American and Canadian poets. Since they are contemporary and from our culture, they usually do not require explanations, as do many Japanese examples. The best source for such poems is *The Haiku Anthology*, edited by Cor van den Heuvel.[2] *The Haiku Handbook: How to Write, Share, and Teach Haiku* contains complete lesson plans for introducing haiku to elementary and secondary students.[3]

I follow the reading with a class discussion about the poems, emphasizing the kinds of things they talk about (content), the way they are written (form), and our responses to them (feelings). In this first session, I encourage students to write a number of haiku, based on things that they can see and hear right now in the room or outside, on things they remember (from as recently as recess or as long ago as when they were little), and on things that sound real but are actually made up. Each student writes at least one of each type, and then another one or two of the kinds they like best: poems of here and now, memory, or fantasy. I move around the room, helping each student shape his or her poems into the classic short-longer-short, three-line rhythm of haiku.

When each student has written at least three or four haiku, I ask them to pick their favorites and read them to the class. In some classes, they want to see everything their classmates wrote, so I encourage them to pass their papers around for everyone to read.

Here are some of the haiku written by the students in those first sessions, from grades four, five, and six, respectively:

Homework
on the floor
sleeping.
   —*Christine Wade*

The ball was spinning
around the rim
for a long, long time.
   —*Roberta Lovato*

A sparrow is chirping
as cars drive up and down
Agua Fria.
   —*Maya Otero*

As these examples demonstrate, haiku do not always have complete sentences, but they exemplify the rule "Show, don't tell." Both haiku and linked poems depend largely on vivid images that may appeal to any of the senses, although sight and sound predominate.

Next, Link and Shift
At the start of the second session, I ask each student to copy out at the top of a fresh sheet of paper a favorite haiku that he or she wrote in the first session. Then we talk about the way many things are connected,

even if we don't see the connection right away. One by one, I ask the students to read their haiku aloud and we all think of things that connect with them.

One thinks of a cat lying on a couch next to the homework, another chases the basketball as it falls; a third sees people skating on the ice rink next to Agua Fria Street.

Now I ask the students each to pass their papers one student to the right. We continue talking about the different ways we can connect one verse to another. For example, kids getting out of school in one stanza might suggest a trip to some faraway place in the next—"vacation" doesn't have to be mentioned. Or one poet talking about someone who is double-jointed might to the next suggest a bent tree. One image can continue to expand in another. A second verse might fill in the scene where the action of the first verse takes place, or the reverse. A word in one stanza—such as *dark*—might suggest a related word in the next—like *black*.

When I feel that they have the idea, it's time for them to read their classmate's haiku and respond to it with a two-line stanza that somehow links with that haiku. Warmed up by the discussion of connections, this doesn't take long. After checking to see that each student has successfully linked a stanza to the beginning haiku, I ask them to pass their papers again to the next person on their right. I explain that the kind of poems we're writing alternate three- and two-line stanzas, so the next should be three lines, like the first. But, and here's the catch, nothing else in the third stanza should remind us of the first stanza, even though it must connect with the second stanza.

A major objective in writing linked poems in the Bashō style is to include as many aspects of life as possible. To get this variety into the poem the poets must avoid staying in the same place or telling a continuous story. Once some person, place, or action has been mentioned in a linked poem, it should not appear again after the very next verse. A well-made linked poem is like a scroll painting, moving from one landscape to another, from season to season, and from distant views to close-ups (or vice-versa) as it unrolls.

I give the class examples like those from Bashō and his friends, showing how each stanza links with the one before it, but also shifts away from connecting with the one before that. We try a few stanzas verbally, using some of the work we've already written and adding possible third stanzas.

When it seems most of them have the idea of both linking and shifting, I tell them to go ahead and write some possible third stanzas on pieces of scrap paper. In a few minutes I start visiting the students, one at a time, helping them to decide which of their trial verses is the best at both linking and shifting; I also help them figure out the best places to break their stanzas into three lines. For some, we combine ideas from two of their trial verses. Sometimes one of their stanzas is the obvious choice. Here are three sets of opening stanzas—again, from fourth, fifth, and sixth grades, respectively. Note the elements in the third stanzas that carry each sequence in a new, unexpected direction:

> The moon
> so bright it guides me
> through the night.   (*Nicholas Trujillo*)

> Walking in the forest
> I hear the water running.   (*Shannon Martinez*)

> A pretty rock
> in the blue stream—
> I put it on another.   (*Gina Chavez*)

Gina transforms the night into day, and moves from passive response to action.

> Carlsbad Caverns
> is fun
> to visit.   (*Iliana Perez*)

> I wish I knew
> how to drive.   (*Jimmie Rylee*)

> Riding a bike, fast
> on the afternoon street
> tilted air.   (*Julieta Olivas*)

Although technically the verse beginning "Carlsbad Caverns" is not very imagistic and does not qualify as a haiku, since my objective here is to let the students have fun—and clearly this was a fun thing for Iliana to write—I did not push too hard for a rewrite at this stage. Rather, I waited to see what the next student would do with Iliana's verse. Obviously, Jimmie's response also does not present a strong visual image. But the reader can sense the increasing tension of desire in these verses; they are very well matched and quite powerful in their effect. And without them, the amazing poetry of Julieta's verse might never have happened. Sometimes the workshop leader must withhold judgement, let "observing the rules" go, and give the students enough room to welcome the great accident of inspiration when it comes.

> At a night club
> eating hamburgers
> and drinking coke.   *(Jason Borrego)*
>
> The dog stole something
> from the dumpster.   *(Nicole Salazar)*
>
> Sneaking around
> to find something—
> it is scary.   *(Maya Otero)*

Here the major change appears in the emotions involved, moving from the pleasures of food and socializing to the almost comic image of the dog foraging, and then the sense of "sneaking" and fear. Once the image train is rolling, an occasional direct statement of emotional reaction may be accepted, so long as the following stanza makes use of it by returning a new image to justify the emotion, and the session does not spiral into a sequence of named feelings.

When all have added their third stanzas to the first two, it's time to pass their papers again. I remind them of the rhythm of three lines and two lines, and tell them again to link their verses with the preceding stanzas, but to be careful to avoid connecting with either of the stanzas before that. Again, they do preliminary work on scrap paper.

Putting It All Together

Creating a long poem of eighteen stanzas on each of these pass-around sheets would take several sessions if we continued this way, so we do pass-around linking for only one more session. In the three sessions we manage to go all around the table at least once in each class, creating as many poem-sections of six stanzas each as there are students.

In the fourth session, we read our work aloud, and then we examine the first and last stanzas of each section, looking for connections that might link them. We also look for striking verses in the first position, which might serve as excellent starting-verses for the final long poem. In each class we find three sections that connect well into one long poem and that do not repeat images or events between one section and another. We make a few minor adjustments to the verses connecting the sections, where needed, to make them fit together well. Since each student participated in each section at least once, this means that each has at least three stanzas in the final eighteen-stanza piece put together this way. The remaining sections are not included in the final long poem, but we put them up on the bulletin board so we can all enjoy them, too.

In one or two classes, our sections from the first three sessions do not reach the full six stanzas, so we put together the three sections we think fit best and then add stanzas from the others that seem to fit, or we write some new stanzas to fill out the end.

In one class, three students fluent in both English and Spanish volunteered to translate the eighteen-stanza poem into Spanish. This done, they read the Spanish version aloud, to the great enjoyment of all. (Japanese and American poets have written *renku* together, in their own languages, with immediate translations provided stanza-by-stanza by bilingual members of their groups. I have used the same process with high school students, some of whom did not speak English, some of whom were bilingual.)

How Much Like Bashō?
There are some rules of traditional linked poetry in Japan that we did not try to observe. For example, traditionally a poem starts with an image from the current season, and there are rules for including images from the seasons in other stanzas. Linking and shifting are often governed by additional rules. And some special topics normally appear in specified stanzas. But we did observe the three main aspects of linked poetry in the Bashō style: collaboration, linking stanzas in a variety of ways, and shifting from one topic to another.

Finishing Touches
When my work was done, professional artists worked with the students and the materials to produce the portfolios of broadsides mentioned earlier. Students made their own portfolio covers and each received a full set of the six broadsides, which were color-copied onto fancy paper provided by a local printer. One set of the broadsides was framed and exhibited for a month at a public library, beginning with an opening reception

where the artists and students described their experiences with the project to parents and friends. Portfolios were also given to the artists, teachers, agencies, and donors involved.

Here is one of the final *renku*:

A Big Frog

A big frog
on the porch
of my house.

It gets cold
when it rains.

An old woman is walking
on the street looking
at the schoolyard.

Bell rings
kids get out.

Carlsbad Caverns
is fun
to visit.

I wish I knew
how to drive.

Riding a bike, fast
on the afternoon street
tilted air.

Those boys are fighting
in the cold breeze.

Snowman
melting to water
by the heater.

I spilt coke
on my baby brother's feet.

Feels like glue
different colors—
mix it.

There goes Jim Carrey
and his career.

A baby bird
was falling out
of a tree nest.

Can't fly an airplane—
never learned.

My grandma
is getting
married.

A rabbit alive
and hopping.

The ball
is bouncing up and down
the sidewalk.

A trampoline is very still
through a glass window.

—*Iliana Perez, Julieta Olivas, Hilda Perez, Marcos Garcia, and Jimmy Rylee*

For Further Reading

The most accessible group of Bashō's linked poems is in *Monkey's Raincoat: Linked Poetry of the Bashō School with Haiku Selections*, translated by Lenore Mayhew (Rutland, Vermont: Charles E. Tuttle Co., 1985). It reads well and is not overburdened by scholarly apparatus. (There are other, scholarly translations of the Bashō-era collection *Monkey's Raincoat*.)

Several linked poems from various periods appear in *From the Country of Eight Islands: An Anthology of Japanese Poetry*, edited and translated by Hiroaki Sato and Burton Watson (various editions; available in most larger public libraries). Sato's prosy translations give each stanza as only one line, however, obscuring the rhythms of the originals.

My own book, *The Haiku Seasons: Poetry of the Natural World* (Kodansha International, 1996), from which some translations in this article are taken, includes excerpts from linked poems of three different eras with comments on linking and shifting, and discusses the seasons in linked poetry.

Excerpts from linked poems by American poets and students appear in the article "Renga" in *The Teachers & Writers Handbook of Poetic Forms*, edited by Ron Padgett (Teachers & Writers Collaborative, 1987), which also includes the related articles "Haiku" and "Senryu."

Notes

1. The project was funded by grants from the City of Santa Fe Arts Commission and the Albertsons Foundation, with additional support from local businesses and the artists involved.

2. Any of its three editions—published by Doubleday (1974), Simon & Schuster (1986), and Norton (1999)—will do.

3. By William J. Higginson with Penny Harter, McGraw-Hill (1985) and Kodansha International (1989).

Laura Gamache

Pictures of a Gone World

Using Keats's "Ode on a Grecian Urn"
And Shelley's "Ozymandias"

FOR THE PAST SIX YEARS, I have been leading poetry workshops in Lynn Black's fifth and sixth grade classroom at Lake Washington Community School in Kirkland, Washington. My classes always tie in to the school's year-long focus of study. This year, they are studying ancient Egypt and Greece.*

My first day, freshly ruined pottery shards dotted the windowsill, a Grecian temple entrance projected from the far wall, twenty-eight foam-core buildings were rising from blueprint floorplans, and Grecian urn shapes drawn with colored pens were taped under the window as examples of symmetry. I was to come in for two $1^1/_2$-hour sessions per week for four weeks. The lengthy sessions allowed ample time for me to read aloud a poetry model, have kids talk about it, present the writing assignment, give everyone time to write, and have time left for them to read what they wrote.

The first day I talked about the time we would spend together, took in what was displayed around the room for clues to what they were studying, and asked them to tell me what they had found most interesting in their study of the ancient world. I used what they told me to create the poetry lessons. Among the things they mentioned were pharaohs, hieroglyphics, Egyptian art, and the desert. All of these together made me think of Percy Bysshe Shelley's "Ozymandias." The kids also were interested in Greek pottery and painting, which reminded me of John Keats's "Ode on a Grecian Urn." I decided to use both poems on the same day, since Keats and Shelley were contemporaries and friends, and because the poems had similar themes and subject matter. Reading the two together

---

* See Addendum for my eight-visit curriculum.

would serve to point these things out without my having to say anything. In his book, *Making Your Own Days,* Kenneth Koch wrote:

> Much of what I have learned about poetry . . . has come about . . . unconsciously, without my knowing it, as a result of my reading and of my feelings. This combination, working in secret, accomplishes a lot for a writer.

My poetry teaching method is based on osmosis, the unconscious acquisition of poetry knowledge through reading poems and having feelings about them. I give kids experiences with poems that really move me and that I think will really move them, and with a minimum of editorial comment, have them write, inspired by that source. I find that what they write shows they have absorbed new ways of using language from a model poem, and have been able to filter their own feelings through language, all in the course of twenty-five or thirty minutes of in-class writing time.

For our experience with Keats's "Ode on a Grecian Urn" and Shelley's "Ozymandias," I gave the kids copies so they could follow as I read the poems aloud. I believe that seeing as well as hearing the writing is important, that how a poem looks on the page, where the line breaks are, and even spelling teaches kids more about how to make poems. I read with attention to the sounds and the pleasure I got from them, sometimes taking the liberty of repeating certain lines.

Both of these poems are very visual. "Ode on a Grecian Urn" depicts the different scenes painted on an ancient Greek vase. "Ozymandias" describes an enormous statue of ancient Egypt's Ramses II, and includes a powerful paraphrase of its inscription. The urn and the statue are real historical objects.

Before I read "Ozymandias," I told the kids what I discovered from the footnote in my *Norton Anthology of British Literature,* that Ozymandias was the Greek name for Ramses II, Pharaoh of Egypt in the thirteenth century B.C.E., and that the hieroglyphics on his ancient tomb had been translated just a few years before Shelley wrote his poem. The hieroglyphics translated to:

> I am Ozymandias, king of kings; if anyone wishes to know what I
> am and where I lie, let him surpass me in some of my exploits.

I read the poems once each, and then asked the kids to draw a picture of an image from one of them. Then, as they drew, I read the poems again. I wanted the language of the poems to flow over the kids, and I knew that drawing would free them not only to see the pictures the poets were making with their words, but also unconsciously to take in Keats's and Shelley's ways of using language. Also, I freely expressed my liking of the poems. While they drew, I wrote on the board:

"Beauty is truth, truth beauty,"—that is all
Ye know on earth and all ye need to know.

   —*John Keats*

Next to that I wrote:

My name is Ozymandias, king of kings:
Look on my works, ye Mighty, and despair!

   —*Percy Bysshe Shelley*

I read those lines twice out loud for emphasis.

I had to read the "happy, happy boughs . . . happy, happy love!" section of "Ode on a Grecian Urn" a couple of extra times because the kids really liked it:

Ah, happy, happy boughs! That cannot shed
Your leaves, nor ever bid the Spring adieu;
And, happy melodist, unwearied,
Forever piping songs for ever new;
More happy love! More happy, happy love!

Although I prefer to let the poems' meanings seep in through rereading, rather than by explaining, I did talk a little about how the ancient world had opened up to Europeans in Keats's and Shelley's time, how Lord Elgin had recently brought ancient Greek sculptures back to England from the Parthenon, and how Keats had written about that. I mentioned that the British thought nothing of this looting of Greece's history. The kids had read about the Rosetta Stone, which facilitated the first translation of Egyptian hieroglyphics only about thirty years before "Ozymandias" was written. I talked about how both these poets were fascinated by the ancient world, whose artifacts were so recently accessible, and interested in the permanence of artifacts and the impermanence of human beings. I pointed out that they had both died young. While I did say that these men were writing in the English of the early nineteenth century, which was why their work might sound somewhat old-fashioned, I didn't dwell on that. After twenty minutes or so, I asked the kids to write a poem about the drawing they had made.

I didn't want the model poems to be heard as museum pieces. Having the kids make art while listening, then write their poems in response to their own artwork, helped keep them from writing stilted late twentieth-century translations of second-generation British romantic poetry. They also were able to have fun and stay engaged while drawing, which shows in their writing. A month before this lesson I had used a short-lined ode by Pablo Neruda as a model poem. As is obvious from the poems that follow, many of these kids continued to write skinny poems that creep down the left margin.

POEMS INSPIRED BY "ODE ON A GRECIAN URN"

As the wind rustles your
hat, O Piper, an ox is
slaughtered in honor of a
god. I would be happy
if I was you, piping and
playing away in the gentle
breeze. . . .

  —Joe Jennings, fifth grade

The Piper

There he was,
the piper with
his smooth pipes
tucked under his
arm. Then he sat
down under the
nearest tree
and started
his morning
song (a-ra a-ra)
he piped as the
birds chirped
and as the chipmunks
scuttled through
the underbrush.
Then as the sun
was blazing overhead

he started his
afternoon song (a-ral a-ral)
he piped as the
squirrels munched
on nuts and as
fish dove in the
river. Then as the
sun was coming
down he started
his evening song (a-rale a-rale)
he piped as
the owl lunged
and as the mice
ran through
the woods.
Then when the
moon was overhead
he stood up and
left. Waiting for
the next day.

  —Adrienne Nova, fifth grade

Ode to a Piper

Oh there he sits
beneath the tree
piping oh so merrily.
His pipe is made of
oak, and is the color
of his cloak.

  —Ian O'Donnell, fifth grade

There,
under a small tree
sits a piper
piping notes only
he can hear.
As he sits
the wind shuffles
the leaves on
the branches
of the tree he sits

under. Only
he can
hear the shuffling.
While he plays
his pipe
he hears the
birds
chirping on the
branches
above him. Only he
can hear the
chirping.
While he sits in
the green grass playing,
he hears the
music of
crickets while they
rub their legs
together. Only he
can hear the music. Only
he.

—*Elizabeth Spouse, fifth grade*

This Is a Tree That Will Never Be Bare

This is a tree
that will
never be bare unless
I erase the
leaves from it.
This is a tree that
will never be bare
unless the wind
blows hard.
This is a tree that
will never be
bare unless it
falls and dies.
This is a tree
that will never
be bare unless
I pick the leaves.

—*Arielle Albinger, fifth grade*

POEMS INSPIRED BY "OZYMANDIAS"

In the darky dusk of dusky dawn
there is a statue in the distance.
The black bluey black blue of
the statue against orange sky.
The orange sky is so yellow it
is orange. The sword and shield
say "This is my place, stay clear."
I still wonder where its head
is and what that weird stone is.

—*Mac McKenna, fifth grade*

Ozymandias Lives

During the year of
1800
I was exploring
in one of
Egypt's
greatest deserts
when
I came upon
a
traveler
who said,
"Two vast and
trunkless legs of stone
stand in the
desert. . . ."
When the
traveler left me in
silence I went
to explore
what
the traveler was
talking about.
There, on the
sand
half sunk,
a shattered visage lies
whose frown
and wrinkled lip
and sneer of cold command

tell that its sculptor
well those passions
read
which yet survive.
Ozymandias,
King of Kings,
Lives.

  —Katie Lombard, sixth grade

The headless and
bodyless statue stands
there proud and short
for it has only legs,
the rest of it buried
deep in the sand.
Its head detached
from its body and
its body detached
from its head.
His hand on the
pedestal that bears
ancient hieroglyphics. I
stand there looking
blank. What should
I think what should
I say? I say it's headless,
that's great! Its body neck-
down in the sand struggling
to breathe.

  —Emily Shields, sixth grade

Ye broken head upon the sand resting
near the feet. I wonder how they thought
of you oh great and ancient statue.
You hear the wind and feel the sun.

  —Christine Bull, sixth grade

Ozymandias

Across the vast stretch of land,
on its side,
lays a cracked head,

it is sneering with evil.
Its ancient seat is atop,
really far up,
two thick pillars.
They made the legs
of some Egyptian guy.
On his sand-worn pedestal
is a piece of writing.
No one knows what it says,
so I decided it says
blah blah blah.
Once in awhile
out of the vast echo of blah,
squeaking is heard saying
words like surpass,
exploits,
and Ozymandias.

    —Ashwin Kumar, sixth grade

The Mad Man

There is a so-called
thing in the middle of the
desert that has
a head in the ground and hard mad
legs on a tilted platform that
is sunk into the sand
and he has big buff arms
and big buff legs; he was a
big buff man.
All the people of his time
must have been scared of
him I was and I didn't even live
there at that time.
But right above it is
a good-looking
stained-glass sky and his pants
are stained glass too.

    —Donn Buck, fifth grade

Oh Statue

Oh statue!
reaching out to the blazing hot sun.
Oh statue!
how you have aged.
Oh statue!
how the head that you lost stares at me.
Oh statue!
your bronze body in a sea of sand.
Oh statue!
your inscription, 'tis so interesting
that king scorpion is looking at
it.

—*Angus Tierney*

Ode on a Grecian Urn

1

Thou still unravish'd bride of quietness,
  Thou foster-child of silence and slow time,
Sylvan historian, who canst thus express
  A flowery tale more sweetly than our rhyme:
What leaf-fring'd legend haunts about thy shape
  Of deities or mortals, or of both,
    In Tempe or the dales of Arcady?
  What men or gods are these? What maidens loth?
What mad pursuit? What struggle to escape?
    What pipes and timbrels? What wild ecstasy?

2

Heard melodies are sweet, but those unheard
  Are sweeter; therefore, ye soft pipes, play on;
Not to the sensual ear, but, more endear'd,
  Pipe to the spirit ditties of no tone:
Fair youth, beneath the trees, thou canst not leave
  Thy song, nor ever can those trees be bare;
    Bold Lover, never, never canst thou kiss,
Though winning near the goal—yet, do not grieve;
    She cannot fade, though thou hast not thy bliss,
  Forever wilt thou love, and she be fair!

3

Ah, happy, happy boughs! that cannot shed
  Your leaves, nor ever bid the Spring adieu;
And, happy melodist, unwearied,
  For ever piping songs for ever new;
More happy love! more happy, happy love!
  For ever warm and still to be enjoy'd,
    For ever panting, and for ever young;
All breathing human passion far above,
  That leaves a heart high-sorrowful and cloy'd,
    A burning forehead, and a parching tongue.

4

Who are these coming to the sacrifice?
  To what green altar, O mysterious priest,
Lead'st thou that heifer lowing at the skies,
  And all her silken flanks with garlands drest?
What little town by river or sea shore,
  Or mountain-built with peaceful citadel,
    Is emptied of this folk, this pious morn?
And, little town, thy streets for evermore
  Will silent be; and not a soul to tell
    Why thou art desolate, can e'er return.

5

O Attic shape! Fair attitude! with brede
  Of marble men and maidens overwrought,
With forest branches and the trodden weed;
  Thou, silent form, dost tease us out of thought
As doth eternity: Cold Pastoral!
  When old age shall this generation waste,
    Thou shalt remain, in midst of other woe
Than ours, a friend to man, to whom thou say'st,
  "Beauty is truth, truth beauty,"—that is all
    Ye know on earth, and all ye need to know.

—*John Keats, 1820*

Ozymandias

I met a traveler from an antique land,
Who said: Two vast and trunkless legs of stone
Stand in the desert . . . Near them, on the sand,
Half sunk, a shattered visage lies, whose frown,
And wrinkled lip, and sneer of cold command,

Tell that its sculptor well those passions read
Which yet survive, stamped on these lifeless things,
The hand that mocked them, and the heart that fed:
And on the pedestal, these words appear:
"My name is Ozymandias, king of kings:
Look on my works, ye Mighty, and despair!"
Nothing beside remains. Round the decay
Of that colossal wreck, boundless and bare
The lone and level sands stretch far away.

  —Percy Bysshe Shelley, 1818

Addendum: Ancient Egypt and Ancient Greece Curriculum
(*Eight Sessions*)

1. Monday, April 20. Introductions by telling something that matters. I wrote responses on the board and read total as list poem. I asked them about their ancient Egypt/Greece study, to gather ideas for the following sessions. They wrote individual "What Matters?" poems and shared them.

2. Wednesday, April 22. *"Smellorama."* The ancient Egyptians and Greeks were enamored of unguents and perfumes. The class smelled coffee, cedar chips, vanilla, lemon peel, and Mentholatum, and took notes.
  I asked: What would this smell be if this smell were—

  a color
  an animal
  an article of clothing
  a place on earth
  weather
  a sound?

What memory comes to you when you smell this?

They wrote a poem from one of their sets of notes, and shared.

3. Monday, April 27. *Miu: The Ancient Egyptians and Their Cats.* I read them "Ode to the Cat" by Pablo Neruda and the cat parts of "Jubilate Agno," by Christopher Smart. Each student got a cat postcard and wrote her or his poem from the cat's point of view.

4. Wednesday, April 28. *It's Ancient Greek to Me.* I read from Homer's *Odyssey*, translated by Richmond Lattimore. I chose the section in which Odysseus's men encounter Circe and are turned into pigs; the part in which Circe (mysteriously kinder and gentler) tells Odysseus about the Sirens, Scylla, and Charybdis; and the scene in which Odysseus has his men, their ears plugged with wax, lash him to the mast so he can hear the Sirens. The kids freewrote for ten minutes. I gave them a handout with Ancient Greek words that are part of the English language (*physician, choir, rhythm, phrase, pneumatic*, etc.). Each chose six words from his or her own writing, and we as a class chose six Ancient Greek words. Using the two lists, they wrote six-line "Process Poems" They wrote six-line poems, using one word from each of the lists on each line, a variation of the "process poem" exercise described in *Poetry Everywhere* by Jack Collom and Sheryl Noethe (Teachers & Writers Collaborative, 1994).

5. Monday, May 4. "Ode on a Grecian Urn" by John Keats and "Ozymandias" by Percy Bysshe Shelley. Students drew a picture based on one of the two poems, and then wrote a poem from the picture they drew. I taught using texts from *The Norton Anthology of English Literature, Volume 2*, fifth edition, but prefer texts from *The Norton Anthology of Poetry*, the revised shorter edition that updates the spelling, replacing "for ever" with "forever," "desart" with "desert," etc.

6. Wednesday, May 6. I read them "Tale of a Shipwrecked Sailor," an ancient Egyptian tall tale in verse from 2000 B.C.E., from *Echoes of Egyptian Voices: An Anthology of Ancient Egyptian Poetry*, translated by John L. Foster. They wrote tall tales, some in verse, some using the frame story from "Tale of a Shipwrecked Sailor," whose first-person narrator uses his tall tale to try to divert his listener from punishing him.

7. Monday, May 18. *The Egyptian Desert.* I read them Florence Nightingale's responses to the desert from her 1849–1850 Egypt correspondence, and desert descriptions from *The English Patient* by Michael Ondaatje. I also read them two contemporary Arab poems about the desert ("Expectation" by Fouzi El-Asmar and "The Lost Mirage" by Ahmad Muhammad al Khalifa) from *The Space between Our Footsteps*, edited by Naomi Shihab Nye.

8. Wednesday, May 20. Everyone chose one or two pieces to read aloud for our end-of-the-year reading at a local coffee house, and up to three pieces to be included in the class anthology. They read their work to each other in pairs and revised, then read aloud to the group, as final practice for the evening reading.

Bob Blaisdell

Sensational von Kleist

Using His Stories

I HADN'T THOUGHT of using Heinrich von Kleist's short stories in my first semester teaching composition at Borough of Manhattan Community College until a few students mutinied against the stories and essays I had assembled in a packet for them.

Michael said, "I like more action."

"More action than a young guy breaking off with his girlfriend while they go fishing?"

"That's not action, professor."

"Okay, okay. But isn't life, presented in this concentrated way, exciting?"

"No."

"Well, then what do you read for fun, Michael?"

He shrugged, then said, "Stephen King."

"Yeah!" erupted three or four students. And for two minutes I let that spontaneously formed reading group throw back and forth: "Remember that part in *It*?. . ."; "What about when, in *The Shining*, the guy? . . ." The students were genuinely excited about having a literary conversation. But since I and the majority of the students couldn't participate, I finally roped it in. Still, it gave me an idea. Who's exciting and literary? Because—call me a snob—Stephen King isn't a serious writer. Once I tried to read one of his novels, but I was too annoyed to go on; you can't be scared if the writing seems amateurish and the emotions conveyed seem unfelt by the author. And I can't teach literature that I feel superior to. On the other hand. . . .

Among students of German literature, Kleist is more famous for his plays, but the stories are extraordinary and sensational, full of catastrophe, vengeance, sexual jealousy, murder—all the makings of the movies and books I knew my students liked.

Kleist himself had a short and sensational life (1777–1811). His career was supposed to lead to one like his father's, a Prussian army officer, but his interests lay elsewhere—almost anywhere else. His father died when Kleist was eleven, his mother when he was fifteen, shortly after he began his life as a soldier. At twenty-one he quit the army to study at the University of Frankfurt, hoping to become an academic. That was not the life for him either, and, while engaged to a conventional daughter of an officer, he decided (to his fiancée's despair) to become a simple farmer. Without ever fulfilling that romantic but impractical dream (or marrying), he started writing plays. Rootless but ambitious, he was travelling back and forth across Europe looking for a career when he was arrested as a spy in France and spent six months in prison, where he continued to write. Returning to Germany, he began composing the fabulous short stories that were published in two volumes. To become a successful playwright he needed the support of Goethe, but the grand man of German letters, who ran the state theater, thought Kleist's work "perverse." The younger man's undecorous intensity seemed to appall Goethe.

Violence and self-destruction are as much a part of Kleist's work as they are of the more delirious moments of Homer, Sophocles, Aeschylus, and Euripides. At thirty-four, he met an incurably ill woman with whom he made a suicide pact. In addition to being in what he considered an insoluble artistic and financial crisis, Kleist had a fatal attraction to dramatic endings. Announcing his suicidal intentions in letters to friends and family, he, along with the woman, prepared a double grave on a hill overlooking a lake. Kleist shot her dead, then himself.

I decided to make photocopies for my students of his story "The Earthquake in Chile."

My biggest mistake was one most teachers wouldn't make: to evangelize him. I more or less told my students, "My guy (Kleist) is better than yours (King)." What I *thought* I was doing, however, was whetting my students' appetites for completing the homework assignment. I handed out the story at the end of class one day and read aloud the first paragraph:

In Santiago, the capital of the kingdom of Chile, at the moment of the great earthquake of 1647 in which many thousands lost their lives, a young Spaniard called Jerónimo Rugera was standing beside one of the pillars in the prison to which he had been committed on a criminal charge, and was about to hang himself. A year or so previously Don Enrico Asterón, one of the richest noblemen of the city, had turned him out of his house where he had been employed as a tutor, for being on too intimate a footing with Asterón's only daughter, Doña Josefa. She herself was sternly warned, but owing to the malicious vigilance of her proud brother she was discovered nevertheless in a secret rendezvous with Jerónimo, and this so aroused her old father's indignation that he forced her to enter the Carmelite convent of Our Lady of the Mountain.[1]

"Now," I said, "read the rest of the story by next time."

"It's long, huh?"

"No! Sixteen pages!"

They groaned.

"No," I repeated. "Come on, it's got everything—love, sex, violence, history, religion . . . and that's just in the first paragraph!"

They laughed. I was sure I had hooked them.

"Sounds very exciting," said Marianne.

"What happens?" asked Michael.

"You have to read it!"

"I know—but I want to know what I'm getting beforehand."

"You'll love it. It's just like that first paragraph, except better." (As sincerely enthusiastic as I was, I should not have worn my heart on my sleeve.)

Michael looked away as if I were teasing him and he shook his head: "Are we going to have to write about it?"

"We'll play that by ear."

"You from California—right, Bob?"

"Yeah."

"Then you know what earthquakes are like. That's why I'm never going there."

"Well, read about this one—but it's probably not going to reassure you, since it destroys most of the city."

The next meeting, while I was getting settled behind the desk a couple of minutes early, I asked Michael, "Did you like the story?"

He shrugged and said, "It was okay."

"Just okay?"

Two of the young women in front of me looked at each other as if to say, "*What* story? Oh, *that* story!" They pulled out their photocopies and started flipping through them.

A quick wave of anxiety passed over the class and then went through me. Assigning reading that doesn't get read is as disappointing as having a party to which the guest of honor forgets to come. As any teacher or quarterback would have, I saw we had a busted play and that I should try to minimize the loss. Looking at my watch, I said, "Let's get started— 'The Earthquake in Chile.'"

"Wait," said Carmen.

"No, we'll start. Don't try to catch up on the reading. It's too long to read in thirty seconds. Since nobody's read it—"

"I read it!"

"All right. One or two of you have read it. What I want you to do, even if you *haven't* read the story—got that?—is to summarize it, tell me the plot, in the next five minutes. And then we'll talk about it, however much we can—okay?"

"Summarize it? Just tell what happened, in general?"

"Yeah, but from start to finish: this happens, then this, then this."

"Three things?"

"However many details you can think of and write in five minutes. It's just like the way you'd tell about a movie, but you're telling somebody about this story. And you want them to keep listening, don't you? So you make it interesting."

Michael waited, hand in the air, till I finished. "What if the story wasn't interesting personally? To me? I'm not saying it wasn't, because I know you yourself enjoy this kind of thing, so I'm just saying, how do you describe something interestingly if it wasn't interesting to you personally?"

"That's a great question. The answer is, I don't know. But, look, you can describe a bad TV show or movie in a really entertaining way, can't you?"

"Teacher . . . Mr. Blaisdell," said Carol, raising her hand, "I should make a confession and say I didn't read the story. I just . . . well, no excuses, I didn't read it."

"I forgot, too," said a couple of other students.

"It doesn't matter! Fool me! Be funny. I'm not grading these. Imagine what a story called 'The Earthquake in Chile' would be like."

This is a possible assignment, by the way—asking students to write a story based on the title of a story they have not yet read. (Some titles are better than others, obviously. "Hills Like White Elephants" might provoke nonsense, while "The End of Something" or "The Battler" might give enough room and direction to get good results.)

"Make it up, then?" said Marianne.

"Yes, exactly."

"Lie, you mean," said Tony.

"No, no, don't lie. If you didn't for some reason read it, you can't possibly know what the story is about, but you can make something of what you know. I read the opening paragraph on Wednesday."

"Oh, that's right."

"So write it, the summary, now?" said Harvey.

"Yes, thank you."

I saw Marianne take out her photocopies and begin reading.

"You don't have time! You can't read it now. I want these back in five minutes and then we'll talk about the real story."

Some of them started to write, others ignored me and peeked at the photocopies.

"Don't try to read it!"

"I'm just reminding myself," said Benita. It was true what she said, as from her summary it was plain that she was one of the three students who had read it. The other two were Michael and Tony. Several students wandered in as the five minutes flew by. I wrote a summary, too, to see how much time it would take me.

I asked for the summaries. The students cried, "Not yet!" So I gave them two more minutes, which I let run to five. Then I collected the papers and read aloud some of the longer summaries, around two hundred words each. A couple were very good—including Benita's and Tony's—though they each got a detail or two wrong. Three students wrote lively, compelling summaries of what they had not read.

Having read aloud one of the accurate ones and then one that was made up, I said, "Which one's the real one?" I got calls for each. "No, it was the first one."

"I like the second better," said Michael.

"But you *read* the real story."

"I know, but I still liked the one somebody else wrote better. I already knew the real way, so the other's more creative."

"I don't know about 'more creative,'" I said, "but this is certainly how fiction—stories, novels—sometimes get written. You guess about things you didn't do or didn't know. And with this, you hear a title, and you can't help imagining some sort of story behind it. You hear 'Antony and Cleopatra,' and you have some idea form in your head what it's about, even if you don't know anything about them."

"Some titles don't tell you nothing."

I nodded, saying, "Yes, or they're deliberately misleading or vague, or the words are being used in an obscure way. But mostly they're useful and suggestive."

"I almost didn't read *The Shining*, because that didn't sound scary," said Michael.

Subna said, "Ooh, and how about *Carrie?*"

"All right, all right," I said, feeling put out by the invasion, once more, of Stephen King. "Let's look at Kleist's story."

I pointed out and read aloud two particularly spectacular parts: Josefa and Jerónimo and their baby reunited after the earthquake; and the brutal scene in Santiago's lone remaining church, where the mob of spiteful survivors destroys the overly optimistic heroes. I was the only enthusiast. "Should I give up?" I said, having given up.

"Give it up, Bob," said Harvey. "And let us go home. Some days it's just not happening."

I hesitated. "Why do you think Kleist was so attracted to inventing stories of life and death passions?"

In response I received a few shrugs and one barely audible and sarcastic "Why not?"

I put off the inevitable for a few minutes by telling them about Kleist's life and death ("You know it almost figures," said Tony, "those creative types commit suicide a lot"). And then I let them go. "Have a good weekend."

*　　*　　*

Having learned my lesson about how *not* to teach "The Earthquake in Chile," I had my students in another composition course simply read the story, and then, before any discussion, I asked them, "What was Josefa's biggest mistake?"

I did not want to repeat my mistake of preaching the word of Kleist and coloring or challenging their initial responses. This was a reactionary experiment, and, for the most part, a successful one. The students were avowedly uninterested in literature, but they showed with their attention to details and their communication of sympathy that they had enjoyed this story. I didn't repeat my error of presenting Kleist as a better alternative to King.

One student, Joe Azcuy, went off on his own tack and wrote Josefa a letter:

"The Earthquake in Chile" by Heinrich von Kleist is an amazing rollercoaster ride of a story. The twists and turns, the chance events, and the misunderstandings multiply to the point where the reader is left in a state of exhaustion. I found the vertigo exhilarating.

Poor Josefa, ruined by love and hope, and left for dead with her lover Jerónimo in the courtyard of a church, your child brought up by someone else—what was your biggest mistake? You fell in love with your tutor, Jerónimo Rugera, in the house of your father, Don Enrico Asterón, one of the richest noblemen of the city. Josefa, didn't you know that one of the duties of money and power is morality? Or at least the pretense of it? You let your brother discover your secret rendezvous with Jeronimo and trigger the catastrophic chain of events that ensued. Look back from beyond the grave—would this be your biggest mistake?

Or was it continuing to see your beloved Jerónimo at the convent, where your father had so outrageously imprisoned you? So there, one night, you consummated your affair. We are told love is the greatest thing on the face of the earth, and this may be, but what everyone fails to mention is that the most dangerous thing on the face of the earth are the consequences. Doña Josefa, did you know that you would give birth to your first, last, and only child on the steps of the Cathedral, at the start of the procession for Corpus Christi, in front of the whole city? This disaster, the consequences of your great love, was this your greatest mistake?

Naturally, in Santiago in 1647, you were condemned to death. The most your family's power could do, after the Abbess' account of your excellent character, was to get the viceroy to commute your sentence from death at the stake to death by beheading! And there are people who say that authoritarian governments are incapable of mercy!

Perhaps your greatest mistake was getting pregnant in 1647, when an earthquake could come along and miraculously free you. Free you to love again, hope again, trust again. This earthquake that freed both you and Jerónimo, he from prison and you on your way to the block, also destroyed the town. In the confusion you managed to save your son from the destroyed convent. Later, in the forest around the town, you found Jerónimo. It was a miracle, Josefa; and the three of you for a little while knew what it must have been like in the Garden of Eden.

For a little while. Josefa, how could you allow yourself to be swayed from your most excellent plan to go to the town of La Concepción, where you had a close friend? From there you could either have gone on to Spain and lived with Jerónimo's relatives, or after a while written to friends in

Santiago to see if it was safe to return. Alas, no. You befriended Don Fernando and his wife Doña Elvira, even suckling their child, and allowed yourself to be seduced by the notion that people are basically good and kind and forgiving. Weren't these seductions the road to your ruin?

Oh, Josefa, how could you agree to go to church and thank God for the miracle of your family's deliverance? Didn't Saint Francis pray and glorify God in the forests of Italy? A Dominican church, at the height of the Inquisition! And when the priest started to justify God's wrath by saying that Santiago was worse than Sodom and Gomorrah, were you really surprised that someone in the crowd recognized you and that the crowd turned against you? Josefa, the madmen murdered both you and your beloved Jerónimo, although your son survived and will be brought up by Fernando and Elvira.

Josefa, your greatest mistake was your innocence, your trust, and your love. But this is who you were. And like Jerónimo I would not change you for the world.

As a summary of the story I think this is neatly and beautifully done; but even better, and more deeply imaginative and sympathetic than any published account of the story I have read, is the evocation of her heroic character. Joe converted what is often a trite exercise ("Write a letter to a character in the story") into the most personal and best kind of literary criticism.

*　　*　　*

When I gave the same class at BMCC that had resisted "The Earthquake of Chile" the first two pages of Kleist's three-page story, "The Beggarwoman of Locarno," I didn't remind them they had read or discussed one of Kleist's other stories. I had a simple trick in mind that didn't depend on their remembering their experience with the author. I had thought of reading them an open-ended story, maybe one of Chekhov's or Hemingway's, and having them continue it, which I had done with more literary students in California. But having reflected on those results, I decided I didn't like distorting a story by "adding" to it; it made me feel disrespectful, for instance, of "The Lady with the Dog" or Hemingway's conception of Nick Adams.

I finally settled on having them complete the last third of "The Beggarwoman of Locarno." I handed out a copy of the first two pages and read them aloud. The fact that it's a ghost story did not produce any scoffing or skepticism. Some of these students, in writing of life back home in the Caribbean or Asia, had already recounted tales of voodoo,

amazing prophecies, and magic. I had been surprised and delighted that
the students wrote, for the most part, with belief and believability about
those supernatural occurrences. Kleist's story is equally unironic.

The last sentence of the second page of the Penguin edition reads,
"When on the third evening the"—that's it. That was the phrase they
had to use to begin the third page.

"I don't know ending!" protested Jan Jan.

"Right," I said. "Nobody here knows the ending—except for me.
Just try to write what you *think* happens. Write it like a story."

"Should we try to write it imitating his style?" asked Edgar.

"In *Kleist*'s style?" I laughed, unable to help myself, because to me
imitating Kleist would be like imitating van Gogh. "I think his style is too
wild and personal to imitate. But sure, you can try. I think you're better
off, though, writing the rest of the story in your own usual style. You
have ten minutes."

"Ten?"

"Okay, fifteen."

There are enough events in the first two pages to make a novel. An
old beggarwoman, sick and using a crutch, comes to a castle; a servant
gives her space on the floor to lie down; the marquis comes home in a
foul mood and orders the old woman to move from that spot to another; she slips, falls, and dies; years later, when the marquis and marquise
attempt to put the castle up for sale, the creakings and moanings of a
hobbling ghost frighten off any potential buyers.

The third page describes their terrible haunted night in the room
where the old woman died; the marquise flees, but the marquis, in a mad
fit, sets fire to the castle and goes up in smoke with it.

I got so anxious watching the students write that I came to feel that
my assignment was ridiculous. Time crawled.

"Ten minutes," I announced. "It's five minutes to go, no matter
what."

And then, "It's fifteen minutes. Time's up."

I collected their versions and read some aloud.

In one, the old woman's ghost, possessed now with incredible
strength and martial arts training, gruesomely murders the marquis with
her crutch-sword and takes over the castle.

In another, the ghost is explained away as a result of the marquis's bad conscience. He sets up a hospital for the disabled, and the ghost, like a good fairy, forgives him.

One student dramatized the old woman's dialogue with the marquis; didn't he know his duty to the homeless? Didn't the marquis have a mother who would one day be disabled? Was it necessary he be so brutal?

An ESL student had the marquis phone for Ghostbusters; the line was busy, so he called the Terminator instead. The hero, spouting "Hasta la vista, baby" and toting hand-held rockets, blasts the castle to smithereens, unintentionally killing the marquis and marquise, with only the old woman's "ghost" (she hadn't really died) surviving.

And, finally, a usually inattentive, impatient student, Robert, irritated as always by having to write, came up with a version that was remarkably similar to Kleist's. The marquis blows up the castle, killing himself and the marquise in the process. The writing even had something of Kleist's gusto.

Shaking my head in wonder, I said, "Except for that first part, where the writer's being deliberately silly, this one's got it!"

Robert tried not to smile.

Then we read Kleist's ending, which we gave more attention, I think, than we would have had we simply read the story straight through. By reading this story, we were all better grounded in describing particular, evocative details of an amazing event. Hoping for more of and more out of their home-country ghost stories, I gave them a writing assignment for the next meeting: "A Ghost Story."

What reading Kleist's ghost story gave them (and me) was more confidence that their tales of what I was calling, with some condescension, voodoo and magic, were legitimate literary topics. I wanted to show them that some of the greatest stories ever written were not slow and uneventful, requiring patience with and appreciation of the everyday. And what I now remember from this class are their fantastic stories of supernatural visions of cows in a Chinese heaven, balls of light in the Guyanese forest, and grinning monsters in the Jamaican bush.

While I made many mistakes with my initial assignment of "The Earthquake in Chile," I keep returning to Kleist's stories for use by my writing classes. In one meeting I can now explode their expectations and prejudices about what that forbidding word *Literature* is made up of, if

I let the students discover for themselves Kleist's unique, overpowering intensity. They are then less hesitant to allow their own writing to venture into the extremes of human experience.

Note

1. Heinrich von Kleist, *The Marquise of O and Other Stories*. Translated by David Luke and Nigel Reeves.

Bibliography

Kleist, Heinrich von. *The Marquise of O and Other Stories*. Translated by David Luke and Nigel Reeves. Hammondsworth, England: Penguin, 1978.

———. *An Abyss Deep Enough: Letters of Heinrich von Kleist*. Edited, translated, and introduced by Philip B. Miller. New York: Dutton, 1982.

Yvonne Murphy

Teaching Elements of Fiction With Mark Twain's *Adventures Of Huckleberry Finn*

ALTHOUGH I AM A POET, sometimes I teach fiction writing, helping students to complete a long story. We usually spend a class period or two (depending on the level of detail and interest of the students) on each element of a story: setting, plot, action, characterization, dialogue, etc. Then we work for a few more days to tie the pieces together into a cohesive whole and to revise.

It can become a rather arduous process. The students, at times, complain that it appears as if they've undertaken an endless project. Ultimately, though, the students feel proud of their stories and gain a real sense of the dedication and hard work that goes into a finished piece. A longer individual project like this also gives them a strong sense of accomplishment, and the faith that they can rely on themselves to see their work through to the end. It is an excellent way, too, for me, a poet, to grow as a teacher and extend my own creative abilities.

Of course, if the students' concentration slips or if a majority of them complain about the length of the project, we take a break and try to do something fresh with our material. For example, in the middle of a long fiction writing project, I might have the students spend a day writing haiku based on their settings. Maybe we'll draw pictures of an important scene, to try to get a new perspective on it. Or we'll write letters from one character to another to uncover motivations and personalities. We might not even write for a day or two, spending class time in teams of two or three, serving as mutual "consultants." As consultants, we take turns reading each other's work and suggesting helpful ideas. Some days, though, we might take a complete break from our project and write another poem or a song. I have a smorgasbord approach to teaching writing: I don't like to go into a classroom and teach only one idea or skill. I much prefer the organic approach of giving access to many potential skills and then sitting back to see what grows. Sometimes I see immediate results; other times an idea will reappear as a brilliant mutation in subsequent works.

This year, in a residency sponsored by Teachers & Writers Collaborative and NBC, I used Mark Twain's *Adventures of Huckleberry Finn* as a model to teach fiction writing to high school juniors and seniors. I've loved *Huckleberry Finn* since my own high school days and have used it before for smaller lessons at a number of grade levels. When I was a teenager, *Huckleberry Finn* enchanted me with its tale of a young outsider, Huck, making his own way downriver in a seemingly vast, dangerous world. Huck's adventure, to me, was made even sweeter by the constant, albeit conflicted, companionship of his one devoted friend, Jim. Many of my own teen days were spent feeling alone and looking for adventure in the form of escape and friendship. Of course, I thought I was all alone in my strangeness. I wasn't all that unusual. From my recent experience teaching eleventh and twelfth graders at Furr High School in Houston, Texas, I am able to understand how normal and vital these feelings actually are.

The NBC residency was an excellent opportunity for me to try something I had long thought of: to use one book, *Huckleberry Finn*, continuously for my longer fiction lessons. In the past, I had always used sections from different books. I was interested to see how an intensive reading of one book would add to the overall experience. It also happened that the classroom teacher I worked with also wanted to teach *Huckleberry Finn*. It was a lucky coincidence that showed the students two different approaches to the same text, each perspective adding to a deeper comprehension of the other and a deeper retention of both.

What follows are a few lessons from my ten-week residency with the students. The dialect, superstition, and parents lessons I describe below could be used as one-time assignments. A perfectly fine story could be written by combining just two of the elements mentioned below. Other writers would certainly highlight elements of fiction I haven't mentioned. There are myriad ways to combine the parts of this project. The trick here is remaining in tune with the class rhythm and knowing when to adjust your plans.

1. Dialects

The first pages of the book are best for this exercise, although dialect from any part of the narrative would suit the purpose here. My edition of *The Adventures of Huckleberry Finn* (see endnote) includes Twain's explanation of his use of dialects. To start the lesson, I read this out loud to my students and ask them if they know what a dialect is. We then stumble through a definition of *dialect* and its difference from the word *vernacular*. To complicate matters, I throw the words *slang* and *jargon* into the mix and we try to give examples of jargon vs. examples of dialect. This part of the lesson is really fun, because I am originally from—as Texans say—"Up North." For this lesson, I try to exaggerate the sounds and particularities of a more general Northern dialect. Then, I offer some dialect from my hometown, Rochester, N.Y. The students give examples of their own dialects, everything from street talk to private family language. We laugh as one student does what he perceives to be a Californian "surfer dude" dialect. Many of my students are familiar with Cajun and Creole dialects, having relatives from nearby Louisiana.

Next, I read from the opening chapter of *Huckleberry Finn*. The class discusses Huck's speech and notes some of the particularities that seem to construct a dialect—phrases, pronunciations, spellings, individual words. For example, in the first paragraph, Huck uses the word *stretchers* to suggest that the book previous to his, *The Adventures of Tom Sawyer*, isn't completely true. The class mulls that word over, comparing it to other words they use or have heard used to mean a white lie. We spend a few more minutes thinking about what makes dialects, and then the conversation turns to the assumptions we make about certain dialects— intelligence, class, race, culture, gender. This turn is emblematic, in my experience, of high school students' thinking: they have an imminent desire to understand the greater social world outside.

The following are some of the dialect pieces written after our class discussion:

My Great-Grandmother

Ma Sha I tell ya, Louisiana is haunted. I tell ya dem plantashuns full wit dem ghosts. Souls of spooks runnin round. I tell ya dey made me play wit dat gul at ha home, and Sha it was a face, of a pritty woman, starin at us. I say look at dat womun, den ha face disapeered. Scared me haf to death. But no Sha, yall got to go see dat big house on da byu. Da snakes, Ohh Sha da snakes came in big groups. One chased me an aunty Lily clean cross da feeld. Lily ran all-da-way ta Tut and Cyset house and dey laffed and laffed at dat fool, oh ye, I was talkin bout dat house, the chilren couldn't sleep in dat house. No, da spirit was takin da cover off da children but da mayd sat, *sho as I'm here you gone let dem alone.* Well, Sha, I'm finsta take my nap ni, good nite Sha.

—*Tiffani Burton*

JUAN: Wuz up, dawg!
JOSE: Chale homes.
JUAN: Say, dawg, let's go cruisin' around in my G-ride.
JOSE: You talkin' about that hooptie?
JUAN: That ain't no hooptie foo. All it need is a paint job, some rims, and a system.
JOSE: How much you got it for?
JUAN: For five bills from that player down the street.
JOSE: Chale!
JUAN For real foo.

—*Juan Alvarado*

Well a sometimes I be on da cut chilling wit my homies and dis fine honey walk up. I be like *yo what's ya name?* So, I'm making her down and thangs and she seems down for whatever. Later on I call the brawd up to see what she bout cause if it's like dat it's all good. We chill and get freaky and thangs so my stomach starts to talk: *it's time to get so vittles up in here.* You heard me! So later on I told da chie I'll holla at her later and I was out the dow. . . .

—*Paul Tatum*

2. Superstitions
This part of our project was charming and delightful. I came into the classroom one morning and started by discussing the word *superstition.* Then I asked the students to spend seven minutes writing down a list of all of the superstitions that either they or their family held. Volunteers then read their lists out loud. Many of us laughed with recognition when we heard "Don't step on a crack, you'll break your momma's back!" and "Say 'bread and butter' when something like a pole comes between you and a friend when you're out walking." We giggled as some very peculiar and idiosyncratic superstitions were read. "I never heard of that!" someone would inevitably shout with glee. "That's *bent!*" Translation: weird.

Next, I read from Chapter Four of *Huckleberry Finn*, in which Huck talks about Miss Watson's superstitions and tells the reader about Jim's auspicious "hairball." The class loved hearing this after our previous discussion. I asked them to spend fifteen to twenty minutes making up their own, unheard-of superstitions. I mentioned that these ideas, besides being pleasurable, might come in handy later, when we would be coming up with character sketches or trying to create a plot twist in our stories. When the students finished writing, I asked again for volunteers to read. Without hesitation, everyone read from their lists. Peals of laughter and amazement ensued.

Here were a few of our invented superstitions:

If you break the frame of your watch, you can expect to age faster.
—*Henry Cantu*

If you say five "n" words in one sentence, your nose will bleed.
—*Derrick Allen*

If you give to the poor, you'll have a good life.
—*Christina Hermosillo*

If a dog looks at you for a long time and doesn't bark, you're going to get a dog bite.
—*Karla Vazquez*

If you wear red on Wednesday, a new love is coming.
—*Erik Alvarado*

Don't sneeze in a church or you will have to change your religion.
—*Firas Hussein*

If you break a glass figurine, you'll have ten days of worrying about your hair being cut off.
—*Jeanette Cantu*

If you use a butter knife to eat a steak, you'll throw up everything you ate that day.
—*Juan Alvarado*

3. Parents

Undoubtedly, one of the more disturbing and real aspects of this novel is Huck's estranged and abusive relationship with his rough, vagrant father. Chapter Five details a rather sudden and violent return of Huck's father, when he berates Huck for going to school and beats him for learning to read. Huck's father accuses him of becoming "swelled-up" with himself and threatens that he'll "learn people to bring up a boy to put on airs over his own father and let on to be better'n he is." Then, he forces him to sit down and read for him. When he is satisfied that Huck can read, he knocks the book out of his hands and says: "Now looky here; you stop that putting on frills. I won't have it. I'll lay for you, my smarty; and if I catch you about that school I'll tan you good." Later on, Huck's dad gets drunk and hallucinates that snakes are attacking him. He then has a fit, going as far as to threaten killing Huck. The chapter ends with Huck's sitting vigil with a loaded gun pointed at his sleeping father.

This scene holds a lot of impact for any young person with a troubled relationship. In any high school, in any town or city, there are teens that understand this scene on an intimate level. After I read this chapter, I don't spend the usual time discussing and analyzing it. The issues seem too raw and all too real. Instead, I read the chapter and clarify any technical questions the students have. Then, I tell them they can write about a real or fictional disagreement between a child and a parent, or about any other troubled or complicated relationship. I do point out the use of dialogue in this scene and stress that they might try incorporating dialogue in their own writing.

Here are two responses:

My T-Jones

My mother: You need to make up your mind on who you want to be with. You're not going to be going out with all those different boys. You are only supposed to have one boyfriend. *Me to my mother*: Momma, I'm not ready to settle down. I haven't found the right person yet. I'm not trying to be like Niecie. *My mother says*: Well, I can't keep up with all these boys, what happened to the boy you brought to the house from Cleveland, TX? What's his name again? *Me*: Who, Marcus? He act like he too busy to call me so I moved on and found someone else. *Momma*: And where is your jacket? You're not leaving this house without a jacket. *Me*: Momma I know, it's right here. You know I never leave the house without it. *Momma*: And some boy called you last night, I forgot his name, there's so many of them. *Me*: Ha ha ha! *Momma*: You know what time to be in the house and if the boy have a pager, give me the pager number and let me know what kind of car he drive. *Me*: O.K., Momma, I'm gone. Bye bye.

—*Charndre Jones*

Midnight

"Jasmine, can't you hear me?" her mother yells while Jasmine stares into the kitchen table, almost seeing through it, she finally realizes someone is speaking to her. "Girl are you deaf or something or are you just plain stupid? You're daydreaming again, it won't get you anywhere girl, I already told you many times. Jasmine, I need you to go to the store for me." "But mom!" "Don't but mom me little girl, just do as you have been told to do so! I swear you're not good for anything Jasmine, all you want to do is complain, Mom this and Mom that, look at you now, you're just sitting there looking awkward. Tell me Jasmine what are you thinking about when you stare off into space?" Her mother won't understand how free Jasmine feels to daydream, she's safe in her own world, trouble-free, no disappointments to face. "Get the hell out of my house." "What?" "You heard me, get the hell out and don't come back until you learn how to take an order." "An order, listen to your drunk ass talk about order. You complain that I don't do anything, well hell at least when I do something I'm sober and not falling all over myself with every step I take. But if this is the way you want it well then so be it. I don't know why I ever left my dad's house." "I'll tell you why, because he didn't want your ass there, this is why little girl." "SHUT UP! I can't stand being here anymore! I have to get out of this hellhole." "Be my guest, this is one less mouth I have to feed." "Oh, you never even feed the ones that you have now. Anyway you want me gone fine, let me just get my things so I can go." "Things, what things? Oh no honey, you didn't buy one piece of clothing, everything that was bought, was bought with my money. Understand, my money. You have worked not one day in your miserable life." "Well then you can take those clothes and shove them up your ass!" As Jasmine walks out the door sobbing like a two-year-old, she turns and looks at her mother for one last time.

—*Jeannette Rubalcava*

4. Setting

In order to help students get started on their long stories, I decided this time to start with settings. I began by asking the class to give their own reasons why a setting is crucial to a story. "Because you've got to know where the story takes place," one person remarked. "It gives the flavor of the story." Another added, "The setting could be a crucial part of the action later on." I stressed that one of the best ways to create a setting is to include strikingly specific details. We spent a minute as a group, deciding what would make a detail "strikingly specific." I asked them if a blue sky is that striking. They said no, too ordinary. I asked if it is specific? They replied that it could be specific, depending on the weather;

however, we agreed that there are ways to make even "blue" more specific. Clear blue, like the color of contact lenses? An ominous, darker blue, like the sky just about to fill up with storming?

I then read from Chapter Nine of *Huckleberry Finn*, where Huck describes his cave dwelling and, subsequently, the outbreak of a heavy thunderstorm. The students were particularly impressed with the ways in which Twain's description mingles the five senses. They also commented on Twain's ability to describe the storm with a certain poetic beauty while maintaining the dialect and integrity of his main character. We discussed the importance of seeing the setting through our characters' eyes. In the following passage, Twain describes the storm through Huck:

> Directly it began to rain, and it rained like all fury, too, and I never see the wind blow so. It was one of these regular summer storms. It would get so dark that it looked all blue-black outside, and lovely; and the rain would thrash along by so thick that the trees off a little ways looked dim and spider-webby; and here would come a blast of wind that would bend the trees down and turn up the pale underside of the leaves; and then a perfect ripper of a gust would follow along and set the branches to tossing their arms as if they was just wild; and next, when it was just about the bluest and the blackest—*fst!* it was as bright as glory, and you'd have a little glimpse of tree-tops a-plunging about away off yonder in the storm, hundreds of yards further than you could see before; dark as sin again in a second, and now you'd hear the thunder let go with an awful crash, and then go rumbling, grumbling, tumbling down the sky towards the under side of the world, like rolling empty barrels downstairs—where it's long stairs and they bounce a good deal, you know. (55–56)

After reading the passage, I asked the students to comment on elements that stood out to them. They shouted out a variety of responses, but we dwelled on the trees being "spiderwebby" and the thunder sounding like "empty barrels." I asked them to consider why these examples worked so well. We discussed how word choices and the senses can affect the physical and emotional impact of an image. We toyed around with different ways to describe a tree: "skeletal," "laughing," "thick-rooted," "smooth." In turn, I encouraged them to concentrate on word choice and description in their own stories.

Below are three brief examples of settings by members of the class:

Corona

Corona is a ranch about nine hours from Houston. I know the place because my cousin lives there, it is a gorgeous place. My cousin stays at a two-story house which is not very far from the river. A block and a half and the river is in your sight. When its current is running, the water is crystal clear. Anything dropped in there could be found. Across the river is the woods which we hunt in. At night it's all real dark, the only light seen is the one from a taco stand which is across from the highway. The way of living there is by growing crops or having animals. My cousin does both. At dawn, my cousin, his father, and I go work at the place where he has oranges and avocados, which is called a *huerta*. The way of irrigation is getting water from the river. The only thing I wouldn't like to happen in Corona is a freeze because all the crops would go to waste. This is what happened with El Niño the last time it struck. My cousins lost their crops and money. Now he is selling cattle in other nearby ranches. There is a *tinaco* that holds water for the little town and mad owls nest in it. Owls don't like to be mocked or aggravated. They will attack you if you whistle like them, or that is what is told. When I go to the plaza to play soccer with all my friends the days go by fast. Then I ask to be walked home 'cause darkness comes and there is no light at all. On the way to my cousin's house I treat to cokes and chips. After I get home I have to shout out so some of my cousins will open the gate and hold the dogs back while I run inside the house.

—*Joe Serna*

Haunted House

Glance at this place and you would think it was abandoned. The path made by its constant visitors is hidden by the yard's abundance of greenery like a rain forest. The houses' entrances and exits are boarded up and sealed, or at least it appears that way. Little dogs and other animals dare not to step into the yard because they know its secrets or maybe because they've been hurt by one of the abandoned syringes. Little kids think of the house as haunted. But these kids must know about the house's secrets because inside the house live the dead. Zombies roam around with eyes that are bloody red all wanting one thing and doing anything for it. The bugs crawl all over the house, with more brains than the inhabitants inside. The air has an old stench of burning because they have no heat. Your vision inside the house is a blur because the action inside the house is immense. You can hear the screaming and shouting of the zombies trying to get what they crave for.

Then, out of nowhere a flood of blinding blue, white, and red lights uncover the hidden secrets of the house and in a flash the blue troops raid the zombies and have exorcised the house from its secrets.

—*Derrick Allen*

The Maze

This place is altogether different. Each corner isn't the same. When you first enter into the maze it seems easy but looks can be deceiving. You have four ways you can go but three out of the four are wrong. These three have something waiting to kill you. You can't climb out, you have to go in with the right choices to make. The walls are gray and are steadily moving. If you try to climb them you slip and fall into quicksand. The things that you meet on the wrong way all lead to death. One is disease, two is drugs, and three, crime. The only right way leads to prosperity and hope. If you can't take the maze of life and try to climb out, you fall into an early grave. It starts out simple but it gets harder and harder as you go and grow in knowledge. You have to make the right choices instead of the wrong ones. The sound comes when someone trips up and is overcome with wrongdoing. This sound is a screaming for help but no one answers the call. You only smell fresh scents of perfume and summer.

—*Paul Tatum*

5. Characterization

Next we turn to characterization. Once we have written a setting for the story, it seems natural to put a person or creature in that place. For characterization, we look closely at what we know about Huck and Jim. I list their names on the board and ask the class to provide information that we know about each character. Since we are already deep into the novel, I don't feel it necessary to read a selection here (if I were to start this project with characterization, I would choose to read any number of descriptions of Huck or Jim from the beginning of the book, when they first are introduced). When we finish our lists, I ask the students to tell me what kind of information is on the board under each character's name. "Their appearance," someone suggests. "Where they're from," I hear another voice say, soon followed by: "name," "age," "race," "physical condition," "hair color," "education," "language," "superstitions," "family situation," "wealth," "marital status," "job" and so on. From this response, I start a new list on the board under the heading of *Characteristics*. We discuss how the word *character* is implicit in that word.

Next, I ask the class if there are any qualities or characteristics of people that we have left off our list. This takes a moment's thought because many of the students are caught up in defining their characters by physical details. "How about their goals in life?" I ask. "What about their fears? Regrets? Loves? Their thoughts? Their capacity to care?" A whole new line of thinking begins: students start suggesting less superficial qualities, such as the way their characters see the world, their characters' inner struggles, ways in which a character is proud of himself or herself. I then suggest that the students use these lists to write a sketch or brief description of their main characters. I take a moment to ask them what a sketch is and how it relates to a larger drawing or painting, and then apply their responses as metaphors for how their character sketches will fit into the creation of their longer stories. I advise them that they might try writing their sketches in the character's voice, from the character's point of view, in order to get a closer sense of them.

Here are some examples of our main characters:

Saint

Saint, yeah, that's what people that know me call me. My real name is Santiago and I'm going to let you in on a little about my life. You know, people may see me and they'll probably think I'm a tough, mean person. And, you want to know something? I am. You're probably wondering: *if this is a tough man as he says he is, then why would he want to talk to me for?* Many times when you're alone and don't have someone to talk to, it's hard. I started living on the streets from the time I was ten years old. You're probably thinking that I'm homeless, but I'm not. For your information, I have my own house. It may not be a fancy house but I would say that I'm a lucky person to have a roof over my head. Many times when I go out in the streets, and by the way I live in L.A., Los Angeles on the South Side in a real bad neighborhood. . . . As I was saying, many times when I go out on the streets it's pitiful to see many of my race, Mexicans, and others living in the street, homeless. Everybody can make a change if they want to, but they choose not to. You know it's all in the mind and attitude of the person. I would have never thought that I would have been around so much pain and suffering.

—*Vicente Magana*

Alzheimer's (My Great Aunt)

I tried to express myself, but couldn't find the
Words. I'd have beautiful feelings and
Moments one minute and the next I didn't

Even remember that I had felt happy or excited.
I felt very confused, almost all the time.
I didn't know how or what to feel.
You cared for me so many years and as you
Were growing up, you saw how my
Mind and memory deteriorated. I wanted to
Give you so much advice and tell you stories
About my life and share my life experiences
With you, and yet, I couldn't even carry on a
Conversation. It's amazing how this disease
Just creeps in slowly, like a thief in the night
And eventually consumes and affects your
Entire life. You can't remember your family
And don't recognize your surroundings.
Then, all of a sudden I'd get brief moments
Of memory and recognition and everything was
Peaceful, but before I knew it I'd have a memory
BLACKOUT and the conclusion would set in
All over again. It was terrible.
I felt like a prisoner in my own body.

—*Nelly Cavazos*

Far from Home

My eyes are at sea level, my body not that much bigger than a fifty-cent coin. My brownish outside helps me blend in with the white sand, but clashes with the muddy dirt. Out here I am open prey, there I had not a care in the world. On the muddy sand seagulls constantly swoop down, and try to grab me for a quick snack. But that is the life of a sand crab far away from home. The beautiful waters of my home brought a hollowed-out log to me. I went exploring on the log and accidentally fell in. My tiny little legs would climb the steep walls, but I would fall due to the massive water decay on the log.

On this voyage I have met fellow sand crabs native to the area. They have taught me how to find food in this strange land. Although I am treated well, I need to find my home. The waters of these parts are too cold for my body to handle. The constant change of weather is too much to bear.

—*Terence Williams*

6. Adding Drama

Next, I make sure that the students understand the difference between plot, drama, and theme. These distinctions are often difficult for the novice writer. The plot, I tell the class, is just a series of events, it's what happened. I give them an example of a plot: my morning so far—I got up, ate cereal, fed the cats, got dressed, left the apartment, got in my car, and drove to school. This is a plot. It moves the story from point A to point B. I tell this example in as bland a tone as possible, to underscore its humdrum quality. However, I add that the *theme* of a story is the meaning or meanings found within the events, while the drama is not what happens in a story, but *how* it happens.

To illustrate this idea, I tell them I am about to read from the beginning of Chapter Fifteen of *Huckleberry Finn*. Jim is on the raft, a fog rolls in, and Huck, in a canoe near the raft, gets separated from Jim but eventually is reunited with him. This plot sounds good, but not overly thrilling. We then discuss the different ways in which Huck might react to this sequence of events. We also take turns describing how the plot might be carried out, what details a writer might or might not choose to dwell on. I tell the students that we are now talking about the drama of the scene. After this, I read the passage and ask the class to close their eyes and imagine the scene as I'm reading it. The scene is full of intense drama. Twain describes the fog in such a manner that the reader is both scared and mystified alongside Huck. At one point, Huck, who has been whooping a call out into the night in hopes that he'll find Jim, insists, "I couldn't tell nothing about voices in a fog, for nothing don't look natural nor sound natural in a fog." I read this section in a dramatic and suspenseful manner. The scene lends itself perfectly to this kind of reading and it keeps students on the edge of their seats. Sometimes I stop reading before the end of the scene, causing students to beg me to finish. I don't do this to be cruel, but rather to illustrate to the young writers how suspense or drama will keep their readers moving from paragraph to paragraph, turning page after page.

After I finish reading, I ask the students to try to create a scene for their story that incorporates more drama. I suggest that they look back over what they've written so far and decide how they could intensify the action or suspense of the plot. Is there something dramatic that could happen with the setting, between the characters, in the dialogue? I remind them that their goal is to try to keep the reader wanting more, to keep them literally "on the edge of their seats."

Below are some excerpts from longer stories written in the class. I hope they keep you wanting more!

Watcher in the Woods

My favorite place is the woods. The woods at night are creepy and scary. Stepping into the woods at night was like stepping into a closet and closing the door behind me because the trees cover the moonlight. The trees felt like they were right behind me. Leaves and branches hit against me feeling like I'm catching a beating. When the branches were swinging from one side to the other you can hear a little whistling sound because of the wind blowing. Owls in trees look scary because you can only see their eyes, which look like headlights.

I could tell I wasn't alone because I could hear steps. It sounded like someone or something was stepping on popcorn. As I walked slowly it walked slowly, too, making it sound like we were stepping on firecrackers. When I turned around to see what it was, it was just a measly raccoon who at first I thought was a skunk. I decided to still continue through the woods. Although I was scared, it just felt like an adventure to me and I wanted to continue. Pacing along the trail I felt myself trembling like it was cold, thinking anything I heard from now on would be a raccoon but I was soon wrong. When I ran into a big bear I didn't think the bear saw me at first but when I tried to run it heard me and stood up growling. I knew then that I had to stop from whatever I was doing and try not to make a sound. Each sound the bear made, I stepped away thinking that it wouldn't hear me. One time it did and it ran up on me, literally throwing me into a tree. After that, I didn't know what hit me but I knew if I was to play dead the bear would let me be. . . .

—*Cheryl Woodley*

Neighborhood Life

It's dark, gloomy. For some reason it's always raining. People are on the corner hanging out. Many of the houses are torn down, some are boarded up. Haze is everywhere, also. Not a sunny day seems to pass. Homeless men try to warm themselves up by using old barrels to start fires to keep warm. Gunshots are always heard at night, also with screams that follow. Police sirens are heard, too.

There is a young boy who wishes he could get out. He saw his older brother die in front of him. Ever since that he has been scared for life. Ten years had passed and the boy, Arron and his friends are chilling on the corner, smoking weed. Juan asks Javier what's going down this weekend. Arron answered that the party's at Brenda's house. All of a sudden, a blue car pulls out in front of them, a group of guys pull out, giving Arron and his homeboys a mean look. Just about when they are getting ready to fight, a couple of cop cars pull up and the young men in the blue car leave. Arron and his friends all go to the store. When they walk up to the store, Arron sees Brenda, "Hey, what up girl!" "Nothing much Arron, still coming to my party?" "Yeah, I'll be there." They stared at each other for a while then said goodbye. Javier: "Hey, man how come you didn't mac† to her?" "It ain't like that." Juan: "Why not?" "Even though I've known her since eighth grade, it's just been hard for me to talk to her in that way." Javier: "Man, you're just scared of what she'd tell you." Arron: "Besides, she got a man." Juan: "F**k that, that's never stopped you before." Javier: "Yeah, what is it, our player has just met love and it's with that girl?" Arron: "Man, let's drop this and get the 40 oz. and roll. . . ."

—*Erik Alvarado*

† Slang for "put the moves on."

Bibliography

Twain, Mark. *Adventures of Huckleberry Finn*. New York: Signet Classic, 1979.

Mimi Herman

If I Had Wings

Classics and Creative Writing
In a Middle School Classroom

ON A COLD MONDAY in the middle of March, we gathered around tables in the media center of Madison Middle School: thirty-three eighth graders—mostly born and raised in the mountains of western North Carolina—and me.

For the past eight years, I had worked as a writer-in-the-schools, teaching students from ages ten through eighteen and their teachers; working with poetry, fiction, and journal writing. But since I usually only had a week in each school, I rarely got to look at great works of literature with my students, to get them excited about the writers who had inspired me as I was growing up.

When I first heard of the Classics in the Classroom project, I thought immediately of Madison County, North Carolina, where I had spent a semester as writer-in-residence the previous year, working with teachers to incorporate writing into their curriculum. The project seemed particularly appropriate for Madison County, since its only middle school had recently lost funding for special programs for gifted students, and needed to offer these students educational challenges that would interest them. Rather than limit this project to students who had been labeled gifted, however, I chose to expand our idea of giftedness and open up the project to any eighth grade student interested in attending.

"What makes a 'classic?'" I asked these students on our first day together. "What makes it different from an ordinary book?"

"It's popular," one said.

"It was written by a well-known author," said another.

And a third, "It's been a top-selling book for a while, *at least* two or three weeks."

"Okay," I said, "so why should I read a classic, instead of going out hunting or riding my four-wheeler? Write me a letter, convince me it's worth my time."

"If you don't put anything in your head, nothing will come out. No reading, no ideas," one of the two Davids wrote in his letter.

"If you read a book it will stay in your brain for a very long time," wrote the other David.

That sounded convincing enough to me, so we continued from there. I had collected my own favorite classics for these students to read. I wanted to use these works to inspire the kids to write their own poems and stories. The works I'd chosen had a common bond: they all dealt with how to live wisely and well in a world that is not always wise or good. I was asking these kids to read some pretty tough stuff: Aesop and Jean de la Fontaine, Confucius and François de la Rochefoucauld, Ovid, and Horace. And of course, the writing assignments were equally demanding: translating la Fontaine's fables and writing their own, examining the personae of Midas, Daedalus, Icarus, and Atalanta to write from their points of view, and creating original odes and aphorisms.

It might help, I decided, if we had some muses floating around to inspire us. So, on the second day, we talked about the Muses, and muses in general, and then we invented some, trying to coax them into our own lives through help-wanted ads, "personals," and simple descriptions:

My muse has the wings of a falcon, the head of a reptile, and his back feet have large spurs of ivory. He loves adventure and that's what I write. My muse helps me in my writing. His fiery breath burns the words in my heart and I put them on paper. His reptile body slips through my head and helps me think.

—*David Messer*

Help Wanted

Someone who understands, cares, and is loyal. Someone who can teach and share and listen. Someone different, loving, and kind; someone with lots of energy and talent, with common sense, intelligence, trustworthy. Someone fun to be with.

—*Shane Franklin*

Emily Dickinson inspired me to write. The way she sees the world, the things that happen all around her. She can make the most traumatizing accident seem romantic. The way she can make the most boring thing turn into action. The way she puts down her words, that's how she inspired me to write.

—Miranda Sawyer

Help Wanted

Need someone great at encouraging writers. Need someone who is very patient because it may take a while to catch on and start writing. Someone who knows how to solve problems that may come to me while writing. I want someone who doesn't mind staying with me for long hours to help, because it may take a long time.

—Jason Penland

On that day, I asked each of the students to choose a book they considered a classic, that they would read in addition to the work we were doing in class. We had such a short time together, and I wanted to expose them to a number of different writers and writing styles. But I also wanted them to experience the feeling of falling in love with a classic. I figured the best way to make this possible was to allow them to choose their own books. I also asked them to keep reading journals, containing brief summaries of what they'd read, as well as words and ideas that had intrigued them. This way they were able to engage more deeply in the books they read, and I got a sense of how their reading was progressing.

In the months preceding the residency, I'd put a great deal of thought into how I could immerse these students in the possibilities offered by language. I wanted them to have the opportunity, early in the first week, to think about the sounds of words as well as the meanings. I also wanted them to play with language as if it were a puzzle. So I prepared an unusual exercise for them. I asked them to translate Jean de la Fontaine's "Le corbeau et le renard" ("The Raven and the Fox") into English.

> Maître Corbeau, sur un arbre perché,
>   Tenoit en son bec un fromage.
> Maître Renard, par l'odeur alléché,
>   Lui tint à peu près ce langage:
> "Hé! bonjour, monsieur du Corbeau.

Que vous êtes joli! que vous me semblez beau!
　　Sans mentir, si votre ramage
　　Se rapporte à votre plumage,
Vous êtes le phénix des hôtes de ces bois."
A ces mots le Corbeau ne se sent pas de joie;
　　Et pour montrer sa belle voix,
Il ouvre un large bec, laisse tomber sa proie.
Le Renard s'en saisit, et dit: "Mon bon Monsieur,
　　Apprenez que tout flatteur
　　Vit aux dépens de celui qui l'écoute:
Cette leçon vaut bien un fromage, sans doute."
　　Le Corbeau, honteux et confus,
Jura, mais un peu tard, qu'on ne l'y prendroit plus.

　—Jean de la Fontaine

"You *did* hear about the French requirement for this class, didn't you?" I teased them, straightfaced, as I handed out the poem in the original. "You *are* all fluent?"

Stunned, they looked everywhere but at me. Some glanced down at their notebooks, wondering whether they should just pack it in and go back to their regular classes.

"Oh, it's okay," I assured them. "Just do the best you can."

We looked at the rhyme scheme of the poem. They listened as I read. I'd expected at first that they would "translate" the French into English words that sounded similar, so that their poems would approximate the sound of the original, but would vary in meaning. A few did, but most surprised me by wanting to do a direct, accurate, word-for-word translation. "*Monsieur* means *mister*, right?" they asked. "Is *phénix* the same as *phoenix*?"

After a while of letting the students muddle through, I pulled out a cheat sheet, a glossary with the English equivalents of about half of the words in the poem. I hadn't planned to give it to them until they'd finished their mock translations, but they were so intent on getting everything exactly right that it seemed a shame not to offer it to them.

"As a reward for working so hard," I told them, "I'll bring you some translations of this poem tomorrow." I decided that if I made them work hard on the translation, reading the poem in English would be an easy pleasure.

They labored over the assignment, taking it home with them and bringing back their translations the next morning, which were delightful in their aptness and language.

One student, Shana, translated the poem in this way:

Sir Raven, on a tree
Sitting with cheese in his beak.
Sir Fox, how are you today?
Very fine, thank you.
Hey, you speak my language.
Hey, Hello, Sir Raven,
Said the fox.
Did you know you are very handsome
Without a mention of your feathers?
It is very bright.
You are the most loving animal
And you have a beautiful voice
For having such a large beak.
You are on my foot.
Move it, my good sir.

—Shana Jarvis

We went on to look at translations of la Fontaine I had brought in, as well as two translations of the Aesop version of the same fable. "Why are the translations different?" one student asked. "Shouldn't they be the same in English if it's only written one way in French?" We discussed the difficulties of translation, how a literal word-for-word translation might be transformed into a variety of different poems, depending on the rhythm and rhyme and syntax of the English version that each poet created.

After translating from French, writing in English was easy. We started the third day by brainstorming for proverbs they'd heard growing up, which could be used as the morals of their own fables:

A man's work begins with the sun, but a woman's work is never done.
The early bird catches the worm.
You can't stay up with the owls if you want to soar with the eagles.
If it ain't broke, don't fix it.

In a short time we came up with over fifty. To give them a sense of aphorisms from other cultures I tossed in a few from Confucius, such as:

The cautious seldom err.

To go beyond is as wrong as to fall short.
Recompense injury with justice and recompense kindness with
    kindness.

I also added the cynicism of la Rochefoucauld, gems like these:

Self-love is the greatest of all flatterers.
We all have strength enough to endure the misfortunes of others.

The students were surprised to find how many of Confucius's sayings
from *The Analects* had become part of our contemporary Western culture. They were amused at the maxims of la Rochefoucauld, and found
a great deal of truth in them. I saw a number of heads nodding in agreement as we read these out loud.

Next, I gave the students some of Aesop's fables to use as models. We
discussed how fables worked, using animals to tell a brief, pointed story
that resulted in a moral. Then I suggested they might use any of the
proverbs we'd discussed to create their own fables, using either the verse
style of la Fontaine or the prose style of Aesop.

They made me laugh, these kids, when they came back the next day
with their fables. One student, Julia Hood, wrote a story of a daredevil
duck and a chicken chicken. The chicken—who gets its feathers singed
and a swift kick from a mule for following the duck's lead—finally draws
the line when the duck suggests a flying race across the lake while lug-
ging bricks attached to them by ropes. The duck, sadly, falls into the
lake and drowns. The moral? "It's better to be a live chicken than a dead
duck." Julia was kind enough to provide a postscript: "No live animal
was harmed in the writing of this story."

Another student, Miranda, adapted Aesop's "The Fox and the Goat."
She chose a different pair of animals from those in Aesop's tale, although
she put them in the same well. In the end, Miranda decided to offer her
own moral.

Dog and Cat

One time after a rainstorm, a cat tripped and fell into a well. The cat only
stayed alive by staying on an island of concrete. The well smelled of a musty
smell and was as wet as a small lake, and the young cat hated it.

   As a dog passed, he heard the cat singing to himself.

   "Say, Cat. What are you doing in that well?" he asked.

"Oh, haven't you heard? All the water on the earth is going to dry up! I'm staying where there is water! Nobody is going to have water but me!" he replied.

"Oh, dear! Cat, may I please join you? There will soon be no water up here! Please?"

"All right. Jump on down. But be careful, it's slippery."

"Oh, thank you, Cat!"

The large brown dog jumped into the well and again thanked the cat.

"No, Dog. Thank *you*."

"Because you were lonely?" he guessed.

As he hopped onto Dog's back, the cat said in reply: "No, dear Dog. I had fallen into the well and couldn't get out. Until a dumb dog—you, my dear friend—came along and helped me get out, only you didn't know it. Now my dear friend, I leave you with some words of advice: Never trust the advice of a man with difficulties."

At this, the cat jumped out of the well and ran off into the street.

—Miranda Poncier

Richard deserted the animal kingdom altogether. He also came up with a contemporary fable, one suited to this neck of the woods, about whether Chevy or Ford makes the better truck.

The Chevy said to the Ford, "I can beat you today."
The Ford just smiled and said, "There is no way."
The Ford said, "Let's race and see."
And the Chevy made his brags, "You'll never catch me."
Then there came a Pontiac to talk to the two,
And he said, "I can beat both of you."
The Chevrolet said, "You will not beat me."
The Pontiac said, "Just wait and see.
I will beat you from the start
Because I will race while you go down to Wal-Mart."
The Ford kept quiet because deep down he knew,
"I can beat both of you."
They were off as they all spun a wheel
And the Ford passed them both like they were sitting still.
The Ford won in a breeze
As the Chevrolet and Pontiac were doing just fifteen.
The lesson to be learned from this fable of mine
Is that the Ford will always beat a Chevy or any other kind.

—Richard Reese

Being a Chevy person myself, I tried to argue Richard out of his conclusion, but with no success.

Between the first week of the residency and the second, we had a month apart, in which I taught elsewhere and the students continued to read the classics they'd chosen and to write in their reading journals.

We began our second week with the myths of Ovid. I chose the Rolfe Humphries translation of Ovid's *Metamorphoses*, because it seemed both lyrical and accessible to a middle school reader. (I thought briefly about having them do their own translations, but decided that it might be a bit much to ask them to tackle both French *and* Latin in a month!) I chose three pieces from Ovid: the stories of Midas, Daedalus and Icarus, and Atalanta. I was fairly certain they would be familiar with the first, thought some of them might have heard of the second, and assumed the third would be new to them.

We read Ovid aloud in class. These teenagers at first read tentatively, then with increased confidence, taking great pleasure in the language. We read all three tales, discussing each in depth: clarifying unfamiliar language; talking about what various lines meant, how the characters must have felt. Then I asked them to write their own pieces based on the *Metamorphoses*. Each student chose a character from Ovid, either one of the principals—Midas, Bacchus, Daedalus, Icarus, Atalanta, Venus, Hippomenes—or one outside the story's frame—such as the fisherman watching Daedalus and Icarus as they flew or the soldier of Minos who saw the father and son escape. Using what they previously knew of these myths, what they'd learned from Ovid, what they'd learned of love and parents and children and life in their thirteen or fourteen years, the students wrote persona poems, telling the stories as if they were the characters.

> I touch a tree and watch the leaves.
> All the fiber the gold weaves.
> It starts down the lively branches.
> On the average day, what's your chances?
> Down the branch—and to the roots
> Further and further the gold shoots.
> After that I went a-walking
> Everything I touch, gold stalking,
> All the people pointing, talking.
>
> —Sarah Leonard

I know now
that such a gift was foul.
It brought me such great pleasure, such riches:
Lovely streets with golden ditches.

   —*Stephanie Fain*

The students spent that day working on their persona poems and sharing them. The next day, we looked at Horace's ode, "Better to Live, Licinius." We examined the ode form and discussed line breaks and ambiguity. Then each student chose someone who might benefit from advice and wrote odes in the style of Horace. The poems we did in these two days proved to be the richest of all the pieces we did together.

Fortress of Loneliness

Always on the loose,
Like a snake that sheds its skin
Will one day crawl under a rock to hide from itself.

Like a hoot owl's worst nightmares,
Endless nights and restless days.
Will the bad dreams ever be gone?

Like a dog with disease,
Driving itself mad,
Going in circles, turning, turning.

And poof, everything is gone
When they bury you.

   —*Miranda Sawyer*

Rescue from Drugs

I wish I knew why you would
like to be this way. I hope
you will listen to what I'm saying.

Clumsy and forgetful is the
path you want to take. Trying
to run from your mistakes.

Like a house flooded and
washed away. You have no control.
Please come back to me.

   —*Kim Gunter*

Toward the end of the residency, I still had so much I wanted to share with these students. So I decided to offer a couple of days in which they could choose what they wanted to write from a variety of centers. On one table, I placed clippings from *The Weekly World News* and *The National Enquirer*, offering the students the opportunity to transform the myths they had read into tabloid stories. Midas seemed to be one of the more popular characters to interview. One student, Holly Rector, wrote, "'People had to feed me,' sobs Midas."

"'I'm very thankful that I have my life back, even though I don't have a lot of gold,'" wrote another, Lydia Briggs.

On another table I placed bookmaking materials and offered students the chance to write and illustrate children's books of the fables they had written. At a third table the students could write myths to explain why something existed in the world:

Why We Can't Understand the Language of Animals

Once, a long time ago, all the animals and people got along with each other and understood each other's languages. But somewhere along the way they got into arguments over who does what and how things are done. Their gods got tired of all the bickering, so they eliminated the language of animals and humans to silence the problems. So today the animals have their language and people have their language.

—*Matthew Anglin*

At other tables they could create more persona poems, translate a number of passages from the maxims of la Rochefoucauld, write additional fables, or transform the fables they had written into poems.

Finally, on our last day, we chose the poems that would be included in an anthology, peer-edited, and revised them. We finished the residency with a reading and celebration of the work we had done. It was an exciting conclusion, leaving us sad to make our good-byes and looking forward to the next time we'd meet.

These kids, unlike Icarus, understood how their wings worked and how to use them wisely:

I was alone in my boat
resting for awhile
when I heard a strange rustle
on the nearby isle.
As I looked over I saw
a man and his son building wings.

I looked off
starting to get back
to my fishing
but then a shadow
was cast
on my boat.
As I looked up toward the sky I saw the boy
with the large feathers on his back.

He started to tremble
as if he would fall. With fear in his eyes
he drew near
to the dark blue water
now close by.
He shrieked one last time before
he plunged deep below.
All that's left
is the wings of death
floating on with no regrets.

—*Rebecca Edwards*

Bibliography

Aesop. *Aesop and Company*. Translated by Barbara Bader. Boston: Houghton Mifflin, 1991.

———. *The Caldecott Aesop*. Translated by Alfred and Randolph Caldecott. Garden City, N.Y.: Doubleday, 1973.

Confucius. "Sayings from *The Analects*" in *World Literature*. Translated by James Legge. Mission Hills, Calif.: Glencoe/McGraw-Hill, 1991.

La Fontaine, Jean de. *Fables of la Fontaine*. Translated by Elizur Wright, Jr. Boston: Tappan and Dennet, 1841.

———. *Fifty Fables of la Fontaine*. Translated by Norman R. Shapiro. Urbana, Ill.: University of Illinois, 1988.

———. *Selected Fables*. Translated by James Michie. New York: Viking, 1979.

Horace. "Better to Live, Licinius" in *World Literature*. Translated by Joseph P. Clancy. Mission Hills, Calif.: Glencoe/McGraw-Hill, 1991.

Ovid. *Metamorphoses*. Translated by Rolfe Humphries. Bloomington, Ind.: Indiana University Press, 1955.

Norman Weinstein

Magnifying Powers

Using Milton, Ovid, Diogenes, Homer, and Hesiod

THERE ARE MANY REASONS for bringing the classics into classrooms, but this essay focuses upon one of the most unrecognized. I am referring to integrating the classics into creative writing lessons based on themes of magnifying one's personal powers. Here's a secret: before my first day of teaching, I listen intensely to playground conversations (coffeeshop palaver if I'm working at the university level) on the sly. Part of a visiting writer's job is keeping his or her ear close to the ground, savoring the colors, rhythms, textures of language at the work site. As vital as these stylistic surfaces are to the writer, just as significant are thematic currents.

I've been teaching third, fourth, and fifth graders at Lowell Elementary in Boise, Idaho, a school still in its original building, over eighty years old. In some cases the grandparents of the kids I now teach once occupied today's classrooms. It seemed fitting to work with the classics in a school resonating with so much of this century's history. Each class is only one hour long, so that many writing assignments carry over into two class sessions. The school, like much of Idaho, is overwhelmingly white. There's not a single African American, Native American, or Jew in my classes, but there is a stimulating mix of kids from wildly differing socio-economic backgrounds. This means that I have a fair number of kids from economically struggling households. The underclass kids I have taught relish recess games, verbal and nonverbal, which allow them to feel powerful in—if nowhere else in the material world—their imaginations. This magnification of personal power is a survival tool. So I marshalled classics zeroing in on that summoning of power through carefully crafted language.

I want to begin with an example of a wrongheaded approach to teaching the classics, then offer alternatives. I've long been fascinated with the "Garden of Eden" theme, both in biblical and mythological guises, and thought the kids would enjoy mining it. I walked into a classroom of eight-year-olds and had the foolishness to read aloud the following:

> But rather to tell how, if Art could tell,
> How from that Sapphire Fount the crisped Brooks,
> Rolling on Orient Pearl and sands of Gold,
> With mazy error under pendent shades
> Ran Nectar, visiting each plant, and fed
> Flow'rs worthy of Paradise which not nice Art
> In Beds and curious Knots, but Nature boon
> Poured forth profuse. . . .

That is a crucial passage from Book IV of Milton's *Paradise Lost* describing the Garden of Eden, but to my class of students it could have been an unintelligible message from another galaxy. There are fifty-seven words in the above excerpt; the students failed to understand nearly a quarter of them, and they were quick to shout out their confusion. "*Mazy?*" "*Crisped?*" "*Boon?*" What kind of garden was this? Surely not one they would ever see—or write about. So I quickly translated Miltonic verse into kid talk:

> This Garden is awesome, so awesome there aren't words
> for it. It has way clear blue streams, shining golden sands,
> a red fountain. It's all neatly organized, but not too neat,
> just overgrown enough. . . .

Of course, the ghost of John Milton was standing beside me in the classroom, furious at my anti-poetic travesty. So I did feel a twinge of guilt. Then again, there is a tradition of rewriting Milton for one's own era. William Blake wrote his epic poem *Milton*, having the delicious arrogance to correct Milton's "errors," implying he knew what ideas Milton really meant to communicate. The contemporary American poet Ronald Johnson went so far as to erase most of *Paradise Lost*, leaving behind a mere skeleton of Milton's original, revealing it to possess a postmodern, elliptical beauty. But what most gave me courage and focus was the long and honorable tradition of "translating" the classics for children by simplifying the language and compressing narrative. Think of *Tales From Shakespeare* by Charles and Mary Lamb. Shakespeare's exquisite poetry is largely lost in their renditions, but what survives is a lively invitation to visit Shakespearian themes through childhood's imaginings. And my reason for wanting students to hear *Paradise Lost* was not to imitate Milton's language in their own writing, a hopeless pursuit irrelevant to their daily lives, but to locate themselves as a first man or woman holding forth in a perfect environment—to feel as powerful as Adam or Eve before the Fall.

I had them begin by drawing a map of how they would travel from their school to the Garden of Eden. I prefaced a number of assignments by encouraging them to literally or metaphorically map their ideas at the top of the page they would begin writing upon. Drawing seemed to free the energy caught up in fright or self-consciousness about writing. How often I would hear from students, "I can't write . . . but wanna see the cool drawing I can make?" So this assignment provoked no resistance. And I discovered that their elation at imaginatively inhabiting such a perfect place, their very own paradises, was strongly colored by melancholy. The painful contrast between everyday life and paradise led to this shocker of an opening paragraph:

> Have you ever wondered how many mosquito bites it takes for your whole body to swell up? Well, if I had my own Garden of Eden in the jungle, mosquitos would be banished.
>
> *—Anjelica Belcastro, fifth grade*

More common were expressions of regret about separation from family members. It was curious to me how often students chose to leave their parents out of Eden—but missed them nevertheless:

> My place is in the jungle. It is by the ocean and at night whales sing.
> There are beautiful flowers and juicy fruit. You can't see it because big trees cover it. The macaws and wolves make pretty sounds. It's prettier than Egypt. It smells like every great smell in the world. It feels softer than a lamb. Only me and my brother know where it is and we will never tell.
> I would like to stay but my parents will worry.
>
> *—Justin Pagel, fourth grade*

One student imagined that it would take leaving Eden to discover who his parents were, a mysterious twist that caught the attention of many students who shared the fantasy that the couple they knew since birth were surrogates. One's real parents would be discovered after leaving Eden.

> I have been in Eden for 2,000 days.
> I am going to escape tonight.
> I have never seen my Mom and Dad.
>
> *—Jim Eytchison, fifth grade*

Several student papers resonated with these variations on *Paradise Lost*. Rich descriptions of pastoral scenery were common. It was terrific to live amidst such beauty. It felt powerful that only you, or a trusted friend or sibling, knew how to get there, yet your everyday life was a lasso tugging you back to your everyday, un-Edenic world. I regret that I allowed only two class periods for this project. Had I expanded the assignment another hour or more I would have encouraged writing about how the qualities of relationships with friends (who were let as easily into Eden as parents were barred) were altered there. Did your best friend become even a better or different friend in that setting? How exactly? Was the thrill of feeling as mighty as Adam doubled with a friend?

Perhaps student writings most glorying in new-found power centered around the myth of Daedalus and Icarus, a paradox since the myth is so clearly a parable about overreaching. The tale is offered in Book Eight of Ovid's *Metamorphoses*, translated into an American English infused with great musicality by Charles Boer. But Boer's translation presumed an intellectual sophistication my elementary students didn't possess. So I gave them a version tailored to them by Sheri Lewis from her *One-Minute Greek Myths*, reading it aloud, feeling like a kid-sized Joseph Campbell. They listened eagerly. True to her title, Lewis edits the myth's content into a few easily digestible paragraphs, and the text includes an illustration of what those melting wax wings of Icarus might have looked like. When I finished, several hands shot up with tales of their first flights—thanks to United or Delta, stories that needed telling—so I went with that flow. Again, I let them draw their images of Icarus—and themselves as a kind of Icarus figure—before they began writing. I also encouraged brainstorming words connected to their flying, and then placing those words around their drawings as a kind of frame, as a way of spatially organizing their ideas. One student drew himself with giant homemade wings and began writing his story inside the wings. Several boys wrote about flying high enough with homemade wings to distract the pilots of jumbo jets from their destinations. Quite a power trip! But I was most moved by these examples of human flight as a mixed blessing:

> If I could trade some part of my body, I would trade my arms for
>   eagle wings.
> I would soar so high I would fly to school, but I wouldn't be able
> to get in the door. So I would fly around and head back home. . . .

I would love to have wings!

—*Danae Allison, fourth grade*

I would want bird wings to fly to school. . . .
I wouldn't have to take the school bus to school in the morning.
The only thing I hate about wings is I can't write.
And if I can't write in school I will get all "F"s
And I wouldn't pass fifth grade.
I would have to eat bird seed.

—*Audra Morgan, fourth grade*

The students understood *intellectually* the point of the myth. It was simply more fun *emotionally* to write about the power to soar and maintain a bird's-eye view of doings on earth, and to let loose with some repressed thoughts about school. The regular classroom teachers sat or stood in the back of the room while I worked in the front. It was fascinating, when some students read aloud to the class their statements expressing the joy of flying out of school before 3 P.M. or of avoiding school entirely, how after their last sentence they would look nervously in the direction of their teacher to assure themselves that such an outré thought could be acceptable. I had developed enough of a successful working relationship with these teachers that I trusted their acceptance of the value of such student writing. They shared my perspective that part of imaginative power summoned through creative writing was the power to express rebellion.

This power was expanded upon with the next assignment. While I emphasized through the Garden of Eden and Icarus assignments how potently the classics emphasized powerful perspective shifts, I also began to focus on the classics as texts confronting political authority through artful challenge. Poet and critic Guy Davenport's eloquent translation of a timeless poem by the ancient Greek philosopher Diogenes needed no translation into kid-language. They grasped it immediately:

I am Alexander the Great.
I am Diogenes, the dog.
The dog?
I nuzzle the kind, bark at the greedy, and bite louts.
What can I do for you?
Stand out of my light.

Their imitations of this simple dialogical form produced numerous riotous encounters with teachers, American presidents, even English royalty:

I am Queen Elizabeth.
I am Justin, the horse.
The horse?
I kick trees, run fast, and trick animals.
What can I do for you?
Give me some space.

   —Justin Pagel, fourth grade

I am Bill Clinton.
I am Felicia, the tiger.
The tiger?
I play roughly with my friends, I hide in trees.
What can I do for you?
You can run away and leave me be.

   —Felicia Laird, fifth grade

The class particularly liked the last line read aloud, and I was puzzled as to why. How could the President be asked to run away? Several explained to me that they were tired of hearing news about the President on TV so much, in fact, hated TV news in general. So I thought Felicia's telling the President to make himself scarce had less to do with this particular president and more to do with the students' aversion to the adult news-saturated world. Their laughter when these poems were read aloud seemed more intense than for any other assignment. That pleased me. I didn't connect the classics with bellylaughs until I was well into adulthood.

Another use of classics involved having students think about the relation of their senses to writing. It is a truism that students need ongoing encouragement to write utilizing all of their senses, particularly the neglected olfactory and tactile senses, but I was also interested in sensory magnification and deprivation. I knew that my students loved to talk about monsters. What child doesn't? So I gave them my paraphrase of the Cyclops description in Homer's *Odyssey*, lucidly translated by Robert Fitzgerald, but still in need of some simplifications. Also I again dipped into the Boer translation of Ovid's *Metamorphoses*, Book Thirteen, to show that a cyclops could come in a variety of flavors other than Homer's.

I had them shut one eye and describe how the classroom looked through that halved field of vision. Then I introduced the cottus, a monster with fifty heads and one hundred arms, described in the opening of Hesiod's *Theogony*, translated by Dorothea Wender. Next I labelled index cards with different sense organ images—one hundred eyes or half a nose (thank you, Picasso!)—and said that everyone would pick at random one cyclops and one cottus card. A cyclops card would transform them into someone with a fraction of normal sensory acuity to write about. A cottus card would put them into the "power trip" of vastly enhanced sensory perception. I suggested they open their stories about their new identities as a waking from a dream. They loved picking their subjects at random from a deck of cards.

Surprisingly, the cottus cards evoked heavily clichéd writing, barely disguised recastings of Superman or an archetypal Disney hero. But the cyclops cards sparked some heady surrealism:

I woke up and found
I had half a tongue
When my mom saw it
we got my tongue stitched up
the side so it would stop bleeding.
It would make me talk
wrong. I told Miss Marsha
that I would have a hot school lunch
and she thought I wanted one cold.
When I ate lunch
the fork went through
the side of my tongue.

   —*Corey Limani, fourth grade*

When I woke up I needed to add 98 arm-holes to my shirt. Then I put my shirt over half of a head. Nothing was leaking out of my head because there was skin covering that side. My mother did not notice my arms, all 100 of them, or the missing half of my head.

   —*Keith Murphy, third grade*

What seemed curious is how even this writing exercise about losing power also asserted the power of individuality. To have heard Corey read his poem aloud to his class was to realize that simply being half-tongued, however painful, was still an aberration worthy of artful word-slinging.

A common thread running through all of these writing assignments was an imaginative toying with the far reaches of human nature. Two books I recommend for anyone interested in tapping this realm with kids are J. C. Cooper's *Symbolic and Mythological Animals* and Max Ernst's *Une Semaine de Bonté*. Cooper's text is a quick read, a brief dictionary cataloging many of the fantastically bizarre creatures dreamed up by peoples around the earth. I let students randomly pick subjects from Cooper's book to write about, and all seemed to enjoy slipping into the state of having, say, a lion's body and human face. Ernst's book is a surrealistic novel narrated almost entirely through collage, replete with images of humans that are part fantastic animal, another part demonic spirit. Students could always find inspiration in unlikely juxtapositions of the human, the proto-human, the animal. I used the Ernst book years ago in rural West Virginia schools, and remember an appreciative teacher telling me how much students enjoyed temporarily escaping the tedium of their normal lives. The French philosopher Gaston Bachelard's book *Lautréamont* offered a notion that helped me understand why these kinds of assignments could so inspire students. As Joanne Stroud writes in the book's foreword, "Bachelard defines imagination primarily as the faculty which moves dynamically and metamorphoses easily. In following a bestial image through the successive stages of attack, imagination is unshackled." My students revealed that animal or monster or hybrid animal/human images need not be aggressive in order for imagination to be unshackled. They need to be simply out of the ordinary.

To describe writing, poet Robert Creeley uses a haunting phrase that often came to mind as I taught the classics in a creative writing context: "not a presumption of value / but a locus of experience." In the heated political climate surrounding schoolbook adaptation decisions, conservatives insist upon the civilizing impact of teaching the classics. Liberals express concern about presenting the classics in a form addressing current social issues. Both assume the value of the classics, particularly the Greek classics I often utilized, as a "given." But I have never encountered a nine-year-old who felt that a book should be taken seriously simply because it has been taken seriously for centuries. If a classic is the kind of book that makes you feel your own paradise, catapults you over cities, or permits you to talk back to presidents, then students will welcome a classic as a new way of experiencing the world, with magnified power, due to how it can spark imaginative writing. I think of classic literature as those texts that help students to express the liquidity, the plasticity, the far reaches of their natures, where hidden powers dwell waiting to find written form. Come to think of it, I can't recall even using the word *classics* when I gave these assignments.

Part of my own education involved being forced to write in school about my hometown—a city I detested at the time, Philadelphia, a city, as my teachers constantly reminded me, where great historical markers were everywhere downtown. Which meant, from my snotty nine-year-old's perspective, that it was a dead place full of dead, uninteresting people from centuries ago. What I now try in my assignments is to bring the energies of the past racing into the present moment with intense vividness, so students can be filled with at least a little of the power of the gods and spirits.

Bibliography

Bachelard, Gaston. *Lautréamont*. Dallas, Tx.: Dallas Institute, 1986.

Blake, William. *Milton*. Princeton, N.J.: Princeton University, 1994.

Cooper, J. C. *Symbolic and Mythological Animals*. London, England: Aquarian, 1992.

Davenport, Guy, translator. *7 Greeks*. New York: New Directions, 1995. Includes Diogenes.

Ernst, Max. *Une Semaine de bonté*. New York: Dover, 1976.

Homer. *Odyssey*. Translated by Robert Fitzgerald. New York: Vintage, 1990.

Hesiod. *Theogony*. Translated by Dorothea Wender. New York: Penguin, 1976.

Johnson, Ronald. *RADI OS*. Berkeley, Calif.: Sand Dollar, 1977.

Lamb, Charles and Mary. *Tales from Shakespeare*. New York: Signet, 1986.

Lewis, Sheri. *One-Minute Greek Myths*. New York: Yearling, i987.

Milton, John. *Paradise Lost*. Many editions.

Ovid. *Metamorphoses*. Translated by Charles Boer. Dallas, Tx.: Spring Publications, 1989.

Andrea Freud Loewenstein

Following the Flow

Using Charlotte Brontë, Sophocles, Shakespeare, Kafka, and Chaucer

WHEN I ENTERED THE CLASSROOM last semester, it was not unusual to find the students arguing about whether Antigone was a hero or a fool, whether Lear deserved what he got, or whether Jane should have left Rochester. On one memorable occasion, I feared two men might come to blows over the honor of the Wife of Bath. The course is called Masterpieces of World Literature, a daunting title that makes me cringe, but did not seem to bother the students at Medgar Evers College, CUNY, in Brooklyn, New York. As English 300, a one-semester course that follows two semesters of Composition, it is the college's only required literature course, and for many students it represents their first and last academic encounter with imaginative literature.

The students in this particular class, a small section consisting mainly of honors students (those who entered the college needing no remediation) were puzzled when I asked them early in the semester what they thought of the "classics" on the syllabus. Some people, I explained, might have problems with a syllabus that featured Sophocles, Chaucer, Shakespeare, Brontë, and Kafka, moving on to Achebe and Morrison only in the last few weeks. The students might question the relevance of these dead white Western (mostly) men to them, Caribbean and African Americans. Several students grew indignant. "Why would they want us to stop reading these books?" asked Terrence Stephen, from St. Lucia. "Take, for example, modern music, it's only based on what's written previously. There is nothing new under the sun. If you limit yourself to the new you'd be denying yourself." Lynn Forsyth, from Grenada, agreed. "But of course these books are relevant. It is everyday happenings they address. The only difference is the way they put it forth." The majority of students in this class, as in the other classes I teach at Medgar Evers College, are from the Caribbean. Some have lived in Brooklyn for years, others came to New York for a college education. The minority born in the "hood" sometimes complain that their Brooklynese hasn't got a chance among the Caribbean inflections that surround them. Although most of the students at Medgar Evers are older than the average college student, and many balance college with families and full-time work, their maturity has not led to cynicism, at least when it comes to literature.

When I taught at a college in Vermont, I encountered a student who had a set response to any reading. "It's a book," he would reply, with a dismissive shrug that said it all. Most of the students I have taught at Medgar Evers, by contrast, meet the literature we read with an openness of which Sophocles and Shakespeare would surely have approved. These students need no prompting to identify with characters who remind them of friends, enemies, and themselves. They are even old-fashioned enough to find inspiration and warnings in the characters' triumphs and failures. Native New Yorker Larone Koonz, for example, wrote that after he finished *A Doll's House* he had a long talk with his wife. "Communicate before it is too late," he urged his readers in his essay on Ibsen's play. "Do not regard your wife as a plaything," he warned. "When she leaves it will be too late."

Lynn Forsyth found a model in Jane Eyre. "Sometimes when I feel like giving up I think of her," she told me. "The way she never let anyone keep her down. When you told me to do one more draft of my paper I had to think of Jane and what she would do."

And Dyan Harriott, from Jamaica, felt close to Antigone, a hero who didn't let anyone tell her what to think. "When your best friend tends to disagree with you, you feel as if you are alone in the world, and no one is standing by your side," she wrote in her reaction journal. "Even Antigone's sister wasn't on her side, but she still didn't back down. That's like me. I am me and will always be me, no matter what anyone says and does."

Role playing is one of my own favorite activities, but many students find it embarrassing or too personal. At Medgar Evers, where it sometimes seems that everything is personal, my students sometimes begin to role play on their own, spontaneously speaking for a character they feel didn't get fair play, or improvising a final scene after an inconclusive ending. When the idea for a particular role play is mine, I usually need to say no more than, "Well, King Lear, how do you feel about your daughters now?" to get the ball rolling.

My students clearly have no need of reader-response theory to respond freely to works from the canon. And the movement from identification to telling one's own story is equally fluid. More than assignments or directives, they simply need permission to "go ahead and tell it your way." Although I become much more active in the revision stage, sometimes suggesting that a particular piece of prose might work as a poem or vice versa, I encourage each student to select his or her own genre for the initial draft. And just as the best role plays and the best discussions in my classes often happen when I abandon my lesson plan and follow the students' lead, so does the most inspired creative writing. Indeed, in my almost thirty years as a teacher, one crucial lesson I have learned is how to step back and listen to my students. I have found the most thoughtful and innovative assignments to be far less effective than observing the students' body language and listening closely to them as they come into class.

Latasha, a single mother who comes in trailing a reluctant small child, complaining, "Sometime I know just how Medea feel," is ready to write. So is Dwight, who enters class raw and literally twitching from his experience as a messenger in an all-white Wall Street firm. "The way they look at you," he complains, "like they're just waiting for something to jump off. It make you paranoid, man. No wonder Othello act so gullible. They be messing with his mind!"

"They be messing with his mind" is a great first line. All I have to do is speak it aloud several times, expressively, and write it on the board and Dwight is off and writing. On the other hand, as an untenured white faculty member in a majority African American and African Caribbean college, I may not want to write this particular phrase on the board in a class called "Masterpieces of World Literature." In a pattern that Lisa Delpit documents in *Other People's Children*, my forays into creative writing are particularly suspect in the eyes of some of my colleagues. They suspect that I, like other white liberal teachers they have known, am failing to provide these students with the tools they will need to compete in the academic world. In fact, for the most part I share my colleagues' goals for my students. They will be expected to produce formal essays based on their reading in most of their other courses, and all of them will at some time be judged on their mastery of standard English. In English 300, we spend a great deal of time at the beginning of class discussing the politics of and uses of different dialects of English, and then concentrate hard on the standard version. I will probably devote no more than the first ten minutes of class, designated as the time for freewriting and quizzes, to allow Latasha to begin her version of the modern-day Medea and for Dwight to complete his rap on Othello and himself. Typically, we will divide the rest of the class between a close reading and discussion of the text on hand, always including some reading aloud for sound and concentration, and an exercise designed to connect that discussion to the essay writing and revision process, often including a close examination of a student essay.

But my colleagues have a point. Somewhere inside me does reside the rather essentialist belief that writing a poem or a play or a story is an intrinsically worthwhile act that must be encouraged, a chance to create that my students deserve, that is somehow more praiseworthy than the act of writing a critical essay. I will urge Latasha and Dwight to complete their pieces at home and submit them to me for extra credit, and will provide extensive comments and make time to work privately with other students to revise promising pieces. I may even imply that I would be willing to substitute the grade on a sufficiently elegant, carefully revised piece of poetry or fiction for that mediocre in-class essay test Dwight took after that last show-down with his boss, or that uninspired and disorganized essay Latasha handed in during the week both her children had chicken pox. If the end result warrants it, I will ask them to read their finished pieces to the class, or I may read them aloud myself, in my most dramatic voice. One's fellow students are an appreciative and honest audience, and the sharp intake of breath, laughter, tears, and spontaneous clapping are more satisfying to an author than any words. Finally, as faculty advisor to the college literary magazine, I will hold out the apple of publication as an additional motivation.

In my own defense, I do believe that Dwight is more likely to write a strong paper proving that Othello was driven mad by the pressures of racism after he has written a rap on the topic; that is, that fluency is catching, and mastery in one kind of writing carries over to another. Still, the students and I feel that creative writing in the context of Masterpieces of World Literature is a slightly subversive activity. Like all forbidden fruit, creative writing in this setting tastes especially sweet.

The student pieces that follow were all done last semester in the context of literature read in English 300. To provide context, I interviewed the authors, asking them what had inspired the piece and how, if at all, it was connected with the literature we had been reading at the time.

Lynn Forsyth, who had spoken in class about the strict morality imposed on women in her island of Grenada, was especially fascinated by Chaucer's Wife of Bath "from a woman's point of view." In fact, Chaucer's Wife surprised and intrigued all the students, who had figured that women in the "olden days" behaved themselves. Everything about the wife, from the way she spent more time introducing the story than telling it, to the way she used the Bible to justify her sexual proclivities, drew exclamations of "She remind me of my aunt!" "There's a lady like that in my church!"

Lynn, who is twenty-six and from a small village, reflected on the Wife of Bath. "To this day we have women who behave like that, but most women today would probably be ashamed to tell of such a life. The writing is what made it so interesting to me; I liked the rhyme and so I used it as a challenge to myself to see if I could write like that. But I had to change it, as the woman I was thinking of was from my homeland, and I knew the way she would speak when she would relate the story. My narrator does have something in common with the Wife of Bath, as she is not shame either. In her opinion she has good reason for her behavior! In Chaucer's version she loses her hearing when her fourth husband beats her, but in my poem you will see I decided to slant it a bit different."

The Tale of Melda and Sparrow

Melda a she name you know
I did learn that eight years ago
A common-law husband belong to she
Who is responsible for this story.
Five children to him she bore
Yet she say she doh mind a few more.
A fowl coop she call their home
And dis is why these children roam.
Mr. Sparrow is a she husband call
The rum drug is he downfall.
So she all time screw a man for pay
Oh God, I pray, bring her a new day.
For message in town she say she a go,
But all except Sparrow know she juices dem flow.
Let me whisper one incident

that really was an accident.
In de garden Mr. Sparrow go dig some yam.
Was for to eat wid de Christmas ham.
Very sick a Mr. Sparrow get
Too soon him return, enough to see her fete.
De house a tremor and a shake
Lash in she backside he make she take
On the left she rerun him one good blow
That is why today he eye cocky so.

    —*Lynn Forsyth*

If most of the students knew someone who reminded them of the Wife of Bath, they seemed more likely to look within to find Franz Kafka's narrator in "The Metamorphosis." Dyan Harriott, at nineteen the youngest student in the class, came in the morning after the story had been assigned with a look of misery on her face. When I asked her what was wrong, she responded, "I know how that bug feel!" Looking around at some of the other tired, worn faces in the classroom that morning, I discarded the quiz on "The Metamorphosis" and asked the students to freewrite for ten minutes, beginning with the phrase, "When (your own name) woke up that morning, she realized that she had turned into a (whatever animal or object you feel like right now)."

In an interview about her piece, which she continued to work on at home and revised extensively, Dyan remembered that morning: "I was feeling left out and sad, like I was in deep mourning. I was angry at myself for thinking in that way, because I wasn't brought up to think like that and yet I was thinking like that. The reason I was feeling that way, I try to please everybody and I can't please everybody and then I end up not pleasing myself. That's what clicked for me about Gregor. He was doing everything, being so helpful for his family, and they turn their back on him. To tell you the truth I did not, I *could not* feel sorry for him. I felt angry at him because he shouldn't have been so helpful. Just like me, I was too helpful until I forgot about myself. If he hadn't been so helpful maybe he wouldn't have turned into a bug, he wouldn't feel the way he felt. Yes, he reminded me of me and I was mad at him just like I was mad at myself. So I made myself a bug like him, but not a roach—a scorpion. You find a lot of scorpions in Jamaica and one thing you notice about them, when you tread on them and they get ready to sting, they turn from black to red."

That Monday Morning

On Monday morning, Dyan got up and found out that she had turned into a big, black scorpion. Realizing this enormous change, she ran between a crack on the striped green wall, afraid to be discovered. As she crawled around and around she got frustrated, not knowing what to do next, as she was not used to being in such a small body. She turned from black to red over and over again. The black showed that she was unhappy, in mourning for her own soul, and the red showed that she was angry at anyone or any creature who should ever cross her path. "What the hell is this, I feel as if I want to kill those who are mightier and bigger than me," she screamed, tossing her stinger around and around. "I want to feel free again, I want back my soul, I can't take this no more!" she yelled, but it came out in a tiny little hiss.

The feeling that came over the big black and red scorpion at the time was disappointment, as she began to realize that being mad and angry at everyone was not the best solution. She was thinking about suicide. She could let someone step on her, or maybe smoke a pack of cigarettes, but how could she get that giant tube to her sharp little mouth? "I can't believe I had to become so small to realize the danger I am putting myself in," she thought. "I just need to calm down and settle myself."

"Dyan, get your ass out of the bed and get to work," I heard my mother scream.

"She is just a lazy black girl," my father said, not knowing that what he would find when he came in the room would be black but not a girl at all.

—Dyan Harriott

Of all the "classics" I have taught, Charlotte Brontë's *Jane Eyre* may be the one that has inspired the most student writing. The vivid evocation of childhood and above all the way Brontë honors rather than trivializes children's pain reminds us of our own childhood and gives us permission to honor our feelings. The pieces inspired by the childhood section of *Jane Eyre* have little to do with Brontë's novel per se, except in the precise way they evoke childhood experience. Terrence Stephen, twenty-six, from St. Lucia, reflected on the impact of the famous "red-room" scene on him.

"First of all, the mere fact that she was able to bring out or relive an experience that was so frightening for her assisted me to tap into my own memory and bring out things that I was trying not to remember. Right after I read the red-room scene, I stopped and thought of a time I was afraid like that. I didn't want to remember that fear, but it came back. The most painful part of my experience in that pond was that I cried out and my friends didn't come. They didn't really believe I couldn't swim, they didn't believe me. This was just like Jane; she cried out but they didn't believe her, they thrust her back. I could have died. But being doubted when you're telling the truth, that was almost as painful. The other thing about the book that got to me was how Charlotte Brontë touched on every single aspect of her environment, what her surroundings were. It was as if you were right there with her. That helped me to write in a way that was so real, it made me feel homesick. And when others from home read it, they could relate to it, it made them homesick also. The rain, walking barefoot in the mud, having the rain hit your body, those are experiences you can never go back to. You cannot relive your past: the most you can do is bring it out in your writing."

The Day at the Pond

The raindrops caressed our bodies. The air smelled green from all the leaves and mud. The water carried mud and stones as it gushed down the gutters. The road was slippery. There were a few blackbirds sitting on the mango trees, too soaked to fly. The mangoes looked rosy up in the trees. Hubert and his twin brother, Jackson, climbed a mango tree. I decided to remain under the tree as the catcher.

"Terry," Jackson shouted. "Hold dat one for me." He dropped me a sweet smelling julie. A few minutes later we had about seven mangoes. The brothers came down from the tree and we continued walking, sharing the fruits evenly and eating as we walked. Up in the distance, through the trees I saw the Clacks' house, where the shortcut began.

"Jackson, you a scare?" Hubert asked his brother.

"Scare of wha?" Jackson replied. That was their usual conversation on our way to the pond. I am not sure if Hubert never questioned me because he already knew I was scared. He was right. I was really scared of the Clacks' big black dogs. Though they never ran as far as the shortcut, I feared them. The walk through the shortcut seemed different to me every time. There was always something I had not seen before. That day, it was the unusual quietness. Except for the sound of water lashing the leaves, it was perfectly quiet. Not even the wild animals seemed to be moving. The tall trees arched over the path, giving it a sunset feeling. The mud stuck to our boots, slowing down our pace.

"La Jacblesse!" screamed Jackson. We ran as fast as we could, never looking back. In my mind I knew he was bluffing, but I was too terrified to look behind or to stop until we got to the open field. My heart throbbed and my feet trembled, but I was able to appear calm.

"Sa ki we vau gason?" asked Hubert, looking toward his brother.

"Gaa met, ou crapon garson," answered Jackson.

"Yo lass fair papishow, man," I interjected. By now we were all soaked, and our boots were filled with water, but that never seemed important. The sky appeared grey. The wet grass was sometimes knee-high. When we walked past the horses' stables, the air smelled of manure mixed with wet grass. This was a place we all feared because the land belonged to the Catholic priests and nuns. We had never encountered them there, and we never planned to. By the time we reached the end of the field, the rain had turned to a drizzle. Walking through the path, we removed the plastic bags into which we were planning to put our fishes.

Finally, the pond was in sight. Everyone bore a smile as we approached it. The water in the pond was browner than usual due to the rain.

"Yo, let's go to the other side," I said. "We'll catch more dere." On the other side, we filled our bags with water and placed them on the ground, making sure the water did not fall out. We walked into the water and started catching fish for our aquariums. There were guppies, fantails, and some which we did not know. With our bare hands, we caught a lot of fishes. Suddenly there was a loud splash in the water. Terrified, we looked behind us. There it was, long, black, and apparently stuck in the mud. I do not remember how, but we all got out of the water before I was aware of what had happened. When we got to the bank, the creature was gone.

"Wha dat?" I asked.

"An eel," answered Jackson.

"In a pond?" I questioned. "Maybe a snake."

"Nahn, I don't tink so," Hubert replied. "Time to go."

"But I want more fishes," Jackson said. He was always the one to play tough, and I was too proud to show my fear. We proceeded to the other end of the pond, the deep section. While I stood on the slippery edge, I slipped and fell. The next thing I remember was trying helplessly to dig my fingers into the mud bank. I tried as hard as I could, but my fingers kept slipping.

"Help, I can't swim." For some reason, Hubert and Jackson just stood there laughing at me. I was terrified. I tried to forget the idea of drowning as I tried in vain to feel for the bottom with my feet. I remembered the creature and screamed again. They stood there and laughed hysterically. I trembled as the water closed in. I felt the tears rushing to my eyes.

"Get me out!" I shouted again. Hubert finally gave me a helping hand. He leaned over, being careful not to slide in. Then, with his right hand, he grabbed my shirt and supported me so that I was able to slide on my stomach out of the pond. I could not stand because my feet shook like a leaf in the wind. The feeling of relief never faded out of my mind.

—*Terrence Stephen*

Jane Eyre's plight also brought back memories to forty-four-year-old Jamaican Gem Joy Barrett, whose mother came to America, leaving her with relatives who did not want her. In her interview, Gem, who is working on a novel about her childhood, remembered how she felt when she read that part of the novel.

"It made me remember! How when the kids turn on you because you don't have anyone, and then you can't complain to the parents because you are an intruder in their family. Mrs. Reid reminded me of my aunt, the unjust treatment, so cold, my aunt use to do that, lock me off and don't even look, the only way she look is giving me a bad eye. And you know what I envy Jane for? Her strength when she tell the aunt off. When I was reading that I wish I had done that, told my aunt how I felt about her, like how Jane did. I think I would have felt relieved, just like she did. It was like something that was bottled up for years, and I knew if I had said something, even if I were to lose everything, I would have felt a little better. I was saying, 'Yeah, yeah,' when she was telling her off. It show how unprotected a kid can be when they don't have their parents with them. You know what else happen, Andrea, what I like is how she write the story in the child's voice and you can see she pull out all the hurt the child have by writing it like that. With me using a child voice I feel strong, I just feel like everything is real coming out. I feel more relief."

When Is My Time to Play?
(excerpt from a novel in progress)

Room for rent
Apply within
When I run out
Then you run in.

The happy voices of the children playing in the yard sent shock waves of anger all over my body as I looked down in the padded, rusty zinc pan with the giggling baby inside of it. They said it was my time to watch the baby. They said when the baby went to sleep then they would take turns watching her. They—my two older cousins who were outside playing with the children from next door.

"Geee-eee" came a sound from the baby. I looked at her without laughing, and I thought how much I hated this baby, who had taken away my freedom ever since my mother went to America and I had to come and live with them. She was kicking her feet and rolling her arms over her head in a playful manner. "Geee-eeee," she said again, showing pink gum as she laughed at me. I was about to smile back at her when I heard the children.

One, two, buckle my shoe.
Three, four, shut the door.
Five, six, pick up sticks.
Seven, eight, lay them straight.
Nine, ten, a big fat hen-n-n-n.

On that hard wooden bench where I sat in the kitchen, black and slippery with grease, I felt my heart beating extra hard against my chest. "When is it going to be my turn to play?" I asked myself. My cousins chose to watch the baby when she was sleeping and all they had to do was run in and out to see if she was awake. If I started to win a game of jacks, rounders, or jump rope, they would make so much noise that the baby would wake up and start crying, then I would have to stop playing and go watch her. I had developed a hatred for this baby who had become my personal responsibility, and to make matters worse my aunt was doing nothing to stop it. She even added to the situation. Last week she told me that I had to stay home from church and watch the baby because my cousins had to sing in the Sabbath school. "I am going to tell my sister when she comes to visit me," I thought. "I hate this place."

London Bridge is falling down
Falling down
Falling down,
London Bridge is falling down
My fair lady!

"Waaah-waaaaah," wailed the baby. With great annoyance I looked at her, and all I could see was pure ugliness. A big meaty mouth with four teeth, two at the bottom and two at the top, which made her look like a rabbit, a broad nose that frilled off at the bottom, little round eyes, and a huge forehead that hung over her eyes like an umbrella. And she was black; rusty black as if somebody had flung her into a bucket of tar.

My aunt's sudden shout from the kitchen door interrupted my analysis of her child.

"What happen to di baby? Pick har up! Yu sit down a look pan har like yu a examine ghost!"

"She is uglier than ghost," I said in my mind. I bent and picked her up, suppressing my rising anger. The baby cried louder.

"A big twelve-year gal like yu, can't hold a baby properly?"

I think I see
My mother coming far way
Mother, you bring any silver?

No my son.
Mother you bring gold?
No my son
I come to town to see you hang
And hang you must be hang.

My aunt wobbled into the kitchen and the baby started to cry louder. "Why don't she take her ugly child from me?" I looked into her dark brown eyes, searching to find some fairness, but found nothing of the sort. I stood as stiff as a wound-up toy soldier, with the baby kicking and wheedling in my stern arms, hollering at the top of her lungs. My heart beat so fast that my stomach felt tight as I thought how unjust my aunt was. The baby wanted to go to her, but she would not take her, as if that ugly child was mine.

"Go walk har outside, it too hot in the kitchen. Yu common sense could tell yu dat? How you so stupid fi a big gal? Mi sister must did have yu when she did gone a market, ha-ha." Mechanically I went through the kitchen door with the loathsome bundle.

Little Sally water
Sitting in the saucer
Rise, Sally rise
and wipe your eyes
Sally, turn to the East
Sally turn to the West
Sally turn to the very one
You love best.

—*Gem Joy Barrett*

Although I have confined myself here to writing done in the context of one particular class, I regularly use classics as a jumping-off point for creative writing in all my classes at Medgar Evers. A play like *Othello*, for example, is full of possibilities for creative writing. The themes of jealousy, racism, and wife-battering are all too contemporary, and the language can be modernized or "translated" to great effect. An examination of narration and point of view, in particular of an unreliable narrator like Iago, offers a number of authorial choices and chances to "tell it from another point of view." A soliloquy can inspire a wonderful persona poem, and indeed a concentration on any poetic or dramatic form invites imitation. Like Tom Stoppard in his *Rosencrantz and Guildenstern Are Dead* or Jean Rhys in her *Wide Sargasso Sea*, student writers may choose to take off on a situation involving Cassio and his fatal reaction to alcohol, or Desdemona in a less repressive age.

As my students remind me every day, the wall between writer and reader, which those of us who studied under the New Critics learned to construct and maintain, is in fact an unnatural one. Appreciation and understanding of a "classic" need not lead to mystification or respectful distancing. Engaged students like those I teach at Medgar Evers College require little more than permission to respond with a move into the authorial position.

Bibliography

Brontë, Charlotte. *Jane Eyre*. New York: Norton, 1971.

Chaucer, Geoffrey. *Canterbury Tales*. Translated by Neville Coghill. London, England: Penguin, 1951.

Delpit, Lisa. *Other People's Children*. New York: The New Press, 1995.

Hear Our Voices II, III, and IV: The Literary Magazine of Medgar Evers College. Available from Andrea Loewenstein, Dept. of LLCP, Medgar Evers College CUNY, 1650 Bedford Road, Brooklyn, NY 11225.

Kafka, Franz. *Metamorphosis*. Translated by Stanley Cumgold. New York: Bantam, 1972.

Shakespeare, William. *King Lear, Othello*. Edited by Barbara A. Mowat and Paul Werstein. New York: New Folger Library, 1992.

Sophocles. *Antigone, Oedipus the King, Electra*. Translated by H. D. F. Kitto. Oxford, England: Oxford University, 1994.

Pamela Freeze Beal

Creative Explorations

Responding to Traditional Classics and Modern Classics from World Literature

I TEACH SOPHOMORES at a comprehensive high school of approximately 2,250 students, grades 9–12, whose academic program offers both a College Prep and a Tech Prep curriculum. Our student population is fairly diverse: approximately 63% white, 28% African American, 8% Hispanic, and 1% Asian and other.

In 1991, our state redesigned the tenth grade English curriculum and made World Literature—excluding American and British works for the most part—the focus of study. Since then I have had a broad range of literature from which to choose—indeed, I have most of the world!—and the more diverse the students in my classes, the better the time we have.

I choose to teach sophomores because I especially enjoy the enthusiasm they have for school and learning; they are not as jaded as juniors and seniors. An administrative label on a class, whether it is "college-bound" or "tech-prep," makes no difference to me in the selections we read or the assignments we do. Together we take a hero's journey through the ancient world of *The Iliad*, *The Epic of Gilgamesh*, and *The Mahabharata*. We travel with Dante through *The Inferno*. We laugh at the humor and debate the politics in Shakespeare, Kafka, Hesse, and Chinua Achebe.

Learning is serious business, of course. But my students learn best and enjoy the process more when we laugh a little along the way. One of my favorite ways of engaging students in a text is to use dramatic play, in which my students, often attired in "silly," makeshift costumes, act out a text. The poet-narrator's plastic ivy wreath, the villain's lobster-claw gizmo, and the hero's spatula-sword are typical props.

Puppets, simple ones easily constructed out of fabric or paper, are important members of my class. My students make them and wear them on their hands, giving life to Brutus as a bull, perhaps, or Cassius as a fox. I encourage imaginative interpretation of characters as long as students can point out connections to the text. Novelty and surprise evoke laughter and make literary texts, which teenagers may perceive as dead or dull, come alive. After all, teenagers today are accustomed to adventure movies with special effects.

Students open up to the reading of classics when they realize that modern storytellers and ancient storytellers have much in common. The heroes and villains, narrative structures such as the journey, and both external and internal conflicts in an old story such as *Gilgamesh* and a modern story such as *Star Wars,* show us that humans have always shared the same deep concerns.

Within the first two weeks of school, I require my students to find and name an editor (other than me)—mom, dad, grandmother, neighbor, or friend. This editor always gets the first chance to offer suggestions. Then in class, students peer-edit with a designated writing partner, revise, and turn in the work to me for further editing. A piece that is especially engaging because of subject or style or some creative twist may go back and forth from me to the student several times. Students keep all copies during the editing process so that they can see how far they have come when we stamp it "finished."

Psalms

One assignment that I use early in the semester to introduce universal themes is the study of Psalm 23 ("The Lord is my shepherd"). The themes of goodness, mercy, and protection make sense to students as ideas that are important to everyday life and, thus, important to write about. The brevity of the individual psalms helps ease the way into a study of longer ancient texts. Psalm 23 is familiar to many students as a religious text, but few of them have thought about it as literature. Also, because the psalms are filled with imagery, they serve as good examples for creating sharp images. Throughout the semester, I refer to specific word pictures such as "still waters" and active verbs such as "anoint" as reminders of the importance of specific details in any kind of writing.

After I talk about the historical and cultural context of Psalms, we read selected ones aloud, each one more than once. I usually read the psalm first because the King James version in our textbook intimidates some students. They enjoy hearing "good reading" that uses dramatic expression. Usually, it is easy to get a student to read the psalm the second time.

We tap out the beat of verses such as "The Lord is my shepherd; I shall not want" to emphasize the rhythm. Then we focus on Psalm 23 and analyze it as an extended metaphor. We talk about the human need for protection and security. The students make a list of people that offer them protection or security. Next they choose one or two and write down specific places and actions that describe how those people protect and help them. Following the structure of Psalm 23, they finish the assignment for homework. The following day they read their poems to classroom partners; each partner jots down two good points, as simple as a particular word or image he or she liked. Then volunteers read their poems to the entire class. We always applaud! I collect the poems and make my own comments and assessments.

Part of the beauty of this assignment is that it is a painless way for students to learn the art of parallel structure. Here are some examples, the first by Amisty:

> My teacher is my helper;
>> I shall not flunk.
> He makes me to learn
>> so I will not fail.
> He restores my mind;
>> He leads me to the right decisions.
> He prepares me for the many tests;
>> He anoints my head with knowledge.
>> My brain runs over.
> Surely, knowledge and goodness
>> shall follow me all the days of my life,
> And I will overcome the obstacles
>> of the world forever.

Amisty, a student in a lower-skills class, felt so inspired that later in the year she announced that she had decided to go to college and become an English teacher.

Josh, a student in that same class, and his parents were so proud of his poem that his mother had a friend write it in calligraphy so she could frame and display it in their home. His poem is written from the point of view of cotton:

The Farmer watches over me;
    I shall grow.
He plants me in rich soil;
    He waters me with cool water.
He fertilizes my roots
    and plows the grass away from me.
I grow through the shadows of the darkness;
    I will fear no frost; his warmth comforts me.
He will harvest me and lay me in a trailer;
    He will take me to a barn and bale me.
Surely, he will load me on a trailer,
    and carry me to a warehouse where I will dwell.

Matt's poem honors his fireman father:

My Firefighter and Captain will protect me;
    I shall not burn;
He makes me to cool down with water;
    He soothes my walls and makes the fire to burn out.
He walks through the valley of fire with me;
    I fear no evil, for his hose and axe, they comfort me.
He keeps my structure standing
    in the face of my enemy.
Surely, goodness and mercy shall follow me
    and I will stand tall forever.

On Mother's Day, Kecia gave her mother the following poem:

My mother is my helper;
    I shall do no wrong;
She makes rules for me to follow
    to lead me in the right direction.
She restores my confidence;
    she is there through thick and thin.
Even though I mess up every once in a while,
    she helps me learn from my mistakes.
When I am in trouble,
    she always leads me back;
She never lets me down.
    Surely, she will always be there for me,
    and I will respect her forever.

Fables

The fable fits in well in a world literature class because it is a popular mainstay of both Western and Eastern literature and thus provides a way to show students that, no matter what the time or place, humans use stories to pass on bits of good advice. Most students are familiar with stories such as Aesop's "The Hare and the Tortoise" and readily understand the morals of traditional fables. However, many of them are surprised when I introduce Winnie the Pooh and Snoopy as modern beasts whose job is to teach children bits of wisdom. We discuss specific episodes of a Pooh or Snoopy adventure that students recall; students suggest morals that the episodes teach.

Once they see Pooh stories, for example, as fables, they can readily name other modern storybook, cartoon, and commercial characters who fit the fable framework. Students enjoy tagging these examples with moral statements in the manner of Aesop. For example, a popular cat food commercial in which cats phone their owners and request a particular brand of food by singing "meow" over and over may teach the following: sometimes you have to say something more than once to get an adult's attention.

My students enjoy studying traditional and modern fables and then writing one of their own. First, we read traditional fables and discuss them as a reflection of the principles of accepted or ideal behavior in the culture for which they were written. Selected fables include the following:

"The Hare and the Tortoise"—Aesop
"The Dog and the Bone"—Aesop
"The Crow and the Pitcher"—Aesop
"Numskull and the Rabbit"—from the Indian *Panchatantra*
"The Wolf and the Lamb"—Jean de la Fontaine
"The Council Held by the Rats"—Jean de la Fontaine

We then read modern fables by Italo Calvino, such as "The Black Sheep" and "The Flash," and discuss them as allegorical expressions of the world he knew.

Volunteers read traditional fables aloud in class. The modern fables are for silent reading in class or at home. Students are surprised by Calvino's somewhat dismal endings in contrast to the traditional fables. But they like being able to break away from the optimism of the moral lesson of classic fables and try something that fits their world better. We brainstorm problems in our school, community, and society that need to be addressed; then students imagine characters facing those problems and create fables that, like Calvino's, usually offer little consolation.

The fables unit requires two or three days of reading and discussion. Then I give the writing assignment, allowing three days before the fables are due for in-class peer editing. Here are four examples:

The Village of Box-Heads

There was once a village where all the people wore boxes on their heads, except for one boy who was called the village idiot. He had been told by everyone that he should do as they did and put a box over his head; then he would be like everyone else and they would not call him an idiot, but he refused because he enjoyed sitting behind his cottage, watching the water in the brook bubble its way over the rocks and around the bends in the stream. He liked sitting in his porch swing and watching the birds light on the branches of trees; he relished the end of the day when the sun's gold turned shades of pink in the sky. How could the villagers cheat themselves out of such beauty, he thought.

One day he decided to uncover the head of a school friend so that he, too, could see the beauty of the world. He pulled the box off his classmate's head and was startled to see what a handsome face he had. The village idiot was alarmed that his classmate's face was much more handsome than his own. He ran home and searched frantically for a box which he pulled down over his head, never to remove it again.

—*Renee*

The Man without a Brain

There was a man whose brain was not fully developed, so he viewed the world as if he were a child. He played with children. He laughed in the rain, and he made up games and created adventures in his imagination. The adults sighed and considered him deprived. They approached a brain surgeon and asked him to transplant the brain of a monkey into the deprived man's head so that he would be able to think like they did.

Eager for a candidate to experiment on, the surgeon agreed. For a while, the surgery seemed successful; after all, the man with the new brain was physically healthy. His head had not rejected the monkey's brain. Soon he could be seen in the town conversing with other adults about the problems in the world. His face wore a sad expression. He no longer played with the children or ventured into his imagination. He lived the rest of his life full of care and worry like all the other adults in the town.

—*Annette*

Gimp, the Child Frog

Gimp was a child frog, full of energy and curious about the pond where he lived. One day after a full morning of exploring, Gimp decided to take a nap. He found a plump, green lily pad near the edge of the pond and hopped on. Soon, he was dreaming of flying bugs for supper.

While he slept, a five-year-old human child named Incubus, who was also full of energy and curious about the pond, noticed Gimp sleeping on his green pad. Incubus scooped up Gimp and the lily pad and carried him home where he put him inside an aquarium with a clear glass cover on top.

When Gimp awoke from his satisfying nap, he was ready to explore again. Not realizing that he had been kidnapped and put in a glass cage, Gimp took a big leap forward and crashed into an invisible wall of glass. Thinking he was still dreaming, Gimp took a big leap upwards and hit his head hard on the glass cover. He tried several more times but there was no escape from this strange invisible trap. Gimp, worn out and helpless, fell asleep on his lily pad inside the aquarium.

When Incubus's mom came home and saw the poor sleeping frog in the aquarium, she made Incubus take Gimp back where he found him. Incubus placed Gimp and his lily pad carefully at the edge of the pond and left. When Gimp awakened this time, he assumed he was still in the glass cage. He made no attempt to leap or jump. He just sat still, looking sad. His frog friends did not understand Gimp's lack of energy and curiosity. They knew something bad must have happened to him. So they brought him bugs to eat every day to keep him from starving. Gimp never jumped again. He just pined his life away on his lily pad, trapped in his own invisible cage.

—*Matt*

The Bell

I sit at my desk. The bell rings suddenly, piercing my mind and moving me to a new level of consciousness. It is not me that sits at my desk; it is someone else. I am not myself. I have changed. But everyone else in the room looks the same; they are their usual selves. I jump up from my desk and shout, "This is not me! I am not me right now! This place is changing me!"

All I see are blank stares. "Don't you see?" I ask in desperation. "We have to choose. Everybody assumes we are all grounded more than we really are. They think we are each unique when all we want to do is write poems of dreams and stars. Don't you see that?"

"What are you talking about? Are you crazy? Everything is fine here," responds one person as others nod in agreement.

"I can be myself here," says another. "What's wrong with you?" They all stare, waiting for my answer.

I sit back down at my desk while my consciousness disintegrates back into its former state. What was I thinking to jump up and shout like that? I need to keep my mouth shut. I am always wrong.

—*Audrey Jo*

Hermann Hesse's *Siddhartha*

A story about the search for identity is relevant to high school students because it parallels their own experience. As sophomores, my students already have plans to leave home after graduation and go to college or move into an apartment of their own. They have no problem with Siddhartha's determination to leave his father's home. They understand the importance of good friends and relate to the friendship between Siddhartha and Govinda. Most of them know that realizing their dreams may be many years away, and some recognize that they will have hard times as well as good times before they find real satisfaction in their lives.

The end of Siddhartha's journey is the most difficult part to understand because Siddhartha's train of thought is completely philosophical. The final chapter of Hesse's classic describes how the Buddhist concept of "self" includes both animate and inanimate objects and their connections throughout the past, present, and future. In his last speech to Govinda, Siddhartha tells him that he respects and loves a stone because he sees meaning in the stone's surface, in its color, in its sound and smell and taste. To help students understand this difficult concept, I ask students to write poems in which they "become" an inanimate object.

First we write one together as a class. I ask the students to look around the room and call out the names of inanimate objects, such as desk, pencil, eraser, concrete block, notebook. We choose one and give it eyes, speculating on what, for example, an eraser sees. We endow the eraser with feet and students contemplate on what part of the eraser feet would be placed and what characteristics would be required in order for it to walk over surfaces such as chalkboards and notebook paper. Perhaps an eraser's feet would function like suction cups. Next we ponder why, as well as how, an eraser chooses what to erase and what the eraser thinks about the mistakes it makes disappear. In this assignment objects take on thinking power and can make judgments.

I allow five days before the poem is due so that students may continue to bring questions to me about the assignment and their ideas for fulfilling it. Again, we peer-edit and read the poems aloud in class. Here are a few "I am" poems that came out of reading Hesse:

Pouring Perpetuity

Without feet,
I follow a liquid course
through dark, slender passageways.
My body slips against others
who feel, devoid of hands.
Speeding aimlessly,
we join each other,
confused by the downward flow.
Colliding with Earth and her elements,
we dwell bound by earth's forces
until Heaven lifts us up anew
and replenishes our spilled glory.
I am a drop of water.

    —Michael

I Am a Window

I am a window.
I live by the presence of the sun's radiant beams.
My heart, easily shattered and broken,
is the glass that covers me.
I hold no secrets,
for all can see right through me.
I see the world as it is presented to me—
nothing more, nothing less.
My eyes are the latch—
sometimes open, sometimes closed.
My mouth is the frame,
sealed with silence.

    —Kim

Mirror's Image

I live upon a wall; I tell the truth.
My mouth is mute; I do not speak.
I do not move; I show.
My heart is flat, a surface reflection of what I see.
I only see what's in front of me.
I have no memory, forgetting what I see.
Beauty smiles at me, then Beauty disappears.
Ugliness despairs in my image and then dissolves.

I cannot express it; I cannot hold it.
I only reflect it; I get no thanks for it.
I am a mirror.
I see. I show the truth.

   —*Kyle*

Chinua Achebe's *Things Fall Apart*

Things Fall Apart is about a family and a traditional society that experiences tragedy as a result of rapid and drastic change imposed on them from an outside culture. High school students are interested in discussing themes of power, corruption, and double standards. Achebe's novel provides a context for debating if and how a culture can remain true to its traditions when the world demands change.

In order to understand the longstanding traditions of the Ibo, students record Ibo proverbs as they read the novel. The "proverbial poem" response to *Things Fall Apart* occurs after a three-week period of recording the proverbs and the student's interpretation of them in what is called a wisdom chart. The chart contains the proverb, the interpretation, chapter and page references for each proverb, and a brief summary of the narrative event that prompted the saying of the proverb. After daily home readings, we discuss the rich folklore of the traditional Ibo society as recorded in the proverbs. Students identify the figures of speech (simile, metaphor, personification, etc.) and look for the parallel structure in each proverb. In class, we discuss the meaning of each proverb as it applies to the episode in which it is found. We also discuss the universality of each proverb.

To demonstrate the relevance of such proverbs to our culture, students write proverbial poems. First they choose a proverb from Achebe's novel or one that they know from their own culture. Then they write poems that contain a relevant anecdote, ending their poems with the proverb they chose. The poem is due two days after we finish discussing the novel.

Here are three student pieces:

Beauty

Delicate hands
white like a fair maiden's;
Eyes, like moonlit emeralds;
Lips, pouty and demure;

She pulls the bow across the strings
igniting passion,
kindling fires that blaze
with sensual mystery
and burst into sound
that reaches deep into my soul;
I dare to ask,
"Take me to the place
    of beauty from which you come."
She plucks one string,
    then quickly, a glance.
"Beauty," she answers,
    "is in the eye of the beholder,"
as she vanishes like the wind
whistling through the mountains.

    —*Jon-Robert*

Problems?

When a problem arises,
    do not run away,
        seeking unnecessary surprises.
Your troubles will follow you,
    no matter where you trek,
        no matter what you do.
Look at troubles as a gift;
    handle them quickly;
        handle them swift.
Erase them now,
    or before them you will bow.
Never take your troubles to sleep;
You must bail the water now
    while it's only ankle deep.

    —*Eric*

A Touch of Silver

Tumble-rolling rumble-roaring
grey thick-skinned elephants
sabotage a daytime sky;
Apollo's gilded rays
seek refuge
in a black-holed space
where they hide
from insolent thunder

and torrential cloudbursts
until the mammoth monsters
exhaust themselves
and a silver haze
like an unveiled spirit
dismisses their noisy clamor
subdues their spiteful wrath
so that the sterling crown of day
can take her throne
and light up the lives of men again.
Every cloud has a silver lining.

   —Alvan

There is nothing more encouraging to a student than to see his or her writing published either in the school literary magazine or in booklets my students compile, containing the best pieces from their portfolios several times during the year. Student artists design the covers, and they all have a good time autographing their pieces in each other's booklets.

Planning creative activities in response to classics, both old and new, takes a little more effort on a teacher's part, but the rewards for both teacher and students are worth it. Approaching the classics through creative responses as well as the expected analytical ones, students become eager to experiment with language and ideas. The creative connections that students make with the literature are personal, and thus exciting and lasting. If we believe that imagination and creative thinking are important as life skills and that aesthetic experience has intrinsic value for all human beings, we must integrate such creative experiences into our classrooms.

Bibliography

Achebe, Chinua. *Things Fall Apart.* New York: Anchor Books, 1959.

Aesop's Fables. Translated by V. S. Vernon. New York: Avenel Books, 1975.

Calvino, Italo. *Numbers in the Dark.* Translated by Tim Parks. New York: Pantheon, 1995.

Hesse, Hermann. *Siddhartha.* Translated by Hilda Rosner. New York: Bantam Books, 1971.

La Fontaine, Jean de. "The Council Held by the Rats" and "The Wolf and the Lamb." Translated by Elizur Wright. In *World Masterpieces*. Englewood Cliffs, N.J.: Prentice-Hall, 1996.

"Numskull and the Rabbit." From *The Panchantantra*. Translated by Arthur W. Ryder. In *World Masterpieces*. Englewood Cliffs, N. J.: Prentice-Hall, 1996.

Psalm 23. In *World Masterpieces*. Englewood Cliffs, N.J.: Prentice-Hall, 1996.

Notes on Contributors

JANE AVRICH has been teaching English at Saint Ann's School in Brooklyn, N.Y., since 1990. Her short stories have appeared in *Harper's*, *The Paris Review*, and *Story*.

PAMELA FREEZE BEAL, a veteran of twenty-two years in the classroom, teaches world literature at Lee County High School in Sanford, North Carolina. She was recently named Lee County Teacher of the Year as well as North Carolina English Teacher of the Year. Many of her students have won awards for their creative writing. She is presently working on manuscripts for children's books and young adult literature based on childhood experiences on her father's dairy farm.

Now retired from the Detroit Public Schools, TERRY BLACKHAWK works as an artist-in-residence through the Michigan Council for the Arts and serves as director of InsideOut, a literary arts program for Detroit youth that she founded in 1995. She has published poems in *Poet Lore, Louisville Review,* and *College English* and received poetry prizes from PoetryAtlanta, *America, Sow's Ear,* and *Marlboro Review.* Her collection of poems entitled *Body & Field* is forthcoming from Michigan State University Press.

BOB BLAISDELL teaches writing and literature at Kingsborough Community College in Brooklyn, N.Y. He has edited *D. H. Lawrence: Selected Poetry, The Selected Poems of Thomas Hardy,* Hardy's *"The Fiddler of the Reels" and Other Stories,* and *The Imagists: An Anthology,* all published by Dover Books.

CHRIS BRANDT has been teaching reading and writing off and on since 1965. He received an M.F.A. in Playwriting while on a Shubert Fellowship. Brandt is the translator of the poetry of Carmen Valle and Joachin Pasos. The work described in his essay was done in a special residency sponsored by NBC.

JORDAN CLARY lives in northeastern California, where she is contract artist for the William James Association Prison Arts Project and, through a California Arts Council grant, writer-in-residence at Credence Communion High School. She writes fiction and essays as well as poetry, and has been published in many literary journals and periodicals. Recent magazine publications include *Northern Lights, Alcrán, Calliope,* and *Fan Baseball Magazine.*

DALE DAVIS's career as a writer and educator began as one of the founding poets of New York State Poets in the Schools. She co-founded The New York State Literary Center and established a limited-edition private press. Through The New York State Literary Center she has edited and published five hundred anthologies of the writing of young people. A poet, scholar, and non-fiction writer, Davis has published in periodicals such as *The Iowa Review* and the *New York Times.* She is a member of The National Faculty and conducts teacher development programs throughout the country. She has served as a consultant to The Children's Dignity Project, ABC network.

JEFF S. DAILEY is Assistant Principal, Supervision, in charge of English, Music, Art, and Library at Grover Cleveland High School in Ridgewood, N.Y. He holds degrees from Wagner College, the College of Staten Island, and New York University. His research on *Beowulf* was originally made possible by a NEH grant provided through the Council on Basic Education. He thanks Professor Hal Momma of New York University for teaching him Old English and English teacher Brian Blayer for allowing him to try out some of the *Beowulf* writing assignments in his class.

CHRISTOPHER EDGAR is a poet, fiction writer, translator, editor, and teacher. He coedited *Educating the Imagination, Old Faithful,* and *The Nearness of You: Students and Teachers Writing On-line,* all published by Teachers & Writers. He has taught poetry at P.S. 157 in the Bronx and the School for Physical City in Manhattan, and is Editor at Teachers & Writers Collaborative. He edits *The Hat,* a literary magazine, with Jordan Davis.

MARGOT FORTUNATO GALT is a poet who has taught imaginative writing at all levels. She received a Ph.D. in American Studies from the University of Minnesota. Her most recent book, an oral history/memoir of Ojibway artist George Morrison, is *Turning the Feather Around: My*

Life in Art (Minnesota Historical Society Press, 1998). She is author of
The Story in History: Writing Your Way into the American Experience
(Teachers & Writers Collaborative, 1992), and a contributor to Teachers & Writers Collaborative's *Old Faithful* and *The Teachers & Writers
Guide to Frederick Douglass*. Her collection of poems is entitled *The
Country's Way with Rain* (Kutenai Press). Galt teaches at Hamline University in St. Paul, Minnesota.

LAURA GAMACHE teaches creative writing to students of all ages
through the Washington State Arts Commission's Arts in Education Program and through Seattle Arts & Lectures' Writers in the Schools. She is
also Director of the Writers-in-the-Schools Program for the University of
Washington. Her work has appeared in many publications, including
The North Atlantic Review, Bellowing Ark, and the anthology *In My
Life: Encounters with the Beatles*. It has also been heard on KUOW,
NPR's Seattle affiliate. She makes her home in Kirkland and Chelan,
Washington, with her husband and two daughters.

BARRY GILMORE teaches eighth grade English and Latin at All Saints
Episcopal Day School in Carmel Valley, California. He has been a teaching artist and guest writer for the Memphis Arts Council, the Nashville
Institute for the Arts, the Tennessee Humanities Council, and other organizations. He is the author of *Creative Writing through the Visual and
Performing Arts* (Calendar Islands Publishers).

KEVIN GRIFFITH is an associate professor of English at Capitol University in Columbus, Ohio, where he teaches creative writing, film, and
composition. His poetry has appeared in *Chelsea, College English, The
Quarterly, The Southern Review, Yankee*, and elsewhere. In 1996 he was
awarded an Ohio Individual Artist's Grant in poetry. His first book,
Someone Had to Live, was published by San Diego Poets Press; his second book, *Paradise Refunded*, won the Backwaters Prize and is forthcoming from Backwaters Press in Omaha, Nebraska.

MIMI HERMAN received her M.F.A. in Creative Writing from the Warren Wilson M.F.A. Program for Writers. She has been a writer in the
schools for the past eight years, working with over 9,000 students, teachers, and administrators. Her passion for writing and education have continually led her to investigate the most successful ways to make learning

as enjoyable and challenging for students as possible. She works with students and teachers throughout North Carolina and Tennessee, providing writing residencies, teacher workshops, and curriculum reform.

WILLIAM J. HIGGINSON made his living for many years as a visiting poet and writing consultant to schools in New Jersey and New Mexico. His work as a translator and literary historian resulted in *The Haiku Handbook,* written in collaboration with his wife, poet Penny Harter; *The Haiku Seasons,* spelling out the connection between haiku and nature; and *Haiku World,* an anthology of more than 1,000 poems from fifty countries, with commentary in the Japanese manner. He lives in Santa Fe and heads the English department at the New Mexico Academy for Science and Mathematics.

ANDREA FREUD LOEWENSTEIN is Associate Professor of English at Medgar Evers College, City University of New York. She is the author of two novels, *This Place* and *The Worry Girl,* and a critical study, *Loathsome Jews and Engulfing Women.*

YVONNE MURPHY taught creative writing in Houston through Writers in the Schools. She has been a Stegner Fellow at Stanford University and received an M.A. in English from New York University. Recently, she moved to Manhattan where she is completing her Ph.D. in English and Creative Writing. She has published poems in *Epoch, Gulf Coast, Passages North,* and *Black Warrior Review.*

RON PADGETT's most recent books are *New & Selected Poems* (Godine); *Creative Reading: What It Is, How to Do It, & Why* (National Council of Teachers of English), a handbook for teachers; and *Albanian Diary* (The Figures), a travel memoir. He edited *The Teachers & Writers Handbook of Poetic Forms.* The recipient of a Guggenheim and other fellowships, Padgett teaches Imaginative Writing at Columbia University and serves as Publications Director of Teachers & Writers Collaborative.

CAROL F. PECK, M.A., was Writer-in-Residence at Sidwell Friends School in Washington, D.C., for thirteen years. She taught poetry writing at University of Maryland University College for over thirty years and still does workshops as one of Maryland's original Poets in the Schools. Currently she is specializing in giving voices to fringe populations: people in nursing homes and hospices, as well as teens at risk. She has published poetry, critical essays, and articles in numerous literary and educational journals and is the author of a book, *From Deep Within: Poetry Workshops in Nursing Homes.*

ELENI SIKELIANOS has published four books of poems, including *To Speak While Dreaming* (Sun & Moon Press) and *The Book of Tendons* (The Post-Apollo Press). Her poems have appeared in *Zoum-Zoum, Grand Street, Sulfur, The Quarterly*, and other magazines. She has received many awards, including a National Endowment for the Arts Creative Writing Fellowship and a Gertrude Stein Award for Innovative American Writing. Sikelianos has a B.F.A. in Poetics and an M.F.A. in Writing and Poetics from the Naropa Institute in Boulder, Colorado. She lives in New York City, where she teaches writing for Teachers & Writers Collaborative.

NORMAN WEINSTEIN is a poet, critic, and educator. His poetry books include *Nigredo: Selected Poems 1970–1980; Albedo*; and *Suite: Orchid Ska Blues.* His books of criticism include *A Night in Tunisia: Imaginings of Africa in Jazz* and *Gertrude Stein and the Literature of Modern Consciousness.* He works as a visiting poet at Lowell Elementary School in Boise, Idaho.

OTHER T&W BOOKS YOU MIGHT ENJOY

The Teachers & Writers Handbook of Poetic Forms, edited by Ron Padgett. This T&W bestseller includes 74 entries on traditional and modern poetic forms by 19 poet-teachers. "A treasure"—*Kliatt*. "The definitions not only inform, they often provoke and inspire. A small wonder!"—*Poetry Project Newsletter*. "An entertaining reference work"—*Teaching English in the Two-Year College*. "A solid beginning reference source"—*Choice*.

Poetry Everywhere: Teaching Poetry Writing in School and in the Community by Jack Collom and Sheryl Noethe. This big and "tremendously valuable resource work for teachers" (*Kliatt*) at all levels contains 60 writing exercises, extensive commentary, and 450 examples.

Luna, Luna: Creative Writing Ideas from Spanish, Latin American, & Latino Literature, edited by Julio Marzán. In 21 lively and practical essays, poets, fiction writers, and teachers tell how they use the work of Lorca, Neruda, Jiménez, Cisneros, and others to inspire students to write imaginatively. *Luna, Luna* "succeeds brilliantly. I highly recommend this book: it not only teaches but guides teachers on how to involve students in the act of creative writing"—*Kliatt*.

Sing the Sun Up: Creative Writing Ideas from African American Literature, edited by Lorenzo Thomas. Twenty teaching writers present new and exciting ways to motivate students to write imaginatively, inspired by African American poetry, fiction, essays, and drama. Essays in the book discuss work by James Baldwin, Gwendolyn Brooks, Zora Neale Hurston, Jean Toomer, Aimé Césaire, Countee Cullen, Lucille Clifton, Jayne Cortez, Rita Dove, and others.

The T&W Guide to Walt Whitman, edited by Ron Padgett. The first and only guide to teaching the work of Walt Whitman from K–college. "A lively, fun, illuminating book"—Ed Folsom, editor of *The Walt Whitman Quarterly*.

The Teachers & Writers Guide to William Carlos Williams, edited by Gary Lenhart. Seventeen practical and innovative essays on using Williams's short poems, fiction, nonfiction, and long poem *Paterson*. Contributors include Allen Ginsberg, Kenneth Koch, and Julia Alvarez.

Personal Fiction Writing by Meredith Sue Willis. A complete and practical guide for teachers of writing from elementary through college level. Contains more than 340 writing ideas. "A terrific resource for the classroom teacher as well as the novice writer"—*Harvard Educational Review*.

Educating the Imagination, Vols. 1 & 2, edited by Christopher Edgar and Ron Padgett. A huge selection of the best articles from 17 years of *Teachers & Writers* magazine, with ideas and assignments for writing poetry, fiction, plays, history, folklore, parodies, and much more.

Old Faithful: 18 Writers Present Their Favorite Writing Assignments, edited by Christopher Edgar and Ron Padgett. A collection of sure-fire exercises in imaginative writing for all levels, developed and tested by veteran writing teachers.

•

For a complete free T&W publications catalogue, contact
Teachers & Writers Collaborative
5 Union Square West, New York, NY 10003-3306
tel. (toll-free) 888-BOOKS-TW
Visit our World Wide Web site at http://www.twc.org